Exploring Mark

An aid for readers and preachers using
Year B of the Revised Common Lectionary

LESLIE J. FRANCIS
AND
PETER ATKINS

continuum
LONDON • NEW YORK

Continuum

The Tower Building   370 Lexington Avenue
11 York Road   New York
London SE1 7NX   NY 10017-6503

www.continuumbooks.com

Sections 1–34 were first published by Mowbray in 1997 as *Personality Type and Scripture: Exploring Mark's Gospel.*

British Library Cataloguing-in-Publication Data
A catalogue record for this book is available from the British Library.

ISBN 0-8264-6562-5

Designed and typeset by Kenneth Burnley in Wirral, Cheshire.
Printed and bound in Great Britain by Bookcraft (Bath) Ltd,
Midsomer Norton, Bath

Contents

	Preface		v
	Index of Sundays (Year B)		vii
	Series introduction		1
1	**Mark 1:1–8**	Advent 2	13
2	**Mark 1:4–11**	Baptism of the Lord	16
3	**Mark 1:9–15**	Lent 1	20
4	**Mark 1:14–20**	Third Sunday before Advent	23
5	**Mark 1:21–28**	Epiphany 4	27
6	**Mark 1:29–39**	Proper 1	31
7	**Mark 1:40–45**	Proper 2	35
8	**Mark 2:1–12**	Proper 3	39
9	**Mark 2:13–22**	Epiphany 8	43
10	**Mark 2:23—3:6**	Proper 4	48
11	**Mark 3:20–35**	Proper 5	52
12	**Mark 4:26–34**	Proper 6	56
13	**Mark 4:35–41**	Proper 7	61
14	**Mark 5:21–43**	Proper 8	65
15	**Mark 6:1–13**	Proper 9	70
16	**Mark 6:14–29**	Proper 10	74
17	**Mark 6:30–34, 53–56**	Proper 11	78
18	**Mark 7:1–8, 14–15, 21–23**	Proper 17	83
19	**Mark 7:24–37**	Proper 18	87
20	**Mark 8:27–38**	Proper 19, Lent 2	91
21	**Mark 9:2–9**	Sunday next before Lent	95
22	**Mark 9:30–37**	Proper 20	99
23	**Mark 9:38–50**	Proper 21	103
24	**Mark 10:2–16**	Proper 22	107
25	**Mark 10:17–31**	Proper 23	111
26	**Mark 10:35–45**	Proper 24	115
27	**Mark 10:46–52**	Proper 25	119
28	**Mark 11:1–11**	Palm Sunday	123
29	**Mark 12:28–34**	Fourth Sunday before Advent	127
30	**Mark 12:38–44**	Proper 27	131

CONTENTS

31	Mark 13:1–8	Second Sunday before Advent	134
32	Mark 13:24–37	Advent 1	138
33	Mark 15:1–39	Palm Sunday, Passion Sunday	142
34	Mark 16:1–8	Easter	148
35	John 1:6–8, 19–28	Advent 3	152
36	John 1:1–14	Christmas Day, Second Sunday before Lent	157
37	John 1:43–51	Epiphany 2	161
38	John 2:1–11	Epiphany 3	166
39	John 2:13–22	Lent 3	170
40	John 3:1–17	Trinity	174
41	John 6:1–21	Proper 12	179
42	John 6:24–35	Proper 13	184
43	John 6:35, 41–51	Proper 14	188
44	John 6:51–58	Proper 15	193
45	John 6:56–69	Proper 16	197
46	John 10:11–18	Easter 4	202
47	John 11:32–44	All Saints' Day	206
48	John 12:20–33	Lent 5	211
49	John 15:1–8	Easter 5	215
50	John 15:9–17	Easter 6	219
51	John 15:26–27; 16:4b–15	Pentecost	223
52	John 17:6–19	Easter 7	228
53	John 18:33–37	Christ the King	233
54	John 19:25b–27	Mothering Sunday	237
55	John 20:19–31	Easter 2	241
	Further reading		247

Preface

Psychological type theory is already being set to work by the Christian churches in a variety of ways. It is being employed to promote personal and professional development among clergy during initial training and continuing ministerial education, to enhance collaborative ministry among local congregations, and to help individual pilgrims find their own preferred pattern of spirituality. This book sets psychological type theory to work in the study of scripture.

There are two very practical ways in which this approach to scripture may be of service to the Christian community. First, this approach provides a disciplined way in which individuals can be helped to meditate on the richness of scripture. It helps them to transcend the more limited focus of their own psychological preferences. Second, this approach provides a disciplined way through which preachers can become more aware of how different members of their congregation may respond to their preaching. It helps them to appreciate how different psychological types may hear and respond to different emphases within the same readings from scripture.

This approach addresses the same four questions to each passage of scripture. How does this passage feed the sense perceptions and establish contact with the reality of the situation? How does this passage feed the imagination and spark off new ideas? What does this passage say about human values and interpersonal relationships? What does this passage do to stimulate the intellect and to challenge the roots of faith? Many Christians may instinctively find one of these questions of greater value and interest than the others. Many Christians may well benefit from experiencing how the scriptures can speak to the totality of their personality, to their senses and their imagination, to their heart and their head.

Readers who are already well versed in type theory will benefit from knowing the psychological type of the authors. Such information may alert them to the strengths and to the weaknesses of each author's own perspective. In the language of type theory, Leslie Francis is an INTJ. This means that he prefers *introversion* (I), *intuition* (N), *thinking* (T) and *judging* (J). Peter Atkins is an ESTJ. This means that he prefers *extraversion* (E), *sensing* (S), *thinking* (T) and *judging* (J). Readers who are not already well versed in type theory will find these concepts defined and discussed in the series introduction.

We planned and revised this book together. Leslie drafted Chapters 1–34 and 49–55. Peter drafted Chapters 35–48. While we critiqued the content of each other's chapters, we have given variety to the text by not writing in the same style.

Index of Sundays (Year B)

Advent 1 ....Mark 13:24–37
Advent 2 ....Mark 1:1–8
Advent 3 ....John 1:6–8, 19–28
Christmas Day ....John 1:1–14
Baptism of the Lord ....Mark 1:4–11
Epiphany 2 ....John 1:43–51
Epiphany 3 ....John 2:1–11
Epiphany 4 ....Mark 1:21–28
Proper 1 ....Mark 1:29–39
Proper 2 ....Mark 1:40–45
Proper 3 ....Mark 2:1–12
Second Sunday before Lent ....John 1:1–14
Sunday next before Lent ....Mark 9:2–9
Lent 1 ....Mark 1:9–15
Lent 2 ....Mark 8:31–38
Lent 3 ....John 2:13–22
Mothering Sunday ....John 19:25b–27
Lent 5 ....John 12:20–33
Palm Sunday ....Mark 11:1–11
Palm Sunday ....Mark 15:1–39
Easter Day ....Mark 16:1–8
Easter 2 ....John 20:19–31
Easter 4 ....John 10:11–18
Easter 5 ....John 15:1–8
Easter 6 ....John 15:9–17
Easter 7 ....John 17:6–19
Day of Pentecost ....John 15:26–27, 16:4b–15
Trinity Sunday ....John 3:1–17
Proper 4 ....Mark 2:23 to 3:6
Proper 5 ....Mark 3:20–35
Proper 6 ....Mark 4:26–34
Proper 7 ....Mark 4:35–41
Proper 8 ....Mark 5:21–43
Proper 9 ....Mark 6:1–13

Proper 10 ....Mark 6:14–29
Proper 11 ....Mark 6:30–34, 53–56
Proper 12 ....John 6:1–21
Proper 13 ....John 6:24–35
Proper 14 ....John 6:35, 41–51
Proper 15 ....John 6:51–58
Proper 16 ....John 6:56–69
Proper 17 ....Mark 7:1–8, 14–15, 21–23
Proper 18 ....Mark 7:24–37
Proper 19 ....Mark 8:27–38
Proper 20 ....Mark 9:30–37
Proper 21 ....Mark 9:38–50
Proper 22 ....Mark 10:2–16
Proper 23 ....Mark 10:17–31
Proper 24 ....Mark 10:35–45
Proper 25 ....Mark 10:46–52
All Saints' Day ....John 11:32–44
Fourth Sunday before Advent ....Mark 12:28–34
Third Sunday before Advent ....Mark 1:14–20
Second Sunday before Advent ....Mark 13:1–8
Christ the King ....John 18:33–37

Series introduction

Exploring Mark's Gospel is part of the Personality Type and Scripture series of books which reflect on scripture in a disciplined way using insights from personality psychology. Readers as yet unfamiliar with the language and theory of personality type may benefit from a brief introduction to that theory. It is for this reason that each volume carries the series introduction, written by Leslie J. Francis.

For the preacher

Looking over the edge of the pulpit into the faces of the congregation, it is not difficult to see that people differ. At the simplest level it is obvious how people differ by age and sex. Most preachers will observe the gender and age composition of their congregation and take this information into account in structuring and delivering their message. Without wishing to sort people too rigidly into categories, it seems just good common sense to recognize that one presentation might be more appropriate for the local Cubs or Brownies, another more appropriate for the Mothers' Union, and yet another more appropriate for the Pensioners' Guild. It is clear that the experience and the expectations of the specific groups have to be taken into account.

In many ways preaching to a homogeneous group like the local Cubs or Brownies may be easier than addressing a large and mixed congregation. In one presentation the preacher is required to address the needs of the ageing widow, to acknowledge the concerns of the business executive, and to capture the attention of the restless child chorister. People differ and the preacher needs to be aware of the differences.

A particularly intriguing and useful account of how people differ is provided by Carl Jung and his theory of psychological type. The theory of psychological type suggests that it is helpful for preachers to take into account not only how the members of their congregation differ in outward ways, but also how they differ in their psychological preferences. Different psychological types may hear sermons in very different ways, and this has important implications for preachers.

For personal study

When a group of people meet to study a passage of scripture, it often becomes clear very quickly how different individuals may study the same passage in very distinctive ways. One member of the group may want to focus closely on the details of the text itself. Another member of the group may want to draw the wider implications from the text and make links with other or contemporary issues. Another member of the group may concentrate on lessons for practical living and for personal relationships. Yet another member of the group may wish to explore the theological implications of the text and the problems and challenges which it raises for faith.

Bible study groups which contain such a rich mix of people can be exciting for many Christians and open their eyes to the different ways in which scripture can enrich the lives of the people of God. When individual Christians meditate on scripture in the privacy of their own home they need to have their eyes opened to the variety of perspectives which can be brought to the same passage by other Christians who see things in a different way.

Carl Jung's theory of psychological type opens our eyes not only to the ways in which people differ, but also to the rich variety of perspectives within ourselves. The theory makes us more conscious of those parts of ourselves which we may undervalue and under-exercise. Type theory concerned with the richness of our own psychological composition has important implications for how we allow ourselves to be nurtured and nourished by scripture.

The Myers-Briggs Type Indicator

It is Jung's theory of psychological type which stands at the heart of the Myers-Briggs Type Indicator, a psychological tool being increasingly used by the Christian churches. This theory identifies two main mental processes. The first process concerns the ways in which we gather information. This is the *perceiving* process. Some people prefer *sensing* (S); others prefer *intuition* (N). According to the theory, these two types look at the world in very different ways.

The second process concerns the ways in which we make decisions. This is the *judging* process. Some people prefer *thinking* (T); others prefer *feeling* (F). According to the theory, these two types come to decisions about the world in very different ways.

Jung also suggested that individuals differ in the *orientation* in which they prefer to employ these two processes. Some people prefer the outer or *extraverting* world (E); others prefer the inner or *introverting* world (I). According to the theory, these two types are energized in very different ways. Extraverts draw their energy from the outer world of people and things, while introverts draw their energy from their inner world.

Finally, individuals differ in their *attitude* to the outer world. Both introverts and extraverts need to deal with the outer world and both may prefer to do this with a *judging* (J) or a *perceiving* (P) process. According to the theory, these two types display very different attitudes to the outer world.

What the theory understands by these preferences now needs to be explained in greater detail.

Introversion and extraversion

Introversion and extraversion describe the two preferred *orientations* of the inner world and the outer world. Introverts prefer to focus their attention on the inner world of ideas and draw their energy from that inner world. When introverts are tired and need energizing they look to the inner world. Extraverts prefer to focus their attention on the outer world of people and things and draw their energy from that outer world. When extraverts are tired and need energizing they look to the outer world. Since this introduction is being written by an introvert, the author prefers to present this perspective first, followed by the extravert perspective.

Introverts like quiet for concentration. They want to be able to shut off the distractions of the outer world and turn inwards. They often experience trouble in remembering names and faces. They can work at one solitary project for a long time without interruption. When they are engaged in a task in the outer world they may become absorbed in the ideas behind that task.

Introverts work best alone and may resent distractions and interruptions from other people. They dislike being interrupted by the telephone, tend to think things through before acting, and may spend so long in thought that they miss the opportunity to act.

Introverts prefer to learn by reading rather than by talking with others. They may also prefer to communicate with others in writing, rather than face-to-face or over the phone; this is particularly the case if they have something unpleasant to communicate.

Introverts are oriented to the inner world. They focus on ideas, concepts and inner understanding. They are reflective, may consider deeply before acting, and they probe inwardly for stimulation.

Extraverts like variety and action. They want to be able to shut off the distractions of the inner world and turn outward. They are good at remembering faces and names and enjoy meeting people and introducing people. They can become impatient with long, slow jobs. When they are working in the company of other people they may become more interested in how others are doing the job than in the job itself.

Extraverts like to have other people around them in the working environment, and enjoy the stimulus of sudden interruptions and telephone calls. Extraverts like to act quickly and decisively, even when it is not totally appropriate to do so.

Extraverts prefer to learn a task by talking it through with other people. They prefer to communicate with other people face-to-face or over the phone, rather than in writing. They often find that their own ideas become clarified through communicating them with others.

Extraverts are oriented to the outer world. They focus on people and things. They prefer to learn by trial and error and they do so with confidence. They are active people, and they scan the outer environment for stimulation.

Sensing and intuition

Sensing and intuition describe the two preferences associated with the *perceiving* process. They describe different preferences used to acquire information. Sensing types focus on the realities of a situation as perceived by the senses. Intuitive types focus on the possibilities, meanings and relationships, the 'big picture' that goes beyond sensory information. Since this introduction is being written by an intuitive, the author prefers to present this perspective first, followed by the sensing perspective.

Individuals who prefer *intuition* develop insight into complexity. They have the ability to see abstract, symbolic and theoretical relationships, and the capacity to see future possibilities. They put their reliance on inspiration rather than on past experience. Their interest is in the new and untried. They trust their intuitive grasp of meanings and relationships.

Individuals with a preference for intuition are aware of new challenges and possibilities. They see quickly beyond the information they have been given or the materials they have to hand to the possibilities and challenges which these offer. They are often discontent with the way things are and wish to improve them. They become bored quickly and dislike doing the same thing repeatedly.

Intuitive types enjoy learning new skills. They work in bursts of energy, powered by enthusiasm, and then enjoy slack periods between activity.

Intuitive types follow their inspirations and hunches. They may reach conclusions too quickly and misconstrue the information or get the facts wrong. They dislike taking too much time to secure precision.

Intuitive types may tend to imagine that things are more complex than they really are: they tend to over-complexify things. They are curious about why things are the way they are and may prefer to raise questions than to find answers.

Intuitive types are always striving to gain an overview of the information around them. In terms of an old proverb, they may prefer to pay attention to the two birds in the bush rather than the one in the hand.

Intuitive types perceive with memory and associations. They see patterns and meanings and assess possibilities. They are good at reading between the lines and projecting possibilities for the future. They prefer to go always for the big picture. They prefer to let the mind inform the eyes.

Individuals who prefer *sensing* develop keen awareness of present experience. They have acute powers of observation, good memory for facts and details, the capacity for realism, and the ability to see the world as it is. They rely on experience rather than theory. They put their trust in what is known and in the conventional.

Individuals with a preference for sensing are aware of the uniqueness of each individual event. They develop good techniques of observation and they recognize the practical way in which things work now.

Sensing types like to develop an established way of doing things and gain enjoyment from exercising skills which they have already learnt. Repetitive work does not bore them. They are able to work steadily with a realistic idea of how long a task will take.

Sensing types usually reach their conclusion step by step, observing each piece of information carefully. They are not easily inspired to interpret the information in front of them and they may not trust inspiration when it comes. They are very careful about getting the facts right and are good at engaging in precise work.

Sensing types may fail to recognize complexity in some situations, and consequently over-simplify tasks. They are good at accepting the current reality as the given situation in which to work. They would much rather work with the present information than speculate about future possibilities. They clearly agree with the old proverb that the bird in the hand is worth two in the bush.

Sensing types perceive clearly with the five senses. They attend to practical and factual details, and they are in touch with physical realities. They attend to the present moment and prefer to confine their attention to what is said and done. They observe the small details of everyday life and attend to step-by-step experience. They prefer to let the eyes tell the mind.

Thinking and feeling

Thinking and feeling describe the two preferences associated with the *judging* process. They describe different preferences by which decisions are reached. Individuals who prefer thinking make decisions by objective, logical analysis. Individuals who prefer feeling make decisions by subjective values based on how people will be affected. Since this introduction is being written by a thinker, the author prefers to present this perspective first, followed by the feeling perspective.

Individuals who prefer *thinking* develop clear powers of logical analysis. They develop the ability to weigh facts objectively and to predict consequences, both intended and unintended. They develop a stance of impartiality. They are characterized by a sense of fairness and justice.

Individuals with a preference for thinking are good at putting things in logical order. They are also able to put people in their place when they consider it necessary. They are able to take tough decisions and to reprimand others. They are also able to be firm and tough-minded about themselves.

Thinking types need to be treated fairly and to see that other people are treated fairly as well. They are inclined to respond more to other people's ideas than to other people's feelings. They may inadvertently hurt other people's feelings without recognizing that they are doing so.

Thinking types are able to anticipate and predict the logical outcomes of other people's choices. They can see the humour rather than the human pain in bad choices and wrong decisions taken by others. Thinking types prefer to look at life from the outside as a spectator.

Thinking types are able to develop good powers of logical analysis. They use objective and impersonal criteria in reaching decisions. They follow logically the relationships between cause and effect. They develop characteristics of being firm-minded and prizing logical order. They may appear sceptical.

Individuals who prefer *feeling* develop a personal emphasis on values and standards. They appreciate what matters most to themselves and what matters most to other people. They develop an understanding of people, a wish to affiliate with people and a desire for harmony. They are characterized by their capacity for warmth, and by qualities of empathy and compassion.

Individuals with a preference for feeling like harmony and will work hard to bring harmony about between other people. They dislike telling other people unpleasant things or reprimanding other people. They take into account other people's feelings.

Feeling types need to have their own feelings recognized as well. They need praise and affirmation. They are good at seeing the personal effects of choices on their own lives and on other people's lives as well.

Feeling types are sympathetic individuals. They take a great interest in the people behind the job and respond to other people's values as much as to their ideas. They enjoy pleasing people.

Feeling types look at life from the inside. They live life as a committed participant and find it less easy to stand back and to form an objective view of what is taking place.

Feeling types develop good skills at applying personal priorities. They are good at weighing human values and motives, both their own and other people's. They are characterized by qualities of empathy and sympathy. They prize harmony and trust.

Judging and perceiving

Judging and perceiving describe the two preferred *attitudes* towards the outer world. Individuals who prefer to relate to the outer world with a judging process present a planned and orderly approach to life. They prefer to have a settled system in place and display a preference for closure. Individuals who prefer to relate to the outer world with a perceiving process present a flexible and spontaneous approach to life. They prefer to keep plans and organization to a minimum and display a preference for openness. Since this introduction is being written by a judger, the author prefers to present this perspective first, followed by the perceiving perspective.

Judging types schedule projects so that each step gets done on time. They like to get things finished and settled, and to know that the finished product is in place. They work best when they can plan their work in advance and follow that plan. Judging types use lists and agendas to structure their day and to plan their actions. They may dislike interruption of the plans they have made and are reluctant to leave the task in hand even when something more urgent arises.

Judging types tend to be satisfied once they reach a judgement or have made a decision, about both people and things. They dislike having to revise their decision and taking fresh information into account. They like to get on with a task as soon as possible once the essential things are at hand. As a consequence, judging types may decide to act too quickly.

When individuals take a judging attitude towards the outer world, they are using the preferred *judging* process, i.e. thinking or feeling, outwardly. Their attitude to life is characterized by deciding and planning, organizing and scheduling, controlling and regulating. Their life is goal-oriented. They want to move towards closure, even when the data are incomplete.

Perceiving types adapt well to changing situations. They make allowances for new information and for changes in the situation in which they are living or acting. They may have trouble making decisions, feeling that they have never quite got enough information on which to base their decision.

Perceiving types may start too many projects and consequently have difficulty in finishing them. They may tend to postpone unpleasant tasks and to give their attention to more pleasant options. Perceiving types want to know all about a new task before they begin it, and may prefer to postpone something new while they continue to explore the options.

When perceiving types use lists they do so not as a way of organizing the details of their day, but of seeing the possibilities in front of them. They may choose never to act on these possibilities. Perceiving types do not mind leaving things open for last-minute changes. They work best under pressure and get a lot accomplished at the last minute under the constraints of a deadline.

When individuals take a perceiving attitude towards the outer world, they are using the preferred *perceiving* process, i.e. sensing or intuition, outwardly. They are taking in information, adapting and changing, curious and interested. They adopt an open-minded attitude towards life and resist closure to obtain more data.

Personality type and preaching

The Myers-Briggs Type Indicator provides information about the individual's orientation (introversion or extraversion), perceiving process (sensing or intuition), judging process (thinking or feeling) and attitude towards the outer world (judging or perceiving). The crucial information for the preacher, however, centres on the two processes, that is to say on the two distinctions between sensing and intuition (the perceiving process) and between thinking and feeling (the judging process).

According to the theory, every individual needs to draw on all four functions of the two processes: sensing and intuition, thinking and feeling. But at the same time one of these four functions is preferred and becomes dominant. The four functions of sensing and intuition, thinking and feeling, when dominant, approach the world in very different ways. These different approaches will be attracted by very different perspectives in preaching.

At its most basic level, the sensing type needs to respond to facts and information, to details and clearly defined images. The intuitive type needs to respond to challenges to the imagination and arresting ideas, to theories and possibilities. The feeling type needs to respond to issues of the heart and to the stuff of human relationships. The thinking type needs to respond to issues of the head and to the stuff of logical analysis.

Of course, left to their own devices preachers will emphasize their own type preference. The preacher who prefers intuition will preach a message full of fast-moving ideas and imaginative associations. The sensing types in the congregation will quickly lose the thread and accuse those preachers of having their heads in the air and their shoes high above the ground. The preacher who prefers sensing will preach a message full of detailed information and the close analysis of text. The intuitive types in the congregation will quickly tire of the detail and accuse those preachers of being dull and failing to see the wood for the trees.

The preacher who prefers feeling will preach a message full of human interest and of loving concern for people. The thinking types in the congregation will quickly become impatient with this emphasis on interpersonal matters and accuse those preachers of failing to grasp the hard intellectual issues and the pressing challenges and contradictions of the faith. The preacher who prefers thinking will preach a message full of theological erudition and carefully argued nuance of perspective. The feeling types in the congregation will quickly become impatient with this emphasis on theological abstraction and accuse those preachers of missing the very heart of the gospel which cries out for compassion, understanding and human warmth.

Responding to the challenge
The theory of psychological types helps to clarify and to sharpen one of the problems confronting the preacher. There is no one simple solution to this problem, although being aware of the problem is itself an important step towards addressing it.

One suggestion is to try to include within the majority of sermons components which will speak directly to each of the four types: sensing, intuition, thinking and feeling. The problem with this solution is that the time generally allowed for preaching makes it difficult to develop all four perspectives in any depth. Evenly distributed, a ten-minute sermon would allow two and a half minutes on each perspective. A second suggestion is to try to vary the preaching style from week to week. In this sense perhaps an ideal preaching team should include four preachers representing the four psychological types. Few churches, however, may have such a resource readily available!

Our aim in this book has been to take 55 gospel passages from Mark and John included in Year B of the Revised Common Lectionary and to interrogate each passage from the distinctive perspectives of the four psychological types. For all 55 gospel passages we have followed the same disciplined pattern of exploring the four functions in the same fixed order: sensing, intuition, feeling and thinking. There is a logic in this order. We need the sensing function to ground us in the reality of the passage of scripture. We need the intuitive function to draw out the wider implications and to develop the links. We need the feeling function to become attuned to the issues of values and human priorities within the narrative. We need the thinking function to face the theological implications and to struggle with the intellectual issues.

We cannot imagine preachers wishing to follow this pattern slavishly week in and week out. But we can imagine preachers using this material in two main ways. On some Sundays we envisage sermons being preached which self-consciously present four different perspectives on the one gospel passage. We envisage congregations, as well as preachers, being aware of the reason for this. We envisage this process leading to a wider and better-informed discussion of the relevance of type theory for appreciating the diversity of perspectives and the diversity of gifts within the local congregation.

On other Sundays we envisage the preacher deliberately targeting one of the perspectives and developing that consistent line of presentation. We envisage individuals in the congregation representative of all four types being challenged to listen and to respond. We envisage this process leading to a deeper spiritual awareness as individuals gain closer contact with the less well-developed aspects of their inner self, and come to appreciate more deeply how the God who created us with diversity of gifts and diversity of preferences can be worshipped and adored through sensing as well as intuition, through thinking as well as feeling.

1
Mark 1:1–8

¹The beginning of the good news of Jesus Christ, the Son of God.
²As it is written in the prophet Isaiah,
'See, I am sending my messenger ahead of you,
who will prepare your way;
³the voice of one crying out in the wilderness:
"Prepare the way of the Lord,
make his paths straight,"'
⁴John the baptizer appeared in the wilderness, proclaiming a baptism of repentance for the forgiveness of sins. ⁵And people from the whole Judean countryside and all the people of Jerusalem were going out to him, and were baptized by him in the river Jordan, confessing their sins. ⁶Now John was clothed with camel's hair, with a leather belt around his waist, and he ate locusts and wild honey. ⁷He proclaimed, 'The one who is more powerful than I is coming after me; I am not worthy to stoop down and untie the thong of his sandals. ⁸I have baptized you with water; but he will baptize you with the Holy Spirit.'

Context

This passage is part of the prologue to Mark's gospel. The complete prologue occupies verses 1–14. In the prologue Mark announces the theme of his book. Like the book of Genesis, Mark opens with the grand pronouncement, 'The beginning'. The theme is to do with the good news (the gospel), Jesus (the new Joshua through whom God saves), the Christ (the anointed one), the Son of God (the new Adam).

Sensing

Be still and open your ears to the sounds of the wilderness. Hear the deep, deep silence of the open spaces. The air is still, the sun is warm, even the creatures are sleeping. But feel the expectancy in the air. The promise of the ages is haunting your memory. The world teeters on the edge of a new revelation. Then prick up your ears and hear the sounds of the distant voice, the voice of one crying in the wilderness. Strain your ears to pick out the sound and to piece together the words,

> Prepare the way of the Lord,
> make his paths straight.

Search your memory banks and find there the scroll of the prophet Isaiah. Look up the text in Isaiah 40:3 and see now that the prophecy is being fulfilled. Feel the blood of excitement race through your veins as the voice stirs your heart.

Be still and open your eyes to the vision of the speaker. Picture the bizarre figure of John the baptizer. See the cloak of camel's hair. See the leather belt around his waist. See his extraordinary lunch box. Taste the locusts and wild honey. Search your memory banks and find the scroll of the books of Kings. Look up the text in 2 Kings 1:8 and see how the prophet Elijah was clothed in the self-same way. Know now for sure that Elijah has returned to prepare the way for the Messiah.

Be still and open your heart to the message of the itinerant preacher. 'Repent,' says John the baptizer, 'repent: turn round and face the other way.'

Intuition

Two words stand at the very heart of the opening verses of Mark's gospel: 'prepare' and 'repent'. What do these words suggest to you?

Take the first word first: 'prepare'. How seriously do you see the need for preparation in the Christian life? Do you make room for periods of preparation? In the pattern of the Christian year, the church has made seasons of preparation before the major festivals of Christmas and Easter. Can you really expect to share in the good news of Christmas Day if you have not waited expectantly through the days of Advent? Can you really expect to share in the new life of the Easter resurrection, if you have not endured the 40 days and the 40 nights of the wilderness and walked the *Via Dolorosa* of the Good Friday cross?

Or to take another example, many of us have been taught during classes for Confirmation or for first Communion of the importance of preparing for meeting Christ in the blessed sacrament of bread and wine, each time we come to receive Communion. I wonder just how much familiarity with the repeated act Sunday by Sunday, or day by day, dulls our expectation and deadens our spiritual awareness. What do you do to keep that sense of preparation alive?

Then take the second word next: 'repentance'. How seriously do you see the need for repentance in the Christian life? Do you make time for periods of repentance? Do you stand back far enough and often enough to see yourself as you really are? Are you aware of the need for repentance and do you ask God's grace to sharpen that awareness? Just think, if you came face to face with John the baptizer and heard afresh his challenge to repentance, what in your life would you wish to change?

Feeling

Have you any idea what it must have been like to be John the baptizer? Go on, step into his sandals, try on his garment of camel's hair for size. What is it like to be driven to proclaim the message of God?

Here is the person who is not only messenger, but the very message itself. Here is the person who has been set apart by the finger of God, to do the work of God. Here is the person whose very life has been taken over, transformed and consumed by the very message of which he is part.

We know that John the baptizer became the person who would not compromise. He would not temper his message to win the sympathy of his hearers. John the baptizer was blunt with the Roman soldiers who sought his advice. John the baptizer was blunt with the Pharisees who tested his message. John the baptizer was blunt with the ruler Herod, who would have preferred a change in the marriage laws. John the baptizer lost his head for the sake of the message.

What do you see there in the heart of John the baptizer? Do you admire a man of cast iron certainty, of resolute conviction? Or are you slightly suspicious of his inflexible dogmatism, of his heartless insensitivity? Do you see a total saint or a slightly dangerous egotist?

And what do you learn from standing in John's sandals about your own calling to live the Christian life? When do you feel that it is right to challenge others to repentance and when do you need to treat others with a gentler message of grace? When would you give priority to sticking your neck out and when would you give priority to keeping your head?

Thinking

The prologue to Mark's gospel focuses clear questions about the kind of author who is writing the book and the kind of book that is being written. Are these opening verses a haphazard stringing together of ideas or are they a carefully crafted masterpiece? And the whole matter is further confused by textual corruption. Some manuscripts complete the first verse with the words 'the Son of God' and others omit these words.

My view is that every word in the opening sentence carries weight and that the rest of the prologue is a carefully constructed commentary on those opening words. Take, for example, the citation attributed to Isaiah. Search Isaiah from beginning to end and you will not find the text, 'See, I am sending my messenger ahead of you, who will prepare your way.' Has Mark got his scriptures wrong? Or is he following proper practice of citing what is in the prophets, 'Prepare the way of the Lord', as commentary on what is in the law? The text missing from Isaiah is there in Exodus 23:20 where it clearly refers to Joshua himself, whose Hebrew name is translated in the Greek as 'Jesus'. Ah, at last I see, Mark is telling me that he is speaking of the new Joshua through whom God saves the people of God. Then, once into the prophecy of Isaiah, my mind trips on with the prophet's words. Mark's one-liner leads to the prophet's promise of bringing *good news*. Indeed, how blessed are the feet of those who proclaim that good news.

What began as an enigmatic opening, 'The beginning of the good news of Jesus' now makes sense because of the skilful setting out of the Old Testament by Mark, the master craftsman of the gospel narrative.

⟫•◉•⟪

2

Mark 1:4–11

⁴John the baptizer appeared in the wilderness, proclaiming a baptism of repentance for the forgiveness of sins. ⁵And people from the whole Judean countryside and all the people of Jerusalem were going out to him, and were baptized by him in the river Jordan, confessing their sins. ⁶Now John was clothed with camel's

hair, with a leather belt around his waist, and he ate locusts and wild honey. [7]He proclaimed, 'The one who is more powerful than I is coming after me; I am not worthy to stoop down and untie the thong of his sandals. [8]I have baptized you with water; but he will baptize you with the Holy Spirit.'

[9]In those days Jesus came from Nazareth of Galilee and was baptized by John in the Jordan. [10]And just as he was coming up out of the water, he saw the heavens torn apart and the Spirit descending like a dove on him. [11]And a voice came from heaven, 'You are my Son, the Beloved; with you I am well pleased.'

Context

This passage is part of the prologue of Mark's gospel, the section which occupies verses 1–14. Abstracted from the prologue, these verses appear to be entirely focusing on the baptism of Jesus. Other interestingly different accounts of the baptism of Jesus are provided by Matthew and Luke.

Sensing

One key image dominates the baptism of Jesus: the image of water.

Take your senses out to play and lose yourself in the sheer joy and richness of water. Paint the picture of the waterfall in your mind's eye. See the water cascading down the hillside. See the rays of light playing on the moving torrent. See the colours and see the shape. See the life-giving force of the living stream. Then let your eyes wander across the green, lush pastures around the foot of the waterfall and see how the living water brings life to the fields.

Hear the many sounds of water. Hear the roar of the water as it rushes over the precipice. Hear the gentle lapping of the slow-flowing water as it caresses the bank of the meandering river.

Stretch out your hands and plunge them into water. Feel the clear cool moisture on the hairs of your skin. And experience how the clear water dissolves the coating of grime and dispels the layer of dust. See how your hand emerges clean and renewed.

Bring the clear cool water to your parched lips and feel the pure liquid moisten your throat. Quench your throat with the living water, and be refreshed with the life-giving draught.

Now fix your eyes on the font. See there, reflected in the water of baptism, all the richness of the waters of the world.

Intuition

In those early days baptism seems to have been a very public and very dramatic affair: adults jumping into flowing rivers, making open confessions of their faith and submitting to total immersion beneath the water.

How do you square all that with what happens in church today: the infant gracefully dressed in christening robes, the gentle splashing with warmed water, the promises made on proxy by sponsors?

What do you remember of *your* baptism? And what does that baptism mean to you? Can you name the place? Can you name the time? Do you recall who were your godparents or sponsors? What part have they played in your life? How have they helped to shape your Christian formation?

Or when have you acted as godparent or sponsor? How many godchildren do you have? What part have you played in their Christian formation? What difference have you made to their lives?

Or as members of a Christian congregation, how many baptisms have you witnessed? How often have you turned to face the newly baptized infant and joined in the liturgical shout, 'We welcome you'? And what have you done to welcome the infants baptized into your congregation? What is your responsibility?

And what line, anyway, should the church be taking on baptizing infants? Should the door be open for all comers, freely to dispense the grace of God? Or should we fence the font and demand certain standards from the parents who bring their infants to baptism? Should we demand regular church attendance and classes of preparation? After all, which is important, what God delivers through the sacramental rite, or what we the people of God do in the name of God?

Feeling

Can you identify with Jesus at that moment of baptism? Can you put yourself in his place? What was it like for him? There in the wilderness, Jesus comes face to face with John the baptizer. Perhaps Jesus already knows something about the relationship between his mother Mary and John's mother Elizabeth? Perhaps the two had met as boys? But now the meeting is really something quite different.

Jesus would know of all the excitement and expectation surrounding John the baptizer. Some rumoured that John was nothing less than the Messiah himself. Others told the tale that John was Elijah returned to prepare the way for the Messiah.

John's words echo through Jesus' ears and stir Jesus' heart. 'The one who is more powerful than I is coming after me . . . he will baptize you with the Holy Spirit.' The people, on the tip-toe of expectation, look round for the one who is coming. Their eyes meet Jesus' eyes. John's eyes meet Jesus' eyes.

Jesus steps down into the water. The heavens are torn apart. The Spirit descends as a dove on Jesus. And the voice speaks from heaven the words of the enthronement psalm, 'You are my Son, the Beloved; with you I am well pleased.'

Anointed with water and with the Holy Spirit, Jesus' vocation is affirmed. He steps out of the water onto the road to ministry and to death.

Can you put yourself in Jesus' sandals and live out that moment of transformation, affirmation and conviction?

Thinking

Two main theological issues are raised by the account of Jesus' baptism. What happened and what does it mean?

To look at what happened we need to compare the different gospel traditions. In Mark, the first of the synoptic gospels, Jesus saw the heavens open and the dove descending. Here the voice addresses Jesus alone, 'You are my Son.' In Luke the passive voice is used, 'the heaven was opened', but the voice still speaks in the second person singular, 'You are my Son.' In Matthew, the account becomes more dramatic, more public, more open. Now when the heavens are opened, the voice speaks to the crowd, 'This is my Son, the Beloved, with whom I am well pleased.' In John's gospel there is no explicit mention of Jesus being baptized, but John the baptizer declares, 'I saw the Spirit descending from heaven like a dove, and it remained on him.' So what did happen? Who saw what? Who heard what?

The fact that Jesus was baptized by John presents a theological conundrum. John proclaimed a baptism of repentance. Surely Jesus, the sinless one, needs no repentance. The problem is spotted first by Matthew who interpolates a conversation between Jesus and John. According to Matthew, John would have prevented Jesus from coming to baptism: 'I need to be baptized by you, and do you come to me?' Jesus' enigmatic answer continues to confound the commentators, 'It is proper for us in this way to fulfil all righteousness.' Then in one of the apocryphal gospels Jesus himself asks the more direct question, 'Wherein have I sinned that I should go and be baptized by him?'

For Mark, however, no such problem exists. Here the baptism of Jesus is no baptism of repentance, but the formal act of anointing. As Elijah *revividus*, John is the maker of Kings, the anointer of Messiahs. Yes, 'You are my Son, with you I am well pleased.'

3

Mark 1:9–15

[9]In those days Jesus came from Nazareth of Galilee and was baptized by John in the Jordan. [10]And just as he was coming up out of the water, he saw the heavens torn apart and the Spirit descending like a dove on him. [11]And a voice came from heaven, 'You are my Son, the Beloved; with you I am well pleased.'

[12]And the Spirit immediately drove him out into the wilderness. [13]He was in the wilderness forty days, tempted by Satan; and he was with the wild beasts; and the angels waited on him.

[14]Now after John was arrested, Jesus came to Galilee, proclaiming the good news of God, [15]and saying, 'The time is fulfilled, and the kingdom of God has come near; repent, and believe in the good news.'

Context

This passage concludes the prologue to Mark's gospel. The prologue opened with the words, 'The beginning of the good news'. The prologue concludes with the words, 'believe in the good news'. This is the theme of the gospel.

Sensing

Push open the door and walk into a well-lit room. Two huge pictures grace the distant wall. Look at them one by one. See the similarities. Spot the differences.

The first picture shows a green lush garden watered by a flowing river. It is rich with greenery and plants. A tall, graceful, fruit-bearing tree rises high and dominates the scene. A man and a woman walk the garden path. Modesty prevents me from describing their lack of clothing. Fig leaves have not yet been crafted into flowing robes. A smiling serpent dances harmlessly through the grass. The woman holds a ripe and tempting fruit.

This first picture portrays the age of innocence when the angels of the Lord inhabit the grounds and the wild beasts come tamely to the man to receive their names and to establish their identity within the created order. See here the first Adam before paradise was lost.

The second picture shows a wild and barren landscape by a parched and cracking river bed. No plant, no tree, no source of food springs from the ground. A solitary man is engaged in inner wrestling, torment and distraction, the Satanic serpent slithering around his feet. Yet in this second picture the mood portrays neither hopelessness nor despair. A sense of victory and hopefulness fills the canvas.

This second picture portrays the age of innocence restored, when once again wild beasts provide comfort to the tormented soul and once more the angels of the Lord inhabit the world of men and women. See here the second Adam in paradise regained.

Intuition

The key idea in this passage is the idea of temptation. What does temptation mean to you?

Begin with your own experience. When would you say that you have felt really tempted? Begin with the trivial examples which you would not mind discussing over tea and biscuits. What about the temptation to over-indulge: a fourth biscuit on a Sunday during Lent, a second or fifth glass of port, a third or sixth can of lager? Or what about the temptation to misappropriate resources: the office paperclip for personal correspondence, or the library book inadvertently removed? Or what about the temptation to exploit other people: the friendship formed for personal gain, or the trust exploited for personal gratification?

What about the less trivial examples, about which you would prefer to remain silent: examples known only to you and to your God; examples so well concealed from your family and closest friends, and not even whispered in the confessional?

So what makes temptation to be temptation in the first place? Somewhere are there objective moral standards against which behaviour is assessed? Where do these standards come from and how do we know that they are right?

And what gives temptation its own unique power and force? With whom do we wrestle when we feel tempted? Do we wrestle with ourselves and conduct the battle wholly within? Or are we caught in a more sinister cosmic conflict between good and evil, between God and Satan?

What does temptation mean to you?

Feeling

It is not always easy to withstand temptation. So can you really blame those who fall? Take a few examples and step inside another's shoes.

Become an adolescent bullied by classmates at school. Feel the isolation, the anguish and the hurt. The only way to gain the respect of the crowd is to accept their way of life, to adopt their standards and to do what they require. The cost of personal acceptance is to accept the dare to break the rules and to become one of the crowd. Step into those adolescent shoes and judge how you would act and feel.

Become the parent of a sick child and your income is inadequate to meet the growing demands of providing adequate care and support. Where fair means of survival fail, foul means of survival appear attractive. Step inside those parental shoes and judge how you would act and feel.

Become an employee working within a corrupt and inefficient organization. However hard you work, all your best efforts will be squandered by your incompetent and unscrupulous head of department. Where integrity is unrewarded and malpractice goes unnoticed, what is to be lost by securing some personal gain? Step inside those employee's shoes and judge how you would act and feel.

And of this we can be sure, the Jesus who walked the wilderness path in the tempter's company is able to sympathize with the temptations which confront our daily lives. He is able to step inside our shoes when the moral dilemma looms large.

Thinking

The gospel account of the temptation of Jesus presents three interesting questions.

The first question is, 'What really happened in the wilderness?'

The original account in Mark provides no details of the temptations themselves. These details are provided only by the later
accounts of Matthew and Luke. Moreover, there are interesting
differences in the way in which the account is given by Matthew
and Luke. From Mark's silence, we can perhaps best assume that
the detail was unimportant to him. What was important for Mark
was the fact that Jesus was tempted by Satan.

The second question is, 'Why was Jesus in the wilderness?'
Mark is clear that it was by no mere accident that Jesus found himself in the wilderness. He was there by divine intention. At the
baptism the Spirit descended on Jesus like a dove of peace and
confirmed the divine anointing. Then the Spirit's very first action
was to drive Jesus into the wilderness. The Greek verb is very
strong. Literally the dove of peace showed no peace. The Spirit
kicked Jesus out into the wilderness.

The third question is, 'Why does Mark describe the temptations at this early stage in his narrative?' Theologically the point
is that Mark is completing his opening definition of what his
theme is really about. In his opening verse, Mark describes his
theme as concerning 'the good news of Jesus Christ the Son of
God'. Here at last the title 'Son of God' is expanded as the second
Adam is set so clearly alongside the first Adam, the Son of God
whose sonship was compromised by the temptation and by the
fall.

4

Mark 1:14–20

[14]Now after John was arrested, Jesus came to Galilee, proclaiming
the good news of God, [15]and saying, 'The time is fulfilled, and the
kingdom of God has come near; repent, and believe in the good
news.'

[16]As Jesus passed along the Sea of Galilee, he saw Simon and
his brother Andrew casting a net into the sea – for they were fishermen. [17]And Jesus said to them, 'Follow me and I will make you
fish for people.' [18]And immediately they left their nets and followed him. [19]As he went a little farther, he saw James son of

Zebedee and his brother John, who were in their boat mending the nets. [20]Immediately he called them; and they left their father Zebedee in the boat with the hired men, and followed him.

Context

Mark sets the beginning of Jesus' ministry in the clear context of John's arrest. This prefigures the fate awaiting Jesus himself. Then Jesus' very first action is the call of his disciples. Mark is the gospel about the creation of a new people of God.

Sensing

Come with me to the edge of the Sea of Galilee. See the blue clear water. Hear the noisy chatter of men at work. Sniff the smell of fish in the air. Taste the fish in the atmosphere. Put your foot into the sea and feel the warm wet water soak between your toes. You have come to the busy heart of the Galilean fishing industry.

Come with me to the edge of the Sea of Galilee and look out across the blue clear water until you spy a little way from the shore a busy fishing boat. Two men are casting a net into the sea. Look into their faces and see the family likeness. As sure as anything, they are sons of the same mother and father.

Now see the wandering preacher call out to these two casters of nets. Hear the urgency in his voice. Hear the strange, haunting, magnetic appeal. Listen to the strange invitation and to the even stranger promise. 'Follow me and I will make you fish for people.'

Now the nets are abandoned and the boat is left. Now the wandering preacher has two followers.

Come with me to the edge of the Sea of Galilee and look out across the blue clear water until you spy a little way from the shore another busy fishing boat. Two men are busy mending their nets. Look into their faces and see the family likeness. As sure as anything, they are sons of the same mother and father.

Now see the wandering preacher call out to these two menders of nets. Hear the same urgency in his voice. Hear the same strange, haunting, magnetic appeal.

Now see a second set of nets abandoned, a second boat left dry on the shore. Now the wandering preacher has four followers.

Intuition

The central theme at the beginning of Jesus' ministry is the call of the first disciples. The idea of call or vocation remains at the heart of the Christian gospel. What does the idea of call mean to you?

Look back over your own experiences. Have you been aware of a call from God, and in what form has such a call been expressed? Perhaps very few Christians claim to hear the divine voice call their names and speak out their future direction. But perhaps the call comes in other ways, in ways more diverse and more subtle?

Why, for example, are you a follower of Jesus today? Did you seek him out and hunt him down? Or did he seek you out and prompt the initial stirrings of your religious quest?

Can you, for example, point to a major encounter which proved decisive in your pilgrimage of life? Did Jesus rock your boat and suddenly challenge you to follow him? Or has your experience been less dramatic than that? Can you point to a growing certainty or just to a developing inevitability of it all? Once Jesus begins to pull the heart strings or pushes on the rudder of your life, it may be incredibly difficult to get away or to ignore the steer.

Or how aware are you of that call today? Are you in a mood to be responsive to the promptings of the Lord? Are you willing to let certain things go and to leave certain things behind? Are you willing to become a new person in the service of the Lord? Or do you prefer to stay put, to hold fast, and to hope that the call will go away?

And what about the so-called vocation to ministry? Is the call to holy orders of any different order from the call to be lay? What do you make of the peculiar role of the ministry of word and sacrament among the people of God? And what if the voice of the Lord is calling you to share in that ministry?

Feeling

Put yourself into one of those two fishing boats and try to see how things felt for the men inside. Become Peter, Andrew, James or John and identify with their feelings. On the outside they are ordinary folk doing an ordinary job. On the outside they are simple fishermen. On the inside, however, they are sophisticated and complex individuals. We shall, of course, never know what was going on in their lives on that eventful day. But we can imagine and feel.

We can imagine and feel their personal anxieties and concerns. The catch had not been good. The nets were wearing thin. The mortgage on the boat was overdue. The aged father was infirm. The mother-in-law was sick. We can imagine and feel their personal hopes and plans. A new style of net will increase the yield. Father's retirement will provide the opportunity to try new techniques. Their own boys are nearly ripe for joining the family business.

On the outside they make a simple, positive and direct decision. On the outside they simply abandon the past and set sights on a new future. On the inside, however, they are human beings wrestling with enormous decisions and accepting huge consequences. We shall, of course, never know what was going on in their minds on that eventful day. But we can imagine and feel.

We can imagine and feel the wrench in leaving behind a well-known and well-established way of life. We can imagine and feel the insecurity generated by abandoning a well-tried trade and regular income. We can imagine and feel the sense of loss as the boat is abandoned to the shore.

But more than this, we need to imagine and feel the implications for those left behind. We can imagine and feel the impact of the young fishermen's decisions on the ageing parents, as their own security and old age was being eroded. Even Simon's mother-in-law must have been disadvantaged by Simon's abrupt departure. We can imagine and feel the impact of the young fishermen's decisions on their wives and children.

And we must ask just how responsible Jesus was being in disrupting family life so violently.

Thinking

The key question for the theologian concerned with gospel studies is this. Why did Mark choose to open his gospel narrative with the account of the call of four disciples, rather than by relating some of the words of teaching or the acts of healing which would logically lead to people wishing to follow him?

The answer is that this opening call set the *structure* for what is to follow. Mark's primary interest is in showing how Jesus constructed around him a new Israel, a new people of God. The clue is given by the way in which the call of the first four followers (Peter, Andrew, James and John) is followed by the call of a fifth follower (Levi). Then there is a general commissioning of the twelve special disciples. The twelve are named and Levi is dropped from the list. The same thing, you see, so often happens in the Old Testament when the twelve tribes of Israel are named. There, too, Levi is often dropped from the list and the number twelve is kept alive by counting separately the two sons of Joseph, namely Ephraim and Manasseh. Mark's intention is clear.

For Mark, the words of teaching and the acts of healing are not there to attract the twelve followers, but to equip them. The teaching and the healing are the object lessons from which they are to learn. Then having learnt, they themselves are sent out to teach and to heal, the very activities which bear witness to the fact that the kingdom of God has come near. Where God reigns, the words of the kingdom and the new life of the kingdom are free for all to receive.

For Mark, therefore, the call of the first disciples is, indeed, the proper opening act for the Jesus who comes proclaiming, 'The time is fulfilled, and the kingdom of God has come near.'

5

Mark 1:21–28

²¹They went to Capernaum; and when the sabbath came, he entered the synagogue and taught. ²²They were astounded at his teaching, for he taught them as one having authority, and not as the scribes. ²³Just then there was in their synagogue a man with an unclean spirit, ²⁴and he cried out, 'What have you to do with us, Jesus of Nazareth? Have you come to destroy us? I know who you are, the Holy One of God.' ²⁵But Jesus rebuked him, saying, 'Be silent, and come out of him!' ²⁶And the unclean spirit, convulsing him and crying with a loud voice, came out of him. ²⁷They were all amazed, and they kept on asking one another, 'What is this? A new teaching – with authority! He commands even the unclean spirits, and they obey him.' ²⁸At once his fame began to spread throughout the surrounding region of Galilee.

Context

Immediately after the call of the first four disciples, Mark presents a sequence of four major healings: a man with an unclean spirit, Simon's mother-in-law who had a fever, a leper, and a paralysed man. Two motifs permeate these stories: Jesus wishes to keep his identity secret. The healings generate controversies with the Jewish authorities.

Sensing

It is a holy day and you are in a holy place. The day is Saturday, the Jewish Sabbath; the place is the synagogue, the Jewish place of meeting. See the men at prayer. Sense the holiness in the air.

The holy day is a time for convention. You know what you can do and what you cannot do on the Sabbath. The holy site is a place for convention. You know what you can expect and what you cannot expect in the synagogue. Sense the security of living with the conventional, of not having to face the unexpected.

Then see an unexpected face occupy the teacher's chair. Hear an unexpected voice fill the auditorium. Listen to an unfamiliar message fill the air. Sense the atmosphere change as the expectations of the congregations are at one and the same time shattered, transformed and re-made. Hear them exclaim, 'What is this? A new teaching – with authority!'

Then see a familiar face within the congregation step into prominence and take on an unwelcome and unwanted role. The unpredictable, unbalanced, unstable madman, so familiar within the congregation, rises to his feet and acknowledges the divine authority of the unfamiliar teacher. Sense the atmosphere change as the worst fears of the congregation are realized and the full powers of madness erupt within their very synagogue.

Then watch the encounter between the teacher with authority and the man with an unclean spirit. See the man convulsed. Listen to the loud cries. Witness the unclean spirit exorcised. Sense the atmosphere change as the drama subsides and as the congregation experiences wholeness and holiness restored. Hear them exclaim, 'What is this? A new teaching – with authority! He commands even the unclean spirits and they obey him.'

Intuition

The main issue raised by the narrative concerns possession. What does possession mean to you? The person who is possessed is not in charge of his or her own destiny. So how can possession be explained to a generation unused to speaking in terms of a transcendent world of demonic powers? What are the new myths generated by a secular age to account for this fundamental human experience of not being in charge of one's own destiny?

A perspective informed by depth psychology will speak in terms of the incalculable power of the deep unconscious controlling and ruling our conscious lives. Debilitating fears and uncontrollable neuroses all take their power from that psychological realm. Can a Jesus who freed first-century men and women (who believed in unclean spirits) from the domination of demonic powers, equally free twentieth-century men and women from the crippling influence of the deep unconscious in which they place their belief?

A perspective informed by sociological analysis will speak in terms of the incalculable power of social conditioning controlling and ruling our conscious lives. Anti-social behaviours and uncontrollable criminal pathologies all take their power from that sociological realm. Can a Jesus who freed first-century men and women (who believed in unclean spirits) from the domination of their demonic power, equally free twentieth-century men and women from the crippling power of social conditioning in which they place their belief?

And how do you account for those aspects of your own lives which seem so often out of your control? And how open are you to inviting Jesus to sort out the mess, irrespective of the nature of the myth through which you choose to account for the situation in which you find yourself placed?

Feeling

One character holds the centre stage of the story. Try to experience and feel the narrative through his eyes. Try to get inside the five stages of his very personal experience.

The first stage is a stage of sickness, disease and unrest. Here is a person whose life is out of control, who is possessed by an unclean spirit, whose personal trauma is exacerbated by the social disdain which his condition attracts.

The second stage is a stage of insight, perception and recognition. Here is a person who looks Jesus in the eye and recognizes Jesus for who he is, whose insight confronts him with the awful realization that Jesus has the power to transform his existence, to heal or to destroy.

The third stage is the stage of confession, acknowledgement and proclamation. Here is a person who is willing to claim as his own the saving grace of God. Here is a person who is not ashamed to shout aloud, 'I know who you are, the Holy One of God.'

The fourth stage is the stage of healing pain, anguish and torment. Before the future can be established the past has to be acknowledged and healed. Here is a person who is convulsed and torn by the very process of healing, who has to experience the depths of pain before embracing the joys of wholeness restored.

The fifth stage is the stage of restoration, healing and salvation. Here is a person who is able to accept the offer of a new beginning held out in Jesus' open hand, who walks away renewed and restored.

One character holds the centre stage of the story. Try to experience and feel the narrative through his eyes. His experience is crucial to the development of the whole gospel narrative, but nobody even thought to record his name. Reflect on how often the gospel is furthered in today's world by the unsung and unnamed saints of God.

Thinking

At this very early point in his gospel narrative, Mark introduces one of his key sub-texts.

This sub-text has been labelled by gospel critics as the *Messianic secret*.

Right from the beginning Mark is concerned to show that the world of men and women failed to recognize Jesus' true identity. Not until chapter 8, at Caesarea Philippi, does one of the disciples, Peter, make the open proclamation of recognition, 'You are the Messiah.'

Nonetheless, while men and women fail to recognize Jesus' true identity, this cannot be concealed from the insightful powers of the world of spirits and of demons. Here in this opening passage of the gospel, the man with an unclean spirit sees right to the heart of the matter and anticipates Peter's much later and more stuttering confession. 'I know who you are,' says the man with the unclean spirit, 'you are the Holy One of God.'

Such public recognition, however, runs counter to Jesus' own intentions. Jesus rebukes the man, saying, 'Be silent.' This command to silence becomes a familiar motif in the following chapters. In spite of the command to silence, however, the passage ends with the telling phrase, 'At once his fame began to spread throughout the surrounding region of Galilee.'

Mark's consistent emphasis on the Messianic secret helps to explain right from the opening chapter of his gospel why it is that this Jesus (proclaimed by the early church to be raised from the dead, the Christ, the Son of God) was not properly recognized during his lifetime and how it came about that the Messiah was rejected and sent to crucifixion by God's chosen people.

Mark, the skilled craftsman of narrative, has this key problem in mind as soon as he picks up his pen to write.

6

Mark 1:29–39

[29] As soon as they left the synagogue, they entered the house of Simon and Andrew, with James and John. [30] Now Simon's mother-in-law was in bed with a fever, and they told him about her at once. [31] He came and took her by the hand and lifted her up. Then the fever left her, and she began to serve them.

[32] That evening, at sundown, they brought to him all who were sick or possessed with demons. [33] And the whole city was gathered around the door. [34] And he cured many who were sick with various diseases, and cast out many demons; and he would not permit the demons to speak, because they knew him.

[35] In the morning, while it was still very dark, he got up and went out to a deserted place, and there he prayed. [36] And Simon and his companions hunted for him. [37] When they found him, they said to him, 'Everyone is searching for you.' [38] He answered, 'Let us go on to the neighbouring towns, so that I may proclaim the message there also; for that is what I came out to do.' [39] And he went throughout Galilee, proclaiming the message in their synagogues and casting out demons.

Context

According to Mark, Jesus' ministry begins with the call of the first
four disciples, Peter and Andrew, James and John. These callings
are followed by acts of healing. First, Jesus heals the man in the
synagogue. He was possessed. Then Jesus heals Simon's mother-
in-law. She had a fever.

Sensing

It is not a long walk, out from the synagogue, along the dusty
street, to the house, but it is long enough. Simon and Andrew
walk in as though they own the place. Well, actually they do own
it. James and John walk in like familiar welcome guests. Well,
actually they are regular visitors to the household. Jesus is there,
too. And you slip in, almost unnoticed.

Look round the room and pick up the signs. It is clearly a
family home. Three generations are living side by side. But it is
a working home as well, the headquarters for a small family
business. There are nets in the yard and the smell of yesterday's
fish still hangs heavily in the air.

Look round the room and pick up the vibes. It is clearly a home
in turmoil. The two brothers have suddenly caught religion. Hear
them chattering about their new-found purpose for living. They
are planning to abandon their boats and to forsake their family
way of life. Now they are planning to hang up their nets and to go
fishing for the souls of men and women.

Look round the room and tune in to the atmosphere. The
matriarch of the house has taken to her bed. Her temperature is
high, her face is flushed, her hands are moist. She is running a
fever. An anxious hush surrounds her fevered presence. Her
daughter dances dutiful attention. Her son-in-law assesses the
seriousness of the situation.

Then see Jesus cross the room, with a quiet deliberate step. See
Jesus stoop to look the matriarch in the eye, to take her hand, and
to lift her up, renewed as from the grave. See the fever exit by the
door. And see the woman transformed from invalid to hostess.

It is not a long walk from the bed of sickness to the kitchen of
hospitality.

Intuition

Well, I wonder what was *really* wrong with Simon's mother-in-law? What kind of fever is it that clears up so quickly? What kind of physician is this Jesus who heals by taking his patient by the hand?

Do you sense just the slightest hint that something psychosomatic may have been afoot? So what do you make of that complex relationship between mind and body, body and soul?

I wonder how much of the illness we see around us today can really be traced to psychological or to spiritual causes? What physical symptoms can be put down to anxiety or to stress? What physical symptoms can be put down to spiritual rootlessness or to spiritual restlessness?

Or, if you dare run the risk of posing the question, when do you become aware of psychological or spiritual roots of physical symptoms in your own body, things like sleeplessness, indigestion, aches and pains?

And what do you do about such symptoms? Do you treat them as if they were purely physical and hope that a physical cure will heal a psychological distress or heal a spiritual malaise? Do you succumb to the view that somehow the physical is real and to be taken seriously, while the psychological and the spiritual are somehow less real and to be taken less seriously?

And what do you learn from Jesus' own example in his ministry of healing to psychosomatic disease? Does Jesus not take seriously the situation that is presented? Is there any hint of either criticism or rebuke? Surely the hand of affirmation is simply extended and the sick soul affirmed.

So how can we, as the hands of Jesus in today's world, extend his healing touch to those whose bodies rebel under psychological pressure or under spiritual unrest?

Feeling

Here is a tale of family life. Try to see it through the eyes of the woman whom Mark excluded from the tale. Grasp how things feel from the daughter's perspective, from the perspective of Simon's wife. Put yourself in the unenviable place of the woman caught between mother and husband. Feel that conflict in her soul.

The daughter's loyalty to her mother is deep and true. It is hard to forget the sacrifices mother made in bringing up her family. After all, times were bad and life was hard for the wife of the Galilean fisherman. Once the daughter was totally dependent on the mother. But now the tables are turned. Late, late in life, the mother is now totally dependent on the daughter. Once her husband brought home the fish, but now the home economy is supported by her daughter's husband.

How can a daughter loyal to her mother's needs see her way of life, her very security threatened by a radical change in the home economy? How can a daughter but sympathize with a mother who retreats to bed in protest or confusion?

The wife's loyalty to her husband is deep and true as well. It is hard to forget the deep-felt love and tenderness which first attracted her to the young fisherman. After all, there had been many fish in the local sea. But the choice had been made and there had been, until now, little reason to regret it. Simon had supported her and her mother, too, through days when fish were plentiful and through days when fish were scarce.

How can a wife loyal to her husband's needs stand in the way, when he hears and responds to the call of God? How can a wife but understand when her husband takes time out to build the kingdom of God?

Here, then, is a tale of family life. Try to see it through the eyes of the woman whom Mark excluded from the tale. Put yourself in the unenviable place of the woman caught between mother and husband. Empathize with the deep conflict in her soul.

Thinking

An issue of church discipline is raised by this ancient story. The issue concerns the relationship between the call to ministry and the demands of family life. Within some denominations the call to priestly ministry is seen as involving a simultaneous call to the life of celibacy.

Had Jesus just given the matter a little more careful thought, would he perhaps never have called the married man, Simon, away from his nets and recruited him as a frontline disciple? Had Jesus just given the matter a little more careful thought, would he perhaps only have called single men to fish souls for the kingdom?

Within other denominations, a married priesthood or a married pastorate is seen as the right and proper identification with the true and real human condition. After all, it is argued, how can ministers really identify with the majority of men and women if they, too, are not fully exposed to the joys and frustrations of family life?

But denominations which encourage (and often expect) a married priesthood must also learn to recognize the growing conflicts between the demands of ministry in a changing church and the demands of family life in a changing world. Denominations which encourage (and often expect) clergy to work from home must also learn to recognize the growing conflicts between the professional expectations of the workplace and the family expectations of the home.

7

Mark 1:40–45

[40]A leper came to him begging him, and kneeling he said to him, 'If you choose, you can make me clean.' [41]Moved with pity, Jesus stretched out his hand and touched him, and said to him, 'I do choose. Be made clean!' [42]Immediately the leprosy left him, and he was made clean. [43]After sternly warning him he sent him away at once, [44]saying to him, 'See that you say nothing to anyone; but go, show yourself to the priest, and offer for your cleansing what Moses commanded, as a testimony to them.' [45]But he went out and began to proclaim it freely, and to spread the word, so that Jesus could no longer go into a town openly, but stayed out in the country; and people came to him from every quarter.

Context
Mark's gospel opens with Jesus calling four disciples (Peter and Andrew, James and John) and performing four major acts of healing. This, the third healing, concerns a leper man.

Sensing
Awake from slumber and find yourself transported back in time, back, back to first-century Palestine. You are travelling the dusty

road on a warm, warm day. Feel the sun beating down on the back of your neck, taste the dust from the road in the back of your throat, smell the parched atmosphere at the back of your nostrils, and see the scorching road running into the distance, peopled with fellow-travellers.

Out there, in the middle of nowhere, your ears prick up and catch a distant sound. You recognize the harsh croak of an untuned voice. You hear an indistinct, but distraught cry. Approaching you along the road is the well-known figure of the leper man.

As the leper man approaches, you see the disfigured unkempt figure. The awful disease has eaten away at self-respect. As the leper man approaches, you hear the distraught cry, 'Unclean, unclean.' The awful disease has eaten away at social relationships and distanced all uncontaminated human contact.

See your fellow-travellers avert their eyes and divert their path. Each traveller, in turn, avoids the leper man and reinforces his sense of loneliness, isolation and distance from the human race.

But there, in the crowd, is a fellow-traveller who disobeys the rules and runs in the face of convention. See Jesus of Nazareth stretch out his hand to touch the leper man who is himself untouchable. Hear the gasp of surprise, the gasp of incredulity, the gasp of horror, as Jesus makes himself unclean by such intimate contact with the leper man, whose disease is so readily communicable, physically, socially and ritually.

See Jesus take up the leper man's cry and shout out his own pollution. See the leper man lay down his leprosy, peel away his disfigurement, slough off his social isolation, and make his way to the priest to proclaim the cleansing and rehabilitation so freely offered.

You have been transported back in time, back, back to first-century Palestine.

Intuition

In the ancient world leprosy was as much a crippling social disease as a crippling disease of the body. The leper was a social outcast. See Jesus' reaction as he embraces the outcast and becomes an outcast himself. Now, in the place of the leper, see the outcasts in today's society, and consider how the hand of Jesus can be stretched out to embrace them.

See the anxious face of the nine year old in the school

playground, the persistent victim of bullying. Ask how the hand of Jesus can be stretched out to restore the battered self-esteem.

See the haunted face of the adolescent trapped in growing substance dependency, avoiding the interrogation of family, friends and the law. Ask how the hand of Jesus can be stretched out to restore the lost autonomy.

See the weary face of the single parent struggling to survive on ever-decreasing benefit, unable to afford life's social pleasures. Ask how the hand of Jesus can be stretched out to restore the lost self-confidence.

See the unshaven face of the middle-aged man grappling with the loss of employment and with the recognition that he is now unlikely to be re-employable. Ask how the hand of Jesus can be stretched out to restore the loss of self-respect.

See the greying face of the ageing widow trapped within the home she can no longer properly maintain, increasingly forgotten by family and friends. Ask how the hand of Jesus can be stretched out to restore the lost peace of mind.

See Jesus embrace the outcast leper man and carry the cost of becoming a social outcast himself.

Feeling

Awake from slumber and find yourself standing in Jesus' shoes as the leper man approaches. Find your own soul torn apart by the range of emotions which plucked at Jesus' own loving heart. In the course of such a short space of time four distinct emotions emerge.

All the ancient texts of Mark are clear that Jesus was *moved* by the sight of the leper man, *moved* by his plaintive plea for help, *moved* by his humble act of kneeling. The translations of scripture which say that Jesus was moved with pity, however, do less than justice to the ancient manuscripts and to Mark's own insight into the loving heart of Jesus.

A preferred reading of the ancient manuscripts says that Jesus was moved first with anger, not with pity. What loving heart could feel anything other than anger at the way in which God's perfect creation is racked with pain and disfigured with disease? What loving heart could confront the leper man with any emotion less than anger? Step into Jesus' shoes and share his emotion of anger for creation racked with pain and disfigured with disease.

But then the anger gives way to compassion. What loving

heart could contemplate the leper man, kneeling there, trembling in hope and anticipation of life renewed and of health restored, without going out in full compassion? What loving heart would not feel compassion in such a situation? Step into Jesus' shoes and share his emotion of compassion for humanity racked by pain and disfigured by disease.

But then the compassion gives way to resolution. The leper man has been healed and Jesus must shape his ministry elsewhere. What loving heart could rest content with one act of mercy and not plan for tomorrow's ministry? With resolution Jesus pushes the man away (again the Greek verb is harsh). With resolution Jesus commands the man to silence. With resolution Jesus is intent that the law of Moses should be observed. Step into Jesus' shoes and share his emotion of resolution.

But then the resolution gives way to frustration. The rumour that Jesus has touched the leper man spreads far and wide. For some, Jesus himself was now unclean. So they banished him from their company. For some, Jesus himself was now the source of all cleansing. So they sought out his company. On both accounts, Jesus could no longer go into a town openly. Step into Jesus' shoes and share his emotion of frustration.

Find yourself standing in Jesus' shoes as the leper man departs.

Thinking

The leper man's conversation with Jesus poses one of the hardest sets of questions confronting the Christian faith. The leper man attributes to Jesus the power of choice. 'If you choose,' says the leper man, 'you can make me clean.' According to the story, Jesus exercises the power of choice. According to the story, Jesus chooses to make the leper man clean and the leper man is cleansed.

The Christian tradition is, of course, committed to a personal view of God. Christians speak of a dynamic and living personal relationship with their God. And any model of personal relationship depends on give and take on each side. Any model of personal relationship presupposes freedom and choice. 'If you choose,' says the leper man, 'you can make me clean.'

But what kind of Jesus does the leper man have in mind, when he makes this request? Can he imagine a Jesus who has the capability of cleansing him, but who would choose not to do so?

The picture of Jesus listening to the leper man's petition and acceding to the request reinforces the gospel message of a powerful and benevolent God. But, if this picture holds true, the obverse must also hold true. The picture of Jesus listening to the leper man's petition and not acceding to the request establishes a message of a God who is either unpowerful or malevolent.

In the case of the Marcan leper man, the issue is purely academic. The choice was made and the leper man was healed. But what of the countless lepers throughout the ages who have voiced the same petition, but who have not experienced the same response?

The leper man's conversation with Jesus poses one of the hardest sets of questions confronting the Christian faith.

8

Mark 2:1–12

[1]When he returned to Capernaum after some days, it was reported that he was at home. [2]So many gathered around that there was no longer room for them, not even in front of the door; and he was speaking the word to them. [3]Then some people came, bringing to him a paralyzed man, carried by four of them. [4]And when they could not bring him to Jesus because of the crowd, they removed the roof above him; and after having dug through it, they let down the mat on which the paralytic lay. [5]When Jesus saw their faith, he said to the paralytic, 'Son, your sins are forgiven.' [6]Now some of the scribes were sitting there, questioning in their hearts, [7]'Why does this fellow speak in this way? It is blasphemy! Who can forgive sins but God alone?' [8]At once Jesus perceived in his spirit that they were discussing these questions among themselves; and he said to them, 'Why do you raise such questions in your hearts? [9]Which is easier, to say to the paralytic, "Your sins are forgiven," or to say, "Stand up and take your mat and walk"? [10]But so that you may know that the Son of Man has authority on earth to forgive sins' – he said to the paralytic – [11]'I say to you, stand up, take your mat and go to your home.' [12]And he stood up, and immediately took the mat and went out before all of them; so that they were all amazed and glorified God, saying, 'We have never seen anything like this!'

Context

This is the fourth of the healings with which Mark opens his gospel. It follows on immediately after the healing of a man with an unclean spirit, Simon's mother-in-law, and a leper. The act of healing leads to controversy with the scribes.

Sensing

You are a practical matter-of-fact sort of person, and you do not let obstacles stand in your way. Relive the way in which you solved the problem on that eventful day in Capernaum.

You will remember that you had been helping out your paralyzed friend, as you so often do. There he is stuck on that couch all day. He can hardly move, poor fellow. You had done some shopping for him, and helped to tidy up the house.

All that talk about Jesus of Nazareth was still fresh and buzzing around in your head. They said that recently Jesus had cured a man of demonic possession, had healed a woman of a fever, and had cleansed a leper. Your friend was none too convinced by that rumour, but you were determined to give it all a try. You find three other able-bodied men game to put the healer to the test. Together you take it in turns to carry your paralyzed friend to the house where Jesus was thought to be.

Picture the sight of the crowd thronging the little house. Sense the despair as you realize that you are never going to enter through that door. You are a practical matter-of-fact sort of person, and you do not let obstacles stand in your way.

Feel the excitement as you and the able-bodied men carry your paralyzed friend to the back of the house. Feel the exertion as you hoist him on to the flat roof. Feel the determination as you dig your way through to the room below. See the astonished faces look up as the roof is uncovered before their very eyes. Hear the astonished exclamations as the paralyzed man is lowered gently to the floor at Jesus' feet. Feel the electric atmosphere as Jesus commands the man to stand up and to walk. Be conscious of your accelerated heartbeat as he walks away, paralyzed no more.

You are a practical matter-of-fact sort of person, and you do not let obstacles stand in your way. Relive that eventful day in Capernaum when you brought your paralyzed friend to the Lord.

Intuition

Here is a story about four people who brought their friend to Jesus. They were unaffected by the encounter themselves, but their friend's life was changed. So where does that leave you and me?

We, too, are called to bring others to Jesus. It is often not an easy task when we are working in isolation, one by one. Just one of the friends would never have got the paralyzed man as far as the threshold. Four of them together raised him to the rooftop and delivered him at the feet of Jesus. Collaborative ministry may achieve what individual ministry fails to do.

We, too, are called to bring others to Jesus. It is often no easy task to bundle our candidates onto a stretcher and to lug them lock, stock and barrel into the presence of Jesus. But we can, at least, begin by carrying them to the Lord day by day in prayer. And this may be more effective than carrying them to the rooftop of the church. The ministry of prayer may achieve what the ambulance ministry fails to do.

We, too, are called to bring others to Jesus. But note carefully, our calling stops right there. The real work takes place face to face, between Jesus and the candidate. We cannot negotiate healing and salvation on their behalf. In the story, the paralyzed man takes responsibility for his own condition. He stood on his own two feet and accepted the gift of mobility.

We, too, are called to bring others to Jesus, but we must always be willing to do so for their benefit and not for our own. In the story, when the healing was complete, the four men vanished from the narrative, thanked neither by Jesus nor by the man who had been healed. They had performed their task and were happy to return to their home. Only hope that they had the courtesy to repair the roof before they left.

Here is a story about four people who brought their friend to Jesus. Pray that we may continue to do the same.

Feeling

Here is a story of human compassion. Lie down on the stretcher and see things through the eyes of the paralyzed man.

Begin by absorbing the feelings of impotence, powerlessness, helplessness, as another long day of immobility stretches out from dawn to sunset. Share in that pain of paralysis.

Absorb the feeling of cynicism, hopelessness and apathy, as tales reach your ears of a demoniac exorcized, of a fever miraculously cured, of a leper spontaneously cleansed. Share in that disbelief of despair.

Absorb the feelings of passivity, acceptance and resignation, as your four able-bodied friends trundle you through the dusty streets to the door of the peripatetic preacher. Share in that surrender of self-determination.

Absorb the feelings of uncertainty, insecurity and anxiety, as you find yourself hustled on to the rooftop and surrounded by the debris of the disintegrating roof. Share in that inner turbulence of anticipation.

Absorb the feelings of self-consciousness, embarrassment and unwelcome disclosure, as you are lowered shamelessly into the midst of the party below. Share in that public humiliation of exposure.

Absorb the feelings of curiosity, inquisitiveness and questioning, as Jesus fixes his eyes on your eyes, and pronounces the unforgettable words, 'Son, your sins are forgiven.' Share in that mixture of uncertainty and acceptance.

Absorb the feelings of release, restoration and wholeness as the legs strengthen and as the body finds renewed mobility. Share in those feelings of forgiveness and of life restored.

Here is a story of human compassion. Pick up your stretcher and see things through the eyes of the forgiven and healed man.

Thinking

This story raises two issues of particular theological interest. The first issue concerns the relationship between sickness and sin. The second concerns the conflict encountered by Jesus' healing ministry.

As it stands the story clearly implies that Jesus shared the current belief of his age that illness is caused by the sufferer's sin. The paralyzed man is presented for physical healing, but Jesus responds by pronouncing the forgiveness of sins.

Elsewhere in the gospels, however, Jesus is portrayed as holding a very different attitude toward the relationship between sickness and sin. According to Luke 13:1–5, Jesus overtly challenges the belief of his age:

Do you imagine that, because these Galileans suffered this fate, they must have been greater sinners than anyone else in Galilee? I tell you they were not.

According to John 9:2–3, Jesus firmly contradicts the view that the blind man's blindness could be traced either to his own sin or to the sin of his parents.

So what do you make of the relationship between sickness and sin?

As it stands, the story clearly implies that Jesus was courting controversy with the scribes. The direct pronouncement of the forgiveness of sins is rightly and quickly challenged by the scribes. The forgiveness of sins, they say, is the prerogative of God alone, and for anyone else to make that claim is blasphemy.

Uncharacteristically, at this point Jesus counters their accusation by claiming the authority to forgive sins on earth and he does so by asserting the title *Son of man*. Elsewhere in the gospels Jesus is not represented as openly claiming this status and the right to act in virtue of it. Elsewhere Jesus does not claim the power to forgive sins by his own *fiat*. Constantly Jesus urges people to repent, so that *God* may forgive them.

So what do you make of this uncharacteristic behaviour so early in Mark's gospel?

9
Mark 2:13–22

¹³Jesus went out again beside the sea; the whole crowd gathered around him, and he taught them. ¹⁴As he was walking along, he saw Levi son of Alphaeus sitting at the tax booth, and he said to him, 'Follow me.' And he got up and followed him.

¹⁵And as he sat at dinner in Levi's house, many tax collectors and sinners were also sitting with Jesus and his disciples – for there were many who followed him. ¹⁶When the scribes of the Pharisees saw that he was eating with sinners and tax collectors, they said to his disciples, 'Why does he eat with tax collectors and sinners?'

[17]When Jesus heard this, he said to them, 'Those who are well have no need of a physician, but those who are sick; I have come to call not the righteous but sinners.'

[18]Now John's disciples and the Pharisees were fasting; and people came and said to him, 'Why do John's disciples and the disciples of the Pharisees fast, but your disciples do not fast?' [19]Jesus said to them, 'The wedding guests cannot fast while the bridegroom is with them, can they? As long as they have the bridegroom with them, they cannot fast. [20]The days will come when the bridegroom is taken away from them, and then they will fast on that day.

[21]'No one sews a piece of unshrunk cloth on an old cloak; otherwise, the patch pulls away from it, the new from the old, and a worse tear is made. [22]And no one puts new wine into old wineskins; otherwise, the wine will burst the skins, and the wine is lost, and so are the skins; but one puts new wine into fresh wineskins.'

Context

After the call of the first four disciples and after the first acts of healing, Jesus calls the fifth disciple, Levi the tax collector. This calling leads to new controversy with the scribes.

Sensing

Picture a wedding banquet that has remained particularly fixed in your memory. Picture the way in which the tables were set out: the cutlery, the glasses, the napkins, the table decorations. Picture the person who sat on your left, and the person who sat on your right. Hear the sounds of their voices and the snatches of their conversation ringing in your ears. Smell the aroma of the food in your nostrils. Taste the richness of the wine on your palate. Stretch out your hands to touch the table to make sure that it is really there.

Picture a wedding banquet that has remained particularly fixed in your memory. Look round the room and see how the event is welding together two distinct families, two separate tribes. See how people who had never eaten together before are at home in the one room, united as part of the one family. Romanticize and dream how the wedding banquet becomes a symbol for life in the kingdom of God.

Picture a wedding banquet that has remained particularly fixed in your memory and allow your imagination to run. The scene changes to first-century Palestine, and the faces of the guests begin to merge with the faces of Jesus' disciples. All sorts of people are there, likely people and unlikely people. Picture the Pharisee who sits on your left, and the tax gatherer who sits on your right. Hear the sounds of their voices and the snatches of their conversation ringing in your ears. Picture a wedding banquet that has remained particularly fixed in your memory and allow your imagination to run.

Look round the room and see Jesus presiding at the Messianic wedding feast, trying to weld together two distinct families, two separate tribes. See how people who have never eaten together before are being introduced one to another in the self-same room. See Levi and the Pharisee face-to-face. Be realistic and recognize how the tension builds. It is risky to put new wine into old wine skins. It is risky to sew unshrunken cloth on an old cloak.

Intuition

Sometimes Jesus calls the oddest of people into leadership in his church. There is really no accounting for Jesus' taste. Sometimes it all seems so irresponsible, all so unnecessary. The call of Levi is a prime example. The acceptance of a tax collector within the kingdom of God was bound to cause controversy. There are no two ways about it.

Sometimes Jesus calls the oddest of people into leadership in his church. There is really no accounting for Jesus' taste. Sometimes it all seems so irresponsible, all so unnecessary. The members of the liturgical commission are a prime example. The rewriting of the prayer book in contemporary language was bound to cause controversy. There are no two ways about it.

Sometimes Jesus calls the oddest of people into leadership in his church. There is really no accounting for Jesus' taste. Sometimes it all seems so irresponsible, all so unnecessary. The call of women to be licensed lay workers, deaconesses, deacons, priests and now bishops is a prime example. The acceptance of women into ministry was bound to cause controversy. There are no two ways about it.

Sometimes Jesus calls the oddest of people into leadership in his church. There is really no accounting for Jesus' taste. Sometimes it all seems so irresponsible, all so unnecessary. The people who campaign for the remarriage of divorced people in church and for the acceptance of divorced and remarried clergy are a prime example. The acceptance of people who make a new beginning in their lives was bound to cause controversy. There are no two ways about it.

Sometimes Jesus calls the oddest of people into leadership in his church. There is really no accounting for Jesus' taste. Sometimes it all seems so irresponsible, all so unnecessary. The people who make a place for lesbians and homosexuals within the church and believe that lesbians and homosexuals can have a place in the ordained ministry are a prime example. The acceptance of people with a different sexual orientation is bound to cause controversy. There are no two ways about it.

After all, religion is the most conservative of institutions and change is never taken lightly. It is risky to put new wine into old wine skins. It is risky to sew unshrunken cloth on an old cloak.

Feeling

Living through times of change is no easy matter, no comfortable experience. Put yourself in the Pharisees' robes and look at things through their eyes.

I wonder how Jesus looked to the Pharisees as he sat down to eat with tax collectors and sinners. In that environment there could be no guarantee that the religious dietary laws were being observed. There was no guarantee that Jesus would not himself become contaminated through the company which he kept. Perhaps it was Jesus' best interests which the Pharisees had at heart. It cannot be easy being old wine skins, when new wine is around.

I wonder how Levi looked to the Pharisees as he sat at the tax booth. With a name like that he was clearly a good Jewish son, but with an occupation like that he had clearly turned traitor, working for the occupying Roman forces. As yet there was no evidence that Levi had turned his back on his chosen way of life. Perhaps it was Levi's best interests which the Pharisees had at heart. It cannot be easy being old wine skins, when new wine is around.

I wonder how Jesus' disciples looked to the Pharisees as they failed to observe the religious fasts. As John's disciples clearly showed, new religious fervour need not necessarily detract from strict religious observance. There was no evidence that it was yet too late for Jesus' disciples to learn from the example of John's disciples. Perhaps it was Jesus' disciples' best interests which the Pharisees had at heart. It cannot be easy being old wine skins, when new wine is around.

Living through times of change is no easy matter, no comfortable experience. Put yourself in the Pharisees' robes and look at things through their eyes.

Thinking

One of the major puzzles of this passage concerns the identity of Levi himself. Here Levi appears to be called as a disciple but, later on, in chapter 3 when the twelve are appointed, Levi's name is dropped from the roll call. So what do you make of that?

Perhaps Mark is not intending to imply from this narrative that Levi had really been called as one of the key disciples. But this view is difficult to sustain, because the story of the call of Levi so perfectly matches the earlier stories of the calls of Peter and Andrew, and of James and John. If those four are core to the team of disciples, surely Levi must be as well?

Perhaps Mark had failed to record that this new disciple is really known by two different names. Here in chapter 2, Mark speaks of Levi as the son of Alphaeus. In the roll call of the twelve in chapter 3, Mark lists the name of James as the son of Alphaeus. So do we have here another example of a pair of brothers called into discipleship, just like Peter and his brother Andrew, or John and his brother James? Or is this a case of one man being known by two names, like Simon Peter. Some early copyists of Mark solved the problem by replacing Levi's name with that of James. Had those copyists got it right?

Or perhaps Mark had confused the name of Levi with one of the other twelve disciples. When Matthew the gospel-writer records the names of the twelve disciples in his gospel, he slips in the description of Matthew as a tax collector. When Matthew the gospel writer retells Mark's story of the call of Levi, he changes the name to Matthew. Had Matthew the gospel writer got it right?

Or is Mark really making the point that Jesus was following the precedent of the Old Testament, by calling the tribe of Levi in a distinctive way and by sometimes omitting the name from the tribal list, as was made so explicit in Numbers chapter 2? Had Mark got it right after all?

So what do you make of the identity of Levi himself?

Mark 2:23—3:6

[23]One sabbath he was going through the grainfields; and as they made their way his disciples began to pluck heads of grain. [24]The Pharisees said to him, 'Look, why are they doing what is not lawful on the sabbath?' [25]And he said to them, 'Have you never read what David did when he and his companions were hungry and in need of food? [26]He entered the house of God, when Abiathar was high priest, and ate the bread of the Presence, which it is not lawful for any but the priests to eat, and he gave some to his companions.' [27]Then he said to them, 'The sabbath was made for humankind, and not humankind for the sabbath; [28]so the Son of Man is lord even of the sabbath.'

[3:1]Again he entered the synagogue, and a man was there who had a withered hand. [2]They watched him to see whether he would cure him on the sabbath, so that they might accuse him. [3]And he said to the man who had the withered hand, 'Come forward.' [4]Then he said to them, 'Is it lawful to do good or to do harm on the sabbath, to save life or to kill?' But they were silent. [5]He looked around at them with anger; he was grieved at their hardness of heart and said to the man, 'Stretch out your hand.' He stretched it out, and his hand was restored. [6]The Pharisees went out and immediately conspired with the Herodians against him, how to destroy him.

Context

Right from the start, Mark's gospel shows the ministry of Jesus generating conflict with the scribes and the Pharisees. Already there has been conflict over Jesus' pronouncement of the forgiveness of sins, over eating with sinners and tax collectors, and over failing to observe the fasts. Now the controversy is over Jesus' attitude toward the Sabbath.

Sensing

Think of the days of the week laid out before you like cards on the table. Now picture each day as a distinctive colour in its own right. What colour do you see Monday? What colour do you see Tuesday? What colour do you see Wednesday? What colour do you see Thursday? What colour do you see Friday? What colour do you see Saturday? What colour do you see Sunday?

So, then, where does Sunday really stand in that array of colours? Do you see Sunday as a bright and positive colour, or as a dull and negative colour? And what is it that colours your attitude towards Sunday?

In your view, is Sunday a bright colour because it means a day off work? Is Sunday a bright colour because, when you go to work, it means double time, or at least time and a half? Is Sunday a bright colour because it means time with the family, or time to get on doing what you want to do? Is Sunday a bright colour because it means less bustle in the city and fewer heavy lorries trundling through the village lanes? Is Sunday a bright colour because it means going to church?

Does your God deserve a bright colour for Sunday? Or in your view, is Sunday a dull colour, because it is a day off work with nothing much to do? Is Sunday a dull colour because you are stuck on your own, or stuck with your family? Is Sunday a dull colour because the banks are shut and the offices and businesses you want to use are closed? Is Sunday a dull colour because the main sporting fixtures are still concentrated on Saturday? Is Sunday a dull colour because it means going to church?

Does your God deserve a dull colour for Sunday?

So where does Sunday really stand in that array of colours, and if you could paint Sunday the way you really wanted it to be, what colour, then, would you choose?

Intuition

The Pharisees were running a campaign to keep the Sabbath special. Jesus fell foul of the way they thought the Sabbath should really be kept. Their campaign to keep the Sabbath special required people to desist from plucking corn. Their campaign to keep the Sabbath special required people to desist from non-emergency healings.

Now, if you could rewrite Sundays the way you would want them to be, where would you draw the line? What provision would you like there to be? Would you keep the hospitals running just like any other day of the week, to get the best return from expensive equipment and highly developed operating theatres?

Or would you try to assign a rest day to a higher proportion of the staff?

If you could rewrite Sundays, would you keep the petrol station open to refuel your car? Would you keep the corner shop open to purchase your paper and the extra pint of milk? Or would you want the staff in these places to benefit from an extra day at home?

If you could rewrite Sundays, would you open the supermarket, the garden centre and the home improvement store, so that much of the day-to-day business could go on undisturbed? Or would you want to signal that such activities are disruptive of family life and of religious sensitivities?

If you could rewrite Sundays, would you see an opportunity for major sporting fixtures, to take the pressure off Saturday and to provide families with something to do? Or would you want to make sure that the churches were operating in a less competitive marketplace?

Now, if you could rewrite Sundays the way you would want them to be, where would you draw the line? What provision would you like there to be?

Feeling

Now see how the whole thing looks to the man with the withered hand.

It must all have seemed so strange to the man with the withered hand. The hand had been like that for years. It had been like that on weekdays; it had been like that on Sabbaths. But never before had the withered hand caused so much controversy.

It must all have seemed so strange to the man with the withered hand. Year in and year out he had longed to come face to face with a real healer who could have made that hand as good as new. But never before had he seen a real healer in that town.

It must all have seemed so strange to the man with the withered hand. Sabbath by Sabbath he had been to that synagogue and no one had as much as noticed that he was there. But today he had been the centre of all attention. The Pharisees and scribes had fixed their eyes on him from the moment he walked in through the open door. Then Jesus had called him to step forward.

It must all have seemed so strange to the man with the withered hand. He stood there on the very edge of being healed, waiting with excitement and expectation. But instead of being at the centre of miraculous healing, he stood at the heart of theological controversy.

It must all have seemed so strange to the man with the withered hand. All he heard was a simple command, 'Stretch out your hand.' All he did was to obey the command. He stretched out his hand and it was restored.

It must all have seemed so strange to the man with the withered hand. As he returned home healed and restored, he heard the whispering conspiracy of the Pharisees. They were plotting to destroy the man who had healed him.

Now see how the whole thing looks to the man with the restored hand.

Thinking

Sinister controversy is at the heart of Mark's gospel. Think through the way in which the theme of sinister controversy has been so steadily and systematically developed throughout the first two chapters. Why, then, is sinister controversy so important to Mark?

Jesus first comes proclaiming the gospel of God in chapter 1. But the context for that proclamation is set by noting that John had already been arrested. The fate of the forerunner prefigures the fate of the one whose way he had come to prepare. What is the significance of this sinister warning?

In chapter 2 Jesus offers healing to a paralyzed man with the authoritative proclamation, 'Son, your sins are forgiven.' The scribes level the accusation of blasphemy, for God alone can forgive sins. What is the significance of this sinister accusation?

Later in chapter 2 Jesus calls Levi into discipleship and sits and eats in Levi's house. When the scribes saw what was going on, they asked, 'Why does he eat with tax collectors and sinners?' What is the significance of this sinister question?

Later in chapter 2 at the time of the fast, the scribes come and ask, 'Why do John's disciples and the disciples of the Pharisees fast, but your disciples do not fast?' What is the significance of this sinister comparison?

Later in chapter 2 the Pharisees see Jesus' disciples plucking grain. 'Look,' they exclaimed, 'why are they doing what is not lawful on the Sabbath?' What is the significance of this sinister exclamation?

And now in chapter 3 the Pharisees watched to see whether Jesus would perform an act of healing on the Sabbath day. What is the significance of their sinister observation?

Sinister controversy is at the heart of Mark's gospel. For now at the beginning of chapter 3 the plot thickens and the dénouement is in sight. The Pharisees went out and conspired how to destroy Jesus.

———————➤◆◄———————

11
Mark 3:20–35

[20]and the crowd came together again, so that they could not even eat. [21]When his family heard it, they went out to restrain him, for people were saying, 'He has gone out of his mind.' [22]And the scribes who came down from Jerusalem said, 'He has Beelzebul, and by the ruler of the demons he casts out demons.' [23]And he called them to him, and spoke to them in parables, 'How can Satan cast out Satan? [24]If a kingdom is divided against itself, that kingdom cannot stand. [25]And if a house is divided against itself, that house will not be able to stand. [26]And if Satan has risen up against himself and is divided, he cannot stand, but his end has come. [27]But no one can enter a strong man's house and plunder his property without first tying up the strong man; then indeed the house can be plundered.

[28]'Truly I tell you, people will be forgiven for their sins and whatever blasphemies they utter; [29]but whoever blasphemes against the Holy Spirit can never have forgiveness, but is guilty of an eternal sin'— [30]for they had said, 'He has an unclean spirit.'

[31]Then his mother and his brothers came; and standing outside, they sent to him and called him. [32]A crowd was sitting around him; and they said to him, 'Your mother and your brothers and sisters are outside, asking for you.' [33]And he replied, 'Who are my mother and my brothers?' [34]And looking at those who sat around him, he said, 'Here are my mother and my brothers! [35]Whoever does the will of God is my brother and sister and mother.'

Context

This passage follows on immediately after Jesus had appointed the twelve disciples. According to Mark, the disciples had been appointed for two purposes: to be Jesus' companions and to be sent out by Jesus to proclaim the gospel and to drive out demons. The controversy over the power to cast out demons, which now confronts Jesus, will also confront the twelve.

Sensing

Today your curiosity has really been aroused. Here you are, part of the pressing crowd, trying to make head or tail of all that is being said about Jesus.

Today your curiosity has really been aroused. Picture yourself in the doorway to Jesus' home. See the crowd of people pressing inside the house. See the crowd of people teeming outside the house. Look into their faces and see the expectancy in their eyes.

Today your curiosity has really been aroused. Sniff the atmosphere and smell the overcrowding. It is a warm day and people are crowding everywhere. You struggle to stay in the doorway where you can see what is happening on the inside and where you can breathe the fresh air from the outside.

Today your curiosity has really been aroused. Feel the people pressing you on all sides. Feel the scribes, who have come down from Jerusalem, pressing you out of the way, so that they may have a better view. Feel the family, who live in the house, pressing you out of the way, so that they might have room to eat.

Today your curiosity has really been aroused. Hear the snippets of conversation going on all around you. Hear the family complain about Jesus, 'He has gone out of his mind!' Hear the scribes who came down from Jerusalem accuse Jesus, 'He has Beelzebul, and by the ruler of the demons he casts out demons!'

Today your curiosity has really been aroused. There you are part of the pressing crowd trying to make head or tail of all that is being said about Jesus.

Intuition

Here is a passage full of loosely connected parables. What ideas do these parables suggest in your mind?

Jesus said, 'How can Satan cast out Satan?' Think for a moment of all the ways in which we try to make the ends justify the means; the ways in which we try to achieve laudable results from dubious strategies. Can Satan really be used to cast out Satan?

Jesus said, 'If a kingdom is divided against itself, that kingdom cannot stand.' Think for a moment of all the ways in which the Church of Christ is divided against itself; the ways in which there are entrenched divisions between denominations, or even within congregations. If a kingdom is divided against itself, can that kingdom really stand?

Jesus said, 'No one can enter a strong man's house and plunder his property without first tying up the strong man.' Think for a moment of all the ways in which you need Jesus to ransack your life and think of the debris that needs to be removed. But have you given Jesus sufficient control to effect that revolution? Can anyone enter a strong man's house or plunder his property without first tying up the strong man?

Jesus said, 'Whoever does the will of God is my brother and sister and mother.' Think for a moment of what it means to be called into Jesus' close and extended family. Think of those within the community of faith whom you find most difficult to embrace as your brother and sister and mother. Must everyone who does the will of God be counted as my brother and sister and mother?

Here is a passage full of loosely connected parables. What ideas do these parables suggest in your mind?

Feeling

Here is a story of family turmoil, confusion and distress. Put yourself in Mary's shoes. What would it all have felt like to her?

Put yourself in Mary's shoes when Jesus came home with twelve new friends, all excited and high on new-found religious fervour. Wouldn't you begin to think that your Jesus had gone out of his mind?

Put yourself in Mary's shoes when the crowds pressed in and around the house, so that there was not even room enough to eat. Wouldn't you begin to think that your Jesus had gone out of his mind?

Put yourself in Mary's shoes when rumour came home that Jesus had embraced the leper man and run the risk of such profound contamination. Wouldn't you begin to think that your Jesus had gone out of his mind?

Put yourself in Mary's shoes when Simon's mother-in-law

came round to tell the tale concerning how Jesus had broken up her family life by seducing her daughter's husband away from the honest trade of fisherman. Wouldn't you begin to think that your Jesus had gone out of his mind?

Put yourself in Mary's shoes when four burly men carried their paralyzed friend onto the roof and began to dig through to the room below. Wouldn't you begin to think that your Jesus had gone out of his mind?

Put yourself in Mary's shoes when the sensible scribes came down from Jerusalem and attributed Jesus' bizarre behaviour to possession by Beelzebul, the ruler of the demons. Wouldn't you begin to think that your Jesus had gone out of his mind?

Here is a story of family turmoil, confusion and distress. Put yourself in Mary's shoes. What would it all have felt like to her?

Thinking

When you are living through times of change, it is not always easy to interpret precisely what is going on. According to Mark, Jesus had initiated a traumatic time of change in first-century Palestine. In the person of Jesus the reign of God was breaking in on the people of God. New and strange things were happening. But how would you have interpreted it all?

On one occasion there was a man with an unclean spirit in the synagogue. A man from nowhere, Jesus, commanded the unclean spirit to come out and the possessed man was made whole. Something new and strange had happened. But could you be sure that it was the work of God and not the trick of some false Messiah?

On one occasion there was a woman in bed with a fever. A man from nowhere, Jesus, took her by the hand and the fever left her. Something new and strange had happened. But could you be sure that it was the work of God and not the trick of some false Messiah?

On one occasion there was a leper man seeking cleansing. A man from nowhere, Jesus, touched him and said, 'Be made clean' and the leper was healed. Something new and strange had happened. But could you be sure that it was the work of God and not the trick of some false Messiah?

On one occasion there was a paralyzed man let down through a hole in the roof. A man from nowhere, Jesus, said, 'Son, your sins are forgiven' and the paralytic got up and walked. Something new and strange had happened. But could you be sure that it was the work of God and not the trick of some false Messiah?

On one occasion there was a man in the synagogue with a withered hand. A man from nowhere, Jesus, said, 'Stretch out your hand' and the hand was restored. Something new and strange had happened. But could you be sure that it was the work of God and not the trick of some false Messiah?

When you are living through times of change, it is not always easy to interpret precisely what is going on. But how would you have interpreted it all?

➤➤◦◦◄

12

Mark 4:26–34

[26]He also said, 'The kingdom of God is as if someone would scatter seed on the ground, [27]and would sleep and rise night and day, and the seed would sprout and grow, he does not know how. [28]The earth produces of itself, first the stalk, then the head, then the full grain in the head. [29]But when the grain is ripe, at once he goes in with his sickle, because the harvest has come.'

[30]He also said, 'With what can we compare the kingdom of God, or what parable will we use for it? [31]It is like a mustard seed, which, when sown upon the ground, is the smallest of all the seeds on earth; [32]yet when it is sown it grows up and becomes the greatest of all shrubs, and puts forth large branches, so that the birds of the air can make nests in its shade.'

[33]With many such parables he spoke the word to them, as they were able to hear it; [34]he did not speak to them except in parables, but he explained everything in private to his disciples.

Context

In chapter 3 (verses 13–19), Jesus appointed twelve disciples to be his companions. Before being sent out in chapter 5 (verse 7), the twelve disciples witnessed Jesus' work of teaching and healing. Chapter 4 provides an example of the teaching, a collection of parables. The present passage follows on after the parable of the sower and the parable of the lamp under the meal-tub.

Sensing

Jesus the master storyteller shaped parables to provide rich food for the senses. Just recall some of the rich pictures Jesus painted.

Paint the picture of the sower in your mind. See the man with the bag of seeds. See the man take a fistful of seeds in his hand. See the man throw the seed purposefully over the ground. Look around and see the variety of terrain on which the seed falls. See the footpath and the birds busily feeding on the seed. See the rocky ground and the young shoots withering away under the blazing sun and lacking true moisture. See the thistles choking and suffocating the corn. See the good and well-nurtured soil and find there the healthy sprouting crops. Pray that the seed may fall on good ground.

Paint the picture of the brightly burning lamp in your mind. See the lamp hidden beneath the meal-tub and sense the darkness grow. See the lamp hidden beneath the bed and sense how the light is lost. See the lamp lifted up high onto the lampstand and sense the darkness dispelled. See the lamp raised high by the torch-bearer and sense how the light is spread abroad. Pray that the light may be seen.

Paint the picture of the tiny mustard seed. Feel the seed lost in the palm of your hand. Paint the picture of the fully-grown mustard tree spreading wide its branches. See the birds of the air coming there to make their nests. Pray that the seed may grow.

Paint the picture of the little piece of yeast. Feel how little it weighs in the palm of your hand. Paint the picture of the rows of newly-baked bread leavened by that tiny yeast. See the bread rise before your very eyes. Pray that the yeast may leaven all the dough.

Just recall some of the rich pictures Jesus painted.

Intuition

Jesus the master storyteller shaped parables to provide rich food for the imagination. Just contemplate some of the rich possibilities and questions Jesus raised.

Contemplate the way in which the sower goes about his work, as an image of the kingdom of God. Is it necessary or even wise to be so wasteful with the seed? Why is it that the kingdom of God is made like that?

Is it necessary for so much seed to fall upon the footpath,

where the birds eat it for their breakfast? Is it necessary for so much seed to fall on rocky ground, where the sun scorches it so soon? Is it necessary for so much seed to fall among the thistles, where the thistles grow up and choke it? Why is it that the kingdom of God is made like that?

Contemplate the way in which the seed grows secretly in the soil, as an image of the kingdom of God. Contemplate the mysterious processes of germination and growth, so central to human survival and yet, in some ways, still so much outside human control. Why is it that the kingdom of God is made like that?

Is it necessary or even wise for the growth of the kingdom of God to be so much outside human control? Is it necessary for us to simply sit back, having sown the seed, and to leave the major work in the hands of God? Why is it that the kingdom of God is made like that?

Contemplate the way in which the mustard seed (the smallest of all the seeds on earth) grows up and becomes the greatest of all the shrubs, as an image of the kingdom of God. Is it necessary or even wise to invest the future of something so large and so useful within such a small beginning? Why is it that the kingdom of God is made like that?

Contemplate the way in which a little piece of yeast is used to leaven so large a lump of dough, as an image of the kingdom of God. Contemplate how the yeast loses its own identity in leavening the lump. Is it necessary or even wise to set the yeast to work in such a way? Why is it that the kingdom of God is made like that?

Just contemplate some of the rich possibilities and questions Jesus raised.

Feeling

Jesus the master storyteller shaped parables to provide rich food for the human heart. Just empathize with some of the human situations Jesus presented.

Put yourself in the place of an ageing father who had two sons. Experience the anguish and drama when the younger son packs his bags and leaves the family home. Experience the hurt, rejection and loss as the younger son disappears over the horizon. Experience the disappointment and frustration as rumours come back home about the younger son's wanton and reckless way of life. Experience the uncertainty and anxiety as the news of famine and hunger spread. Experience the unexpected joy and unlimited jubilation on the younger son's unannounced return. Experience the anguish and the drama when the older son refuses to welcome his brother's return. Put yourself in the place of an ageing father who had two sons.

Put yourself in the place of the good and faithful shepherd who had a hundred sheep. Experience the anguish and drama when only 99 of those sheep are counted in the fold. Experience the uncertainty and anxiety as he contemplates the plight of the missing sheep, lost in a deep ravine or in the jaws of some ravenous wolf. Experience the determination and exertion as every nook and cranny of the open countryside is searched. Experience the unexpected joy and unlimited jubilation as the lost sheep is found. Put yourself in the place of the good and faithful shepherd who had a hundred sheep.

Put yourself in the place of the good and faithful woman who had ten silver coins. Experience the anguish and drama when only nine of those coins are counted in the purse. Experience the uncertainty and anxiety as she contemplates the plight of the missing coin, stolen by an evil thief or hidden by some unscrupulous demon. Experience the determination and exertion as every nook and cranny of the home is searched. Experience the unexpected joy and unlimited jubilation as the lost coin is found. Put yourself in the place of the good and faithful woman who had ten silver coins.

Just empathize with some of the human situations Jesus presented.

Thinking

Jesus the master storyteller shaped parables to provide rich food for the human mind. Just think through the ways in which some of Jesus' parables work.

Think through the parable of the sower. How does that narrative really work to unlock the mystery of the kingdom of God? The storyteller speaks of seed, but informed listeners know they are hearing about the word of God. The storyteller speaks of the birds of the air, but informed listeners know they are hearing about Satan who comes to carry off the word. The storyteller speaks of seed falling on rocky ground, but informed listeners know they are hearing about those whose faith is shallow. The storyteller speaks of seed falling on good soil, but informed listeners know they are hearing about those who hear the word and welcome it, bringing forth good fruit. Without the key, of course, this parable of the kingdom does not work. Here Jesus deploys *allegory* to unlock the mystery of the kingdom of God.

Think through the parables of the mustard seed or the yeast. How do these narratives really work to unlock the mystery of the kingdom of God? The story of the mustard seed reminds us of a basic principle of nature. Seeds always work like that. The story of the yeast reminds us of a basic principle of nature. Yeast always works like that. Without knowing how the natural world functions, these parables of the kingdom do not work. Here Jesus deploys *similitude* to unlock the mystery of the kingdom of God.

Think through the parables of the shepherd searching for the lost sheep or the woman searching for the lost coin. How do these narratives really work to unlock the mystery of the kingdom of God? The story provides an example of how people act. The example generates insight into how Jesus himself behaves and offers a model for us to follow. Here Jesus deploys *exemplars* to unlock the mystery of the kingdom of God.

Think through the parable of the owner of the vineyard whose tenants refused to pay the rent and killed the owner's son when he came to collect his dues. How does this narrative really work to unlock the mystery of the kingdom of God? Jesus turned to the listeners and forced them to make a judgement. 'What,' Jesus asked, 'should the owner of the vineyard do?' 'Punish the wicked tenants and give the vineyard to others,' came their reply. In judging others, they themselves stood judged. Here Jesus deploys the most skilful of *parables* to unlock the mystery of the kingdom of God.

Just think through the ways in which some of Jesus' parables work.

13
Mark 4:35–41

[35]On that day, when evening had come, he said to them, 'Let us go across to the other side.' [36]And leaving the crowd behind, they took him with them in the boat, just as he was. Other boats were with him. [37]A great windstorm arose, and the waves beat into the boat, so that the boat was already being swamped. [38]But he was in the stern, asleep on the cushion; and they woke him up and said to him, 'Teacher, do you not care that we are perishing?' [39]He woke up and rebuked the wind, and said to the sea, 'Peace! Be still!' Then the wind ceased, and there was a dead calm. [40]He said to them, 'Why are you afraid? Have you still no faith?' [41]And they were filled with great awe and said to one another, 'Who then is this, that even the wind and the sea obey him?'

Context

In the earlier part of chapter 4, Mark has portrayed Jesus teaching the crowd in parables. The crowd is clustered on the shore; Jesus teaches from a boat. Now, at the end of the day, Jesus withdraws from the crowd to the other side. The journey by boat provides the context for the first of three major acts of divine power.

Sensing

It has been a long, long day standing there on the shore. Your feet are baked from pressing on the hot sand. Your legs are aching from jostling in the crowd. Your head is spinning from unravelling the parables and pondering the mystery of the kingdom of God. It has been a long, long day standing there on the shore.

But at last, the last words of teaching fade away across the sea and you prick up your ears to hear the master address you by name. 'Let's go across to the other side,' he said. As you take your seat in the little boat, your feet are cooled in the clear water at the bottom of the hull. Your legs are rested from supporting your wearied weight. Your head is cleared from the urgent and intriguing message of the parables. At last, the last words of teaching fade away across the sea.

Feel your muscles tighten as you begin to pull on the oars. Hear the water lapping by the bows as your oars pull the craft across the sea. See the distance put between you and the crowd standing on the shore. Feel your muscles tighten as you pull harder on the oars.

Then all of a sudden the whole atmosphere changes. All your senses become attuned to the impending disaster. See the sky darken and see the smile wiped from your companions' faces. Feel the boat tossed on the growing waves and feel your stomach churn in sympathy with the storm. Smell the atmosphere change and sniff the anxiety of your fellow-travellers. Hear the timbers of the boat creak and listen to the groans of the sailors. All of a sudden the whole atmosphere is changed. It has been a long, long evening riding on the crest of a storm.

Intuition

Two great themes of the Christian tradition permeate this narrative: the theme of faith and the theme of fear. Jesus said to the disciples, 'Why are you afraid? Have you still no faith?' But how can faith address fear in today's world?

Take the example of the young child who fears the dark. There she lies imprisoned in her bed, desperately trying to make sense of a confusing and irrational world. Monsters lurk in the cupboard; fiends dwell under the bed. How can faith address the young child's fear of the dark?

Take the example of the adolescent youth who fears the empty streets. There he hides in prison behind his door, desperately trying to avoid the intimidation and conflict of a hostile world. Gangs lurk round the corner; terrorists dwell in the shadows. How can faith address the adolescent youth's fear of the empty streets?

Take the example of the young adult who fears some crippling illness. There she lives imprisoned within her anxiety, desperately trying to identify and diagnose the symptoms of physical disease. Cancers lurk under every cell. Viruses dwell in every organ. How can faith address the young adult who fears some crippling illness?

Take the example of the middle-aged executive who fears the empty desk. There she works imprisoned by the company, desperately trying to identify the forces for reorganization and rationalization. Takeovers lurk behind every board meeting;

redundancies dwell in every restructuring. How can faith address the middle-aged executive who fears the empty desk?

Take the example of the frail pensioner who fears the hour of death. There he survives imprisoned within the body he dreads to leave, desperately trying to face the certainty of mortality and to embrace the uncertainty of immortality. Black-clothed undertakers lurk in the shadows; long-faced ministers dwell in the attics. How can faith address the frail pensioner who fears the hour of death?

Feeling

It is by no means easy to be always confident that Jesus is in command. Put yourself in the place of the disciple sitting in the bow of the boat. Become attuned to the range of emotions which ran through his heart on that eventful evening.

Share the sense of relief, the sense of release, flooding through you as you are called away from the crowd to join Jesus in the boat. Share the sense of security, the sense of safety as you take your seat in the bow.

Share the sense of growing uncertainty, the sense of growing anxiety, as the sky darkens and as the breeze freshens. Share the sense of increasing despair, the sense of increasing helplessness as the waves beat into the boat and as the water swamps the vessel.

Share the sense of rising frustration, the sense of rising impatience, as Jesus continues to slumber in the stern, as Jesus continues to snore on his pillow. Share the sense of escalating anger, the sense of escalating aggression as the powerful teacher abdicates all power, as the saviour of the universe permits chaos to reign.

Share the sense of profound amazement, the sense of profound wonder, as the commanding teacher rises in the stern, as the authoritative voice rebukes the wind, 'Peace! Be still!' Share the sense of absolute mystery, the sense of absolute awe, as the billowing waves return to calm, as the turbulent wind returns to tranquillity.

It is by no means easy to be always confident that Jesus is in command. Put yourself in the place of the disciple sitting in the bow of the boat.

Thinking

To those well versed in the theology and imagery of the ancient world, there is so much more to this narrative than first would meet the eye.

You see, once long ago there was another storm which raged across the face of the universe, the primordial storm from which the creation itself was called into being. The God who brought order out of chaos controlled the seas and established dry land. Here indeed is the original act of *divine* power. For example, referring to the creation myths in Psalm 89, the psalmist praises God:

> You rule the raging of the sea;
>> when its waters rise, you still them.

You see, in the traditions of the Old Testament, there are many examples of God's chosen people being buffeted by the storms and submerged in the waters. The image of a storm, or of great waters, was used frequently as a metaphor for the evil forces active in the world. The image of a storm, or of great waters, was used frequently for the tribulations of the righteous, from which only the power of God could save them. Here indeed is the continuing act of *divine* power. For example, in a cry for succour in Psalm 69, the psalmist prays:

> Let me be delivered from my enemies
>> and from the deep waters.

You see, in the piety of the traditions, the righteous could always place their complete confidence in the power of God to save them from the most terrible and tumultuous of storms. The righteous could be confident that the God in whom they placed their complete confidence would quell the tempest and calm the storm. Here indeed is the guarantee that this *divine* authority is focused on the person of Jesus. For example, in a shout of confidence in Psalm 46, the psalmist proclaims:

> Therefore we will not fear . . .
> though the waters roar and foam
>> though the mountains tremble.

You see, even the God of the Old Testament was known to slumber at certain decisive moments in the nation's history. Even the God of the Old Testament needed to be roused from sleep to rally to the aid of the people of God. Here indeed is continuity with the salvation history of the past. For example, in Psalm 44 the psalmist cries:

Rouse yourself! Why do you sleep, O Lord?
Awake, do not cast us off forever!

For those well versed in the theology and imagery of the ancient world, there is so much more to this narrative than first would meet the eye.

14

Mark 5:21–43

21When Jesus had crossed again in the boat to the other side, a great crowd gathered around him; and he was by the sea. 22Then one of the leaders of the synagogue named Jairus came and, when he saw him, fell at his feet 23and begged him repeatedly, 'My little daughter is at the point of death. Come and lay your hands on her, so that she may be made well, and live.' 24So he went with him.

And a large crowd followed him and pressed in on him. 25Now there was a woman who had been suffering from haemorrhages for twelve years. 26She had endured much under many physicians, and had spent all that she had; and she was no better, but rather grew worse. 27She had heard about Jesus, and came up behind him in the crowd and touched his cloak, 28for she said, 'If I but touch his clothes, I will be made well.' 29Immediately her haemorrhage stopped; and she felt in her body that she was healed of her disease. 30Immediately aware that power had gone forth from him, Jesus turned about in the crowd and said, 'Who touched my clothes?' 31And his disciples said to him, 'You see the crowd pressing in on you; how can you say, "Who touched me?"' 32He looked all around to see who had done it. 33But the woman, knowing what had happened to her, came in fear and trembling, fell down before him, and told him the whole truth. [34]He said to her, 'Daughter, your faith has made you well; go in peace, and be healed of your disease.'

[35]While he was still speaking, some people came from the leader's house to say, 'Your daughter is dead. Why trouble the teacher any further?' [36]But overhearing what they said, Jesus said to the leader of the synagogue, 'Do not fear, only believe.' [37]He allowed no one to follow him except Peter, James, and John, the brother of James. [38]When they came to the house of the leader of the synagogue, he saw a commotion, people weeping and wailing loudly. [39]When he had entered, he said to them, 'Why do you make a commotion and weep? The child is not dead but sleeping.' [40]And they laughed at him. Then he put them all outside, and took the child's father and mother and those who were with him, and went in where the child was. [41]He took her by the hand and said to her, 'Talitha cum,' which means, 'Little girl, get up!' [42]And immediately the girl got up and began to walk about (she was twelve years of age). At this they were overcome with amazement. [43]He strictly ordered them that no one should know this, and told them to give her something to eat.

Context

After a section of teaching in which Jesus expounds the secret of the kingdom of God through parables, Mark demonstrates God's decisive activity in the world through Jesus. In echoes of the creation story, Jesus calms the raging seas and imparts the gift of human life.

Sensing

By now you have grown accustomed to being part of a crowd. Every time Jesus leaves the boat a crowd assembles. Feel the people crowding round you, jostling, pushing, agitating, trying to catch a glimpse of Jesus, trying to catch Jesus' attention, trying to catch the sleeves of Jesus' cloak. By now you have grown accustomed to being part of a crowd.

By now you have grown accustomed to the kind of people who crowd round Jesus. Every time Jesus leaves the boat, the flotsam and jetsam of society crowd around his feet. See the scarred faces of the people crowding round you; see the injured bodies of the people crowding round you. See the blind, the deaf, the paralyzed, the social outcast. By now you have grown accustomed to the kind of people who crowd round Jesus.

By now you have grown accustomed to the kind of people who stir up trouble around Jesus. Every time Jesus leaves the boat, the holy and the righteous level accusations against him. Hear the voices of scribes accuse Jesus of blasphemy, when he pronounces the forgiveness of sins. Hear the voices of Pharisees accuse Jesus of eating with sinners, when he calls Levi. Hear the voices of holy men in the synagogue accuse Jesus of breaking the Sabbath, when he restores the withered hand. By now you have grown accustomed to the kind of people who stir up trouble around Jesus.

By now you know what you can expect. See Jairus, a leader of the synagogue, approach. Anticipate the conflict. Spot the trouble. But, instead of standing on his dignity, Jairus falls to his knees. Instead of challenging Jesus' authority, Jairus begs Jesus' aid. The tables have turned. By now you no longer know what you can expect.

Intuition

It is easier for some people to come to the feet of Jesus than it is for others. After all, what had the leper man to lose? What had the paralyzed man to lose? What had the social outcast to lose? It is easier for some people to come to the feet of Jesus than it is for others.

Take the case of Jairus. Would not Jairus have looked out of place in a crowd which attracts the flotsam and jetsam of society? Would not Jairus have felt out of place rubbing shoulders with tax collectors and sinners, rubbing shoulders with the mad and the bad? Would not Jairus have sounded out of place begging succour from someone in less authority than himself? Take the case of Jairus as an example. It is clearly easier for some people to come to the feet of Jesus than it is for others.

But then look round your own church. Who is likely to look out of place there? Do all ages look equally at home? Do both genders look equally at home? Do all racial groups look equally at home? It is clearly easier for some people to come to the feet of Jesus than it is for others.

But then listen to the concerns of your own church. Who is likely to feel out of place there? Do all economic groups feel equally at home, neither patronized nor exploited? Do all social classes feel equally at home, neither looked down on nor looked up to?

Do all educational levels feel equally at home, neither spoken down to nor bemused by ideas above their heads? It is clearly easier for some people to come to the feet of Jesus than it is for others.

Take the case of Jairus. In spite of the difficulties, in spite of the improbabilities, Jairus came to the feet of Jesus, driven by the pressing questions of his own condition. Jesus welcomed Jairus and responded to Jairus' need.

Then pray that, in spite of the difficulties, in spite of the improbabilities, others may continue to follow in Jairus' footsteps, and that you and I may be given the grace to respond to them in Jesus' name.

Feeling

The story of Jairus is the story of human life transformed, an epic of human values, priorities and personal transformation, a narrative of life, of death, of life restored. Put yourself in Jairus' robes and feel events from his perspective, as those events unravel through a three-act play.

In act one, picture Jairus the well-established, firmly secure, professional and family man. Socially, he is well positioned in the local community. Religiously, he is well respected, having risen to become the supervisor of the worship in the local synagogue. Personally, he is content to nurture his family and to observe his offspring blossom from childhood into adulthood. In act one, Jairus is the well established, firmly secure, professional and family man.

In act two, picture Jairus the middle-aged man whose world is disintegrating. Socially, his status in the community is in tatters. He has been observed grovelling in the crowd alongside sinners, tax gatherers and lepers. Religiously, his credibility is in ruin. He has been seen kneeling at the feet of an untrained, unlicensed and unauthorized spiritual leader. Personally, his family life has been torn asunder. His little daughter has been given up to death. Already the ritual mourning has taken over his home. In act two, Jairus is the middle-aged man whose world is disintegrating.

In act three, picture Jairus the man whose life has been broken and remade. Socially, he no longer needs the support and the approval of the establishment. Religiously, he has turned his back on the old order and embraced the new life which is in Christ. Personally, he has experienced his young daughter risen from the grave. In act three, Jairus is the man whose life has been broken and remade.

The story of Jairus is the story of a human life transformed, an epic of human values, priorities and personal transformation, a narrative of life, of death, of life restored.

Thinking

Up to this point in Mark's gospel, you could perhaps be forgiven for thinking that the good news of Jesus Christ was for men only. As you recall the great acts of calling, it is the names of men who come readily to the mind: names like Peter and Andrew, James and John, and Levi. As you recall the early acts of healing, it is the faces of men who come most readily to the mind: faces like the possessed man in the synagogue at Capernaum, the leper man on the highway, the paralyzed man lowered through the roof, the man with the withered hand. Up to this point in Mark's gospel, you could perhaps be forgiven for thinking that the good news of Jesus Christ was for men only.

But even such an account is clearly inadequate, since it overlooks the second great act of healing related in chapter 2: the healing of Simon's mother-in-law. Now in a carefully constructed pair of healings, Mark demonstrates that Simon's mother-in-law stood by no means alone. Now the woman who had been suffering from haemorrhages for twelve years is healed. Now the girl who is twelve years old is brought back to life. Beyond this point in Mark's gospel you could *not* be forgiven for thinking that the good news of Jesus Christ was for men only.

But even such an account is clearly inadequate, since it overlooks the major theological significance of the twelve-year-old *girl*. In the primordial story of creation, the first act of divine power was revealed in the stilling of the seas. In Mark's account of the new creation, Jesus has performed the self-same act. In the primordial story of creation, the second act of divine power was revealed in the giving of life to *man*. In Mark's account of the new creation, Jesus restored life first to *woman*. Beyond this point in Mark's gospel, there could be no doubt that the good news of Jesus Christ was also for women.

Mark 6:1–13

¹He left that place and came to his hometown, and his disciples followed him. ²On the sabbath he began to teach in the synagogue, and many who heard him were astounded. They said, 'Where did this man get all this? What is this wisdom that has been given to him? What deeds of power are being done by his hands! ³Is not this the carpenter, the son of Mary and brother of James and Joses and Judas and Simon, and are not his sisters here with us?' And they took offence at him. ⁴Then Jesus said to them, 'Prophets are not without honour, except in their hometown, and among their own kin, and in their own house.' ⁵And he could do no deed of power there, except that he laid his hands on a few sick people and cured them. ⁶And he was amazed at their unbelief.

Then he went about among the villages teaching. ⁷He called the twelve and began to send them out two by two, and gave them authority over the unclean spirits. ⁸He ordered them to take nothing for their journey except a staff; no bread, no bag, no money in their belts; ⁹but to wear sandals and not to put on two tunics. ¹⁰He said to them, 'Wherever you enter a house, stay there until you leave the place. ¹¹If any place will not welcome you and they refuse to hear you, as you leave, shake off the dust that is on your feet as a testimony against them.' ¹²So they went out and proclaimed that all should repent. ¹³They cast out many demons, and anointed with oil many who were sick and cured them.

Context

Since their calling in chapter 3, the twelve apostles have travelled with Jesus and witnessed the teachings, the healings and the conflicts. Now the twelve apostles are sent out two by two to put into practice what they have learnt.

Sensing

Today has begun much as every other day had begun since that momentous day when Jesus went up into the hills and spoke aloud your name, appointing you one of the special twelve. You have grown used to being an integral part of the cluster of twelve apostles, satellites of the one awe-inspiring master. Look round into the faces of your companions and run their names through your mind. Assure yourself that you are there, part of the team. Today has begun much as every other day had begun since you were appointed one of the special twelve.

But then the unexpected happened. Just as Jesus had called the twelve together and appointed them to be his special companions, now he calls them together for a second time. Then the unexpected happens.

See the faces of the twelve change as they learn what is now in store for them. See the comfortable interaction of the group gradually fragment as discrete pairs are formed. Feel the urgency in the air as the staffs are picked up in readiness for the journey. Hear the command to be weighed down or held back by no unnecessary baggage. Watch as the purses are emptied, as the lunch boxes are returned to the kitchen, as the spare tunics are hung behind the door. See the faces of the twelve change as they learn what is now in store for them.

Now set out on your missionary journey, you and your one companion friend. Grasp the staff in your hand. Recognize the lightness in your step, untroubled by superfluous baggage. Recognize the urgency in your heart, motivated by the desire to bring the liberating and releasing power of God to those entrapped by the demons of evil. Now set out on your missionary journey, you and your one companion friend.

Intuition

In preparing for their missionary journey those twelve apostles were forced to re-evaluate their commitment to three fundamental pillars of life: money, food and clothes. Imagine for a moment what these three pillars of life mean to you.

How important is it to you to have money in your pocket, money in your purse? How important is it to you to have money in your bank, money in your building society or in your stocks and shares? Jesus said to the disciples, 'Take no money in your belt.'

How much does money actually influence your life? How much does money determine what you do for a living? How much does money determine how you spend your leisure time? How willing are you to give money away to support good causes and charitable endeavours? Jesus said to the disciples, 'Take no money in your belt.'

How important is it to you to have a well-stocked larder, a well-stocked freezer? How important is it to you to know where the next meal is coming from, what the next meal will be? Jesus said to the disciples, 'Take no food for the journey.'

How much does food actually influence your life? How much time do you take shopping for food, preparing food, cooking food, eating food? How much does food determine how you spend your leisure time? How hospitable are you in inviting others to share your food? Jesus said to the disciples, 'Take no food for the journey.'

How important is it to you to have clothes in your wardrobe? And how much do clothes actually influence your life? How much time do you spend shopping for clothes, deciding which clothes to wear? How much does having the *right* clothes influence where you go and what you do in your leisure time? How generous are you in sharing your clothes with others? Jesus said to the disciples, 'Take no second tunic.'

In preparing for their missionary journey, those twelve apostles were forced to re-evaluate their commitment to three fundamental pillars of life: money, food and clothes. How content are you with your evaluation of these three pillars of life?

Feeling

Here is a story of twelve ill-prepared men being sent out on an impossible mission to a hostile world.

Put yourself in those apostles' sandals, if they have a pair to spare. Imagine what it has been like to live and work together for so long as a closely-knit group of twelve specially chosen companions. Imagine what it has been like to live and work for so long alongside Jesus, such a powerful and such an inspiring leader. Imagine the fellowship, imagine the comradeship. Imagine the interdependence and mutual support.

Put yourself in those apostles' sandals, if they have a pair to spare. Imagine what it is like to see the closely-knit group of twelve broken down into arbitrary pairs. Imagine what it is like to experience Jesus sending you away from his presence. Imagine the trauma, imagine the pain. Imagine the loss and fragmentation.

Put yourself in those apostles' sandals, if they have a pair to spare. Imagine what it is like to be sent out on a mission so ill prepared, so ill resourced. Imagine the empty purse and loss of all financial security. Imagine the empty larder and the loss of all independence over what and when you eat. Imagine the empty wardrobe and the loss of the second tunic for the cold night or for the rainy day.

Put yourself in those apostles' sandals, if they have a pair to spare. Imagine what it is like to be sent out knowing the conflicts and problems which stand in the path. Imagine what it is like to be sent out knowing the misunderstanding and antagonism your mission will cause. Imagine the anxiety, imagine the uncertainty. Imagine the commitment and dedication to do the master's will.

Here is a story of twelve ill-prepared men being sent out on an impossible mission to a hostile world.

Thinking

In this narrative Jesus sends out the twelve leaders of the new Israel to demonstrate that the kingdom of God has dawned. Think through the subtle way in which the twelve have been prepared for their mission.

The story begins back in chapter 3 when the twelve are appointed or formally constituted. And what, do you think, was the rationale for their appointment? According to Mark, they are appointed for two purposes: to be with Jesus and to be sent out by him. And what, do you think, was the rationale for their impending mission? According to Mark, they will be sent out for two purposes: to teach and to cast out demons.

And after their appointment in chapter 3, what, do you think, was the very first experience of these twelve apostles? According to Mark, no sooner had the twelve been appointed than they witnessed Jesus being accused of exercising power through an unholy alliance with Beelzebul, the prince of demons.

And after witnessing this conflict and disbelief, how, do you think, were the twelve apostles prepared for their solo mission? According to Mark, they are prepared in two ways. For their ministry of teaching they are prepared by listening to parables of the kingdom. For their ministry over demonic powers they are prepared by witnessing the dramatic stilling of the storm and the spectacular exorcism of the man known as Legion.

And after hearing the teaching about the kingdom of God and experiencing the power over the forces of evil, what, do you think, the twelve apostles witnessed next? According to Mark, the conflict and the challenge return, this time in Jesus' home town and among his closest family and friends.

Mark's structure is, therefore, clear. The twelve are called and they witness Jesus' rejection. They hear the teaching and they experience the power over the demonic order. They witness Jesus' rejection and they are sent out on their mission. So what kind of reception, do you think, can they expect now?

16

Mark 6:14–29

[14]King Herod heard of it, for Jesus' name had become known. Some were saying, 'John the baptizer has been raised from the dead; and for this reason these powers are at work in him.' [15]But others said, 'It is Elijah.' And others said, 'It is a prophet, like one of the prophets of old.' [16]But when Herod heard of it, he said, 'John, whom I beheaded, has been raised.'

[17]For Herod himself had sent men who arrested John, bound him, and put him in prison on account of Herodias, his brother Philip's wife, because Herod had married her. [18]For John had been telling Herod, 'It is not lawful for you to have your brother's wife.' [19]And Herodias had a grudge against him, and wanted to kill him. But she could not, [20]for Herod feared John, knowing that he was a righteous and holy man, and he protected him. When he heard him, he was greatly perplexed; and yet he liked to listen to him. [21]But an opportunity came when Herod on his birthday gave a banquet for his courtiers and officers and for the leaders of Galilee. [22]When his daughter Herodias came in and danced, she pleased Herod and his guests; and the king said to the girl, 'Ask me for whatever you wish, and I will give it.' [23]And he solemnly swore to her, 'Whatever you ask me, I will give you, even half of my king-dom.' [24]She went out and said to her mother, 'What should I ask for?' She replied, 'The head of John the baptizer.' [25]Immediately she rushed back to the king and requested, 'I want you to give me at once the head of John the Baptist on a platter.' [26]The king was deeply grieved; yet out of regard for his oaths and for the guests, he did not want to refuse her. [27]Immediately the king sent a soldier of the guard with orders to bring John's head. He went and beheaded him in the prison, [28]brought his head on a platter, and

gave it to the girl. Then the girl gave it to her mother. [29]When his disciples heard about it, they came and took his body, and laid it in a tomb.

Context

After sending out the twelve apostles on their missionary journey, Mark reveals nothing of their individual or personal experiences. Instead, Mark interposes the account of the death of John the baptizer. John's fate foreshadows the fate of Jesus himself and the fate of many early disciples.

Sensing

Form a series of pictures of John the baptizer in your mind, and see Mark's account of his life unfold before your eyes.

Picture John the baptizer down by the river Jordan. Picture the young man full of vigour. Picture young John dressed as Elijah the prophet had been dressed before him. See the coat of camel's hair and the leather belt around his waist. Hear young John proclaim the gospel of repentance as he summons his hearers to transform their way of life. Feel young John stir up the waters as he immerses the repentant sinners within the flowing river. Picture John the baptizer down by the river Jordan.

Picture John the baptizer languishing in Herod's prison. Picture the not-so-young man decline in vigour. Picture the not-so-young John brought out of prison to give audience to Herod. Hear him proclaim his unflinching message, so distasteful to Herod's ears. Feel him stir up in Herod's heart a mixture of respect and aggression. Picture John the baptizer languishing in Herod's prison.

Picture John the baptizer ignominiously summoned to the executioner's table. Picture John succumbing to martyrdom. Hear the axe fall and the head roll. See the disciples come to lay his corpse in the tomb. Hear them bewail his death. Feel their anguish and pain. Picture John the baptizer ignominiously summoned to the executioner's table.

Form a series of pictures of John the baptizer in your mind and see how, according to Mark, the forerunner prepares the ground for the Messiah's life and foreshadows the Messiah's death.

Intuition

Here is a narrative about power, Herod's power, Herod's uncontrolled and uncontrollable power. Power, it is said, corrupts. So what ideas spring to your mind when you consider Herod's handling of power?

How do you see power used in the arena of international politics? How do you see power used between rich nation and poor nation? Power, it is said, corrupts.

How do you see power used in the arena of internal politics within nations? How do you see the repression of human rights and the suppression of information? Power, it is said, corrupts.

How do you see power used by the multinational financial institutions? When do you see the proper concerns of the small player totally eclipsed and disregarded? Power, it is said, corrupts.

How do you see power used in the workplace? When do you see the workforce exploited by management? When do you see management brought to its knees by the workforce? When do you see the hopes of individuals trampled roughshod by others? Power, it is said, corrupts.

How do you see power used between the sexes? When do you see women exploited by men? When do you see men exploited by women? How do you see power used between the social classes? When do you see one class exploiting the other? How do you see power used between the different age groups? When do you see the elderly exploited? When do you see the young exploited? When do you see the middle-aged exploited? Power, it is said, corrupts.

But, most of all, how do you see power used in your own two hands? Over whom do you have power, within your family, among your friends, in your place of work, in your place of recreation, within your church? Power, it is said, corrupts.

Pray that God may give you grace to use power wisely and that you may not be corrupted by it.

Feeling

Put on your villain's crown and explore the story from Herod's perspective.

Put on your villain's crown and listen to John's accusation, to John's incisive indictment of your behaviour. Watch John look you in the eye and hear John proclaim, 'It is not lawful for you to have your brother's wife.' What powerful ruler would tolerate such impertinence?

Put on your villain's crown and send your men to arrest John, to confine John to your prison cell. Watch John languish in the prison darkness and hear John's solitary and plaintive cry. What powerful ruler could resist such proper retribution?

Put on your villain's crown and summons John to proclaim his message, to preach his gospel of righteousness. Hear John's passion for truth, watch his unflinching grasp on integrity. What powerful ruler could fail to be moved by such obvious signs of righteousness and of holiness?

Put on your villain's crown and watch the young girl dance. Let your eyes and your heart be seduced by the young girl's grace and guile. What powerful ruler could reward such display with anything less than a lavish reward?

Put on your villain's crown and feel your heart torn asunder by the young girl's request. Let your eyes survey the crowd who witnessed your promise on oath. Let your mind evaluate the options. What powerful ruler could fail to recognize when he has been caught in such an obvious trap?

Put on your villain's crown and command the executioner to act. Let your eyes rest on the platter. Let your mind dwell on the severed head. What powerful ruler could fail to be conscious of his awesome power over life and limb?

Put on your villain's crown and live with the consequences of your act. Let your sleeping hours be haunted with the nightmares of the execution. Let your waking hours be haunted with the fears of John brought back to life. What powerful ruler could obliterate the memory of his guilt?

Put on your villain's crown and explore the story from Herod's perspective.

Thinking

Here is the only narrative in Mark's gospel which is not, in some sense or other, a story about Jesus. I wonder in what sense the story can be said to be true?

Is the story historically true? Well, there is at least some independent account of Herod's involvement in the death of John the baptizer, preserved by the historian Josephus. After reporting a defeat of Herod's army, Josephus wrote:

some of the Jews thought that the destruction of his army came from God, and that very justly, as a punishment for what he did against John who was called the Baptist.

The major difficulty faced in reconciling the two accounts is that Mark's chronology suggests that John was executed in AD 29 or 30, while the defeat referred to by Josephus probably occurred in AD 37. Perhaps God waits for divine retribution, or perhaps the Jews have long memories.

Is the story psychologically true? Think about the other details in the narrative: the banquet, the dance, the sworn promise of up to half the kingdom, the extravagant request prompted by the mother, the solemn entry of the guard bearing John's head on the platter. Debates in the learned commentaries question whether in oriental custom the solo (erotic) dance would have been appropriately assigned to the king's daughter. And technically, Herod, as tetrarch under the aegis of Rome, had no constitutional rights to dispose of a kingdom. Here, surely, are the characteristic motifs of legend and epic which speak deeply to the human heart.

Is the story theologically true? For Mark, the crucial significance of the story is shown by where he chose to place it. In Mark's account of the spread of the kingdom of God, this narrative is purposefully inserted between Jesus sending the twelve apostles on their first missionary journey and Jesus recalling them to give account of their mission. John's execution foreshadowed the death of Jesus himself and foreshadowed the martyrdom of countless Christian disciples.

I wonder in what senses this story can be said to be true?

⟹━◆━⟸

17
Mark 6:30–34, 53–56

[30]The apostles gathered around Jesus, and told him all that they had done and taught. [31]He said to them, 'Come away to a deserted place all by yourselves and rest a while.' For many were coming and going, and they had no leisure even to eat. [32]And

they went away in the boat to a deserted place by themselves.
[33]Now many saw them going and recognized them, and they
hurried there on foot from all the towns and arrived ahead of
them. [34]As he went ashore, he saw a great crowd; and he had
compassion for them, because they were like sheep without a
shepherd; and he began to teach them many things.

[53]When they had crossed over, they came to land at
Gennesaret and moored the boat. [54]When they got out of the
boat, people at once recognized him, [55]and rushed about that
whole region and began to bring the sick on mats to wherever
they heard he was. [56]And wherever he went, into villages or cities
or farms, they laid the sick in the marketplaces, and begged him
that they might touch even the fringe of his cloak; and all who
touched it were healed.

Context

Earlier in chapter 6, Mark related how Jesus sent the twelve
apostles on a missionary journey. Now Mark relates how the
apostles reported back to Jesus. Nowhere does Mark give any
information about their experiences while away from Jesus.

Sensing

In rapid succession Mark presents four sequential images of everyday life in the company of Jesus. Ponder each image in turn.

Open your eyes and see the apostles making their way back to
Jesus. Look to the east and see Peter and Andrew in the distance,
walking towards you. Look to the west and see James and John in
the distance, walking towards you. Look to the south and see
Matthew and Thomas. All are travelling light, staff in hand, as
they return from their missionary journey. There is tiredness in
their step. Here is the first image.

Prick up your ears and hear the apostles talking with Jesus,
telling him all they have done and taught. Listen to Peter and
Andrew as they talk about their work in the east. Listen to James
and John as they talk about their work in the west. Listen to
Matthew and Thomas as they talk about their work in the south.
There is tiredness in their voices. Here is the second image.

Open your eyes and see the twelve apostles making their way
with Jesus to a deserted place. See the tranquillity of the sea and
the wide open spaces of the water. See the tranquillity of the shore
and the wide open spaces of the desert. All are seeking rest and

refreshment. There is relaxation and hope in their hearts. Here is the third image.

Prick up your ears and hear the sounds of the crowd come closer. Hear the splash of the oars on the sea. Hear the clatter of sandals on the road. Hear the crescendo of the chatter. Hopes of relaxation and rest are shattered. Here is the fourth image.

In rapid succession Mark presents four sequential images of everyday life in the company of Jesus. Ponder each image in turn.

Intuition

Two main themes inform this narrative: the need to talk and the need to withdraw. So what ideas do these themes spark off in your mind?

To whom do you talk about the things that *really* matter? Do you talk often enough? Do you talk deeply enough? Or do you prefer to let things bottle up inside? The apostles told Jesus all that they had done and taught.

To whom do you talk about the pressures at work? To whom do you talk about the pressures at home? To whom do you talk about your innermost hopes and fears? To whom do you talk about the joys and frustrations of your Christian faith? The apostles told Jesus all that they had done and taught.

To whom do you *really* listen talking about the things that matter to them most? Do you really listen to your colleagues at work? Do you really listen to your family at home? Do you really listen to your friends in the church? Jesus listened to all that the apostles had done and taught.

How do you make time to withdraw and to listen to the depths of your own being? How do you step back from the intimacy and the immediacy of your working life to listen to what is really going on? How do you step back from the intimacy and the immediacy of your family life to listen to what is really going on? How do you step back from the intimacy and immediacy of your religious work to listen to what is really going on? Jesus said to the apostles, 'Come away to a deserted place by yourselves and rest awhile.'

Two main themes inform this narrative: the need to talk and the need to withdraw.

Feeling

Here in Mark's gospel is the first clinical description of ministry burnout. According to Mark, the original disciples had no leisure even to eat. Jesus' disciples today often find themselves in the same predicament.

Put yourself in the shoes of one of those original disciples. You have forsaken your old family trade and placed your life in the hands of Jesus. You are deeply conscious of the call of Jesus to teach. You are deeply conscious of the commission of Jesus to heal. But the task is never-ending; the demand is overwhelming. When you come home from a missionary journey, the crowds follow you down the street. When you set sail to the distant shore, the crowds arrive there before you. When you long for peace and quiet, the whole region brings out their sick to be healed. According to Mark, those original disciples had no leisure even to eat. How did that feel for them?

Put yourself in the shoes of one of the full-time ministers in today's church. You have forsaken a more regular pattern of work and placed your life in the hands of Jesus. You are deeply conscious of the call of Jesus to teach. You are deeply conscious of the commission of Jesus to heal. But the task is never-ending; the demand is overwhelming. When you come home from hospital visiting, the undertaker has left a message on the answer-phone. When you close the study door to prepare tomorrow's sermon, a distressed family arrives on the doorstep. When you long for peace and quiet, the whole church council crowds into your lounge. In the parsonage you live on the job, unprotected by officious secretary or carefully prescribed office hours. According to Mark, full-time ministers have no time even to eat. How does that feel for them?

Place yourself in the shoes of one of the leading laity in today's church. You have forsaken a more regular pattern of recreation and placed your life in the hands of Jesus. You are deeply conscious of the call of Jesus to teach. You are deeply conscious of the commission of Jesus to heal. But the task is never-ending; the demand is overwhelming. When you come home from work, the minister has left an urgent message on the answer-phone. When you close the door to spend time with the family, a distressed committee member comes ringing the bell. When you long for peace and quiet, the church council persuades you to go on another lay leadership course. According to Mark, the dedicated laity have no time even to eat. How does that feel for them?

Here in Mark's gospel is the first clinical description of ministry burnout. Do you recognize the symptoms?

Thinking

This narrative raises immense questions about fairness, about justice, and about responsibility. So what do you make of the ways in which these issues are treated in the narrative?

Was Jesus being really fair to those original twelve disciples? What do you think? Could Jesus really have expected them to be ready to go on that missionary journey when they had been with him for such a short space of time? Could Jesus really have expected them to cope with the incessant coming and going of the crowds? Was Jesus really being fair in his expectations?

Were the crowds really being fair to Jesus in those early days? What do you think? Could the crowds really have expected such constant teaching and so much attention, when Jesus had only so recently set up in business? Could the crowds really have expected Jesus to cope with row upon row of sick people on mats, wherever he went? Were the crowds really being fair on Jesus?

Was Jesus really being fair to himself in those early days? What do you think? Could Jesus really have expected so much of himself, so constantly teaching, so constantly healing, so constantly aware of power being drained from himself? Could Jesus really have expected himself to cope with so many shepherdless sheep?

And what of the church today? Do you think that the world is being fair in the expectations and demands it places on the church? Do you think that you are being fair in the expectations and demands you place on the church and on the clergy? Do you think that the church is being fair in the demands it places on you?

This narrative raises immense questions about fairness, about justice, and about responsibility. So what do you make of it all?

18
Mark 7:1–8, 14–15, 21–23

[1]Now when the Pharisees and some of the scribes who had come from Jerusalem gathered around him, [2]they noticed that some of his disciples were eating with defiled hands, that is, without washing them. [3](For the Pharisees, and all the Jews, do not eat unless they thoroughly wash their hands, thus observing the tradition of the elders; [4]and they do not eat anything from the market unless they wash it; and there are also many other traditions that they observe, the washing of cups, pots, and bronze kettles.) [5]So the Pharisees and the scribes asked him, 'Why do your disciples not live according to the tradition of the elders, but eat with defiled hands?' [6]He said to them, 'Isaiah prophesied rightly about you hypocrites, as it is written,

"This people honours me with their lips,
    but their hearts are far from me;
[7]in vain do they worship me,
    teaching human precepts as doctrines."
[8]You abandon the commandment of God and hold to human tradition.'

[14]Then he called the crowd again and said to them, 'Listen to me, all of you, and understand: [15]there is nothing outside a person that by going in can defile, but the things that come out are what defile.

[21]'For it is from within, from the human heart, that evil intentions come: fornication, theft, murder, [22]adultery, avarice, wickedness, deceit, licentiousness, envy, slander, pride, folly. [23]All these evil things come from within, and they defile a person.'

Context

Mark drives home the regular motif that Jesus' good actions are followed by conflict with the scribes and Pharisees. In chapter 6 Jesus had fed 5000 men. Now, immediately afterwards, the Pharisees criticized his disciples for eating without ceremonial cleansing.

Sensing

The scribes and the Pharisees gave Jesus a hard, hard time.

Picture the day when Jesus had settled down to teach inside the house in Capernaum. See the paralyzed man make a dramatic entry on a stretcher through a hole in the roof. See the healed man make a dramatic exit on his own two legs through the door. Hear the scribes criticize Jesus for the blasphemy of pronouncing salvation and wholeness. The scribes and the Pharisees gave Jesus a hard, hard time.

Picture the day when Jesus had settled down to dinner in Levi's house. See the disreputable sinner turn his back on his old way of life. See the reformed character become the host of the feast. Hear the scribes and the Pharisees criticize Jesus for eating with sinners and tax collectors. The scribes and the Pharisees gave Jesus a hard, hard time.

Picture the day when Jesus had settled down in the synagogue on the Sabbath. See the man with the withered hand come forward bearing his deformity. See the man with the restored hand returned to his home healed. Hear the Pharisees criticize Jesus for breaking the Sabbath. The scribes and the Pharisees gave Jesus a hard, hard time.

Picture the day when Jesus had settled down to feed the starving crowd. See the 5000 men sit down in groups of hundreds and of fifties on the green grass. See the twelve basketfuls taken up of leftovers remaining from the five loaves and two fishes. Hear the Pharisees criticize Jesus and his disciples for eating with ritually unclean hands. The scribes and the Pharisees gave Jesus a hard, hard time.

Intuition

The key issue raised by this narrative concerns the positive and negative sides of religious rituals and ceremonies. So what examples come to your mind?

Consider the ceremonial washing of hands. For Pharisees in an occupied land, this is surely a strong reminder of their Jewish identity. Or is this observance just another reason to feel superior over the disciples of Jesus?

Consider the weekly attendance at church. For Christians in a secular age, this is surely a powerful witness to the strength of their Christian faith. Or is this observance just another reason to dress more smartly than their neighbours?

Consider the ritual in worship, like genuflection before the blessed sacrament. For devout worshippers approaching the presence of Christ, this is surely a sincere witness to their heartfelt piety. Or is this observance just an outward substitute for the true genuflection of the heart?

Consider the formal pattern of a daily office or set form of prayers. For normal human beings distracted and diverted by the ups and downs of daily living, this is surely a firm rock on which to build a secure relationship with God. Or is this observance just an empty shell shrouding a dead or dying spirituality?

Consider the liturgy of infant baptism. For devout parents anxious to incorporate their newborn infant within the body of Christ, this is surely a clear sign of Jesus' saving resurrection. Or is this observance just an excuse for a christening party?

The key issue raised by this narrative concerns the positive and negative sides of religious rituals and ceremonies. So what examples come to your mind?

Feeling

So often the story is told only from the perspective of Jesus' supporters. Try seeing the situation from the Pharisees' point of view.

Put on the Pharisees' phylactery and return to the house in Capernaum. Listen carefully to the words as Jesus speaks them: 'Son, your sins are forgiven.' Feel the righteous indignation as this unauthorized healer takes to himself the prerogative of God alone. To keep faith with your God, you have no choice but to help the preacher see the error of his ways.

Put on the Pharisees' phylactery and return to the banquet in Levi's house. Look carefully at the assembled company and recall how each tax collector had turned traitor to his country and to his God, by working for the Roman occupation. Feel the righteous indignation as this uninformed teacher takes on the contamination of his companions. To keep faith with your God, you have no choice but to help the teacher see the error of his ways.

Put on the Pharisees' phylactery and return to the synagogue on the Sabbath. Listen carefully as Jesus speaks to the man with the withered hand. Feel the righteous indignation as this unwelcome miracle worker so blatantly breaks the Sabbath observance. To keep faith with your God, you have no choice but to help the miracle worker see the error of his ways.

Put on the Pharisees' phylactery and return to your place

alongside the starving multitude. Look carefully at the twelve disciples as they hand food among the crowd and eat their own meal with hands left ritually unclean. Feel the righteous indignation as this unlicensed victualler flaunts the traditions of the elders. To keep faith with your God, you have no choice but to help the victualler see the error of his ways.

So often the story is told only from the perspective of Jesus' supporters. Try seeing the situation from the Pharisees' point of view.

Thinking

Have you ever considered what a big deal Mark makes of eating, and particularly the part played by bread in his gospel?

Recall how, when Jesus had cured Simon's mother-in-law, she began to serve them at table. I wonder why?

Recall how the reformed Levi invited Jesus to dinner and how the Pharisees criticized Jesus for eating there. I wonder why?

Recall how the disciples plucked grain on the Sabbath, how the Pharisees criticized them, and how Jesus drew on the example and authority of David and the bread of the Presence. I wonder why?

Recall how, when Jesus' disciples were criticized for not fasting, Jesus replied that the wedding guests cannot fast while the bridegroom is with them. I wonder why?

Recall how, when Jairus' daughter was restored to life, Jesus commanded them to give her something to eat. I wonder why?

Recall how, when Jesus despatched the disciples two-by-two on their mission without him, he explicitly commanded them to take no bread. I wonder why?

Recall how, when Jesus had compassion on the crowd, he took five loaves, blessed the loaves, broke the loaves, and distributed the loaves to the people. I wonder why?

Recall how the Pharisees took exception to the way in which Jesus' disciples handled bread without ritual cleansing. I wonder why?

Look forward to the gospel climax, when the Messianic table is spread and the bread is given its new significance in the Messianic kingdom, 'This is my body.' Now do you begin to see why?

19

Mark 7:24–37

[24]From there he set out and went away to the region of Tyre. He entered a house and did not want anyone to know he was there. Yet he could not escape notice, [25]but a woman whose little daughter had an unclean spirit immediately heard about him, and she came and bowed down at his feet. [26]Now the woman was a Gentile, of Syrophoenician origin. She begged him to cast the demon out of her daughter. [27]He said to her, 'Let the children be fed first, for it is not fair to take the children's food and throw it to the dogs.' [28]But she answered him, 'Sir, even the dogs under the table eat the children's crumbs.' [29]Then he said to her, 'For saying that, you may go – the demon has left your daughter.' [30]So she went home, found the child lying on the bed, and the demon gone.

[31]Then he returned from the region of Tyre, and went by way of Sidon towards the Sea of Galilee, in the region of the Decapolis. [32]They brought to him a deaf man who had an impediment in his speech; and they begged him to lay his hand on him. [33]He took him aside in private, away from the crowd, and put his fingers into his ears, and he spat and touched his tongue. [34]Then looking up to heaven, he sighed and said to him, 'Ephphatha,' that is, 'Be opened.' [35]And immediately his ears were opened, his tongue was released, and he spoke plainly. [36]Then Jesus ordered them to tell no one; but the more he ordered them, the more zealously they proclaimed it. [37]They were astounded beyond measure, saying, 'He has done everything well; he even makes the deaf to hear and the mute to speak.'

Context

Mark's gospel presents two accounts of feeding the crowd. In chapter 6, 5000 are fed and twelve baskets of remains collected. In chapter 8, 4000 are fed and seven baskets of remains collected. In the first narrative the Jews were fed and in the second narrative the Gentiles were fed. Jesus' conversation with the Syrophoenician woman marks the point of transition.

Sensing

Mark tells of two great feeding miracles. Let us get the facts right first.

On that first occasion, what did Jesus do? He ordered the disciples to make the people sit down on the green grass. How many people were there in each group? They sat in groups of hundreds and fifties. Then what did Jesus do? He performed four distinct actions: he took the bread, he said the blessing, he broke the bread, he shared the bread with the crowd.

On that first occasion, how many loaves were available? There were five loaves. How many people were fed? There were 5000 men. How many baskets were filled with what was left over? There were twelve baskets filled. What type of baskets were used? In the Greek, the baskets were called *kophinos*.

On that second occasion, what did Jesus do? He ordered the crowd to sit down on the ground. How many people were there in each group? This time Mark does not say. Then what did Jesus do? He performed four distinct actions: he took the bread, he gave thanks, he broke the bread, he shared the bread with the crowd.

On that second occasion, how many loaves were available? There were seven. How many people were fed? There were 4000 people. How many baskets were filled with what was left over? There were seven baskets filled. What type of baskets were used? In Greek, the baskets were called *spyris*.

And between the two accounts of feeding the crowd, hear Jesus say to the Syrophoenician woman, 'Let the children be fed first.' And hear the Syrophoenician woman reply, 'Sir, even the dogs under the table eat the children's crumbs.'

Let us get the facts right first.

Intuition

Mark tells of two great feeding miracles. What is Mark up to? Let us explore the theories.

The first theory suggests that Mark was simply being naïve. In the oral tradition which Mark heard there were two similar, but different, accounts of Jesus feeding the crowd. The original eye-witnesses were rather muddled. Some thought there were 4000 people, and some thought there were as many as 5000 men. Some thought that there were seven loaves, and some thought there were only five. Mark could not make up his mind which tradition to use. So he used both. The first theory suggests that Mark was simply being naïve.

The second theory suggests that Mark was making a profound theological point. In the first of the feedings, Jesus was welcoming the Jewish nation to the Messianic feast. In the second of the feedings, Jesus was opening the table to the Gentile nations as well. And all this was being made explicit through that enigmatic conversation with the Gentile woman of Syrophoenician origin.

If that second theory works, then there is significant symbolism in each component of the narrative. What do you think?

Take the locations where the feedings were set: the first around Galilee and the second around the Decapolis. Surely one suggests a Jewish crowd and one suggests a Gentile crowd?

Take the number of loaves: the first five loaves and the second seven loaves. Surely one suggests the five books of the Jewish law and one suggests the 70 nations of the Gentile world?

Take the number of basketfuls remaining: the first twelve basketfuls and the second seven basketfuls. Surely one suggests the twelve tribes of Israel and one suggests the 70 Gentile nations?

Take the two words for basket: the first *kophinos* and the second *spyris*. Surely one suggests the distinctively Jewish world and the other suggests the Gentile world?

So here is the rich Marcan symbolism. What do you think?

Feeling

It was really quite a day for the Syrophoenician woman.

The day began with the irrefutable diagnosis. Her little daughter was not herself today. She was clearly possessed, possessed by an unclean spirit. The diagnosis was not good. The Syrophoenician woman was filled with despair.

The day continued with the irresistible news. Jesus of Nazareth, it was rumoured, had crossed to the region of Tyre. Jesus of Nazareth was clearly around. The news was good. The Syrophoenician woman was filled with hope.

The conversation with Jesus began with undeniable difficulty. Jesus addressed her with directness and with discourtesy. 'Let the children be fed first,' he said, 'for it is not fair to take the children's food and throw it to the dogs.' In those words she clearly recognized the Jewish disdain for the Gentile people. The opening bid was not promising. The Syrophoenician woman was filled with foreboding.

The conversation with Jesus continued with unmistakable improvement. She addressed Jesus with directness and with determination. 'Sir,' she said, 'even the dogs under the table eat the children's crumbs.' Recognizing her status and accepting the insult, she pleaded her case. Her response was not fainthearted. The Syrophoenician woman was filled with determination.

The day ended with unforgettable reward. Jesus accepted her persuasion and complimented her perception. 'For saying that,' he said, 'you may go – the demon has left your daughter.' And the girl was made well. The Syrophoenician woman was filled with wonder and with gratitude.

It was really quite a day for the Syrophoenician woman.

Thinking

Really there is no point in trying to dodge this issue. Here is a story about unfairness and about injustice.

It is, after all, hardly fair that the young girl should have been invaded and possessed by an unclean spirit. She had no choice in the matter. She was clearly the unfortunate victim of the demonic realm. What kind of justice guides a world like that?

It is, after all, hardly fair that the Syrophoenician woman should have been taken to task for being of Gentile descent. She had no choice in the matter. She was clearly the unfortunate victim of the situation of her birth. What kind of justice guides a world like that?

It is, after all, hardly fair that Jesus should have addressed the woman with such discourtesy and disdain. The age-old history of conflict between Jews and Gentiles was not of her making. She was clearly the unfortunate victim of racism and ethnic stereotyping. What kind of justice guides a world like that?

But then, at last, when God acts decisively in the story, the injustice is reversed. The Syrophoenician woman is treated like one of the children and is no longer left outside like one of the dogs. The young girl is freed from the unclean spirit and is no longer left victim to demonic possession. What kind of God intervenes in a world like that?

This is a story not only about unfairness and about injustice, but about God's decisive activity as well.

20

Mark 8:27–38

²⁷Jesus went on with his disciples to the villages of Caesarea Philippi; and on the way he asked his disciples, 'Who do people say that I am?' ²⁸And they answered him, 'John the Baptist; and others, Elijah; and still others, one of the prophets.' ²⁹He asked them, 'But who do you say that I am?' Peter answered him, 'You are the Messiah.' ³⁰And he sternly ordered them not to tell anyone about him.

³¹Then he began to teach them that the Son of Man must undergo great suffering, and be rejected by the elders, the chief priests, and the scribes, and be killed, and after three days rise again. ³²He said all this quite openly. And Peter took him aside and began to rebuke him. ³³But turning and looking at his disciples, he rebuked Peter and said, 'Get behind me, Satan! For you are setting your mind not on divine things but on human things.'

³⁴He called the crowd with his disciples, and said to them, 'If any want to become my followers, let them deny themselves and take up their cross and follow me. ³⁵For those who want to save their life will lose it, and those who lose their life for my sake, and for the sake of the gospel, will save it. ³⁶For what will it profit them to gain the whole world and forfeit their life? ³⁷Indeed, what can they give in return for their life? ³⁸Those who are ashamed of me and of my words in this adulterous and sinful generation, of them the Son of Man will also be ashamed when he comes in the glory of his Father with the holy angels.'

Context

Peter's confession that Jesus is the Messiah marks the watershed or pivotal point in Mark's gospel. Up to this point the emphasis had been on preserving the secrecy of Jesus' Messiahship. From this point onwards the emphasis is on redefining Jesus' Messiahship in terms of suffering.

Sensing

Jesus' Messiahship had been a well-kept secret.

Recall how, in the early chapters of Mark's gospel, people kept wondering who Jesus really was. Remember how, in chapter 1, in the Capernaum synagogue they kept on asking one another, 'What is this? A new teaching – with authority!' Remember how, in chapter 4, they said one to another, 'Who then is this, that even the wind and the sea obey him?' Remember how, in chapter 6, even King Herod was asking the question.

Remember how, in the early chapters of Mark's gospel, only the world of spirits and demons recognized who Jesus really was. Remember how, in chapter 1, the man with an unclean spirit cried out, 'I know who you are, the holy one of God.' Remember how, in chapter 3, whenever unclean spirits saw Jesus they fell down before him and shouted, 'You are the Son of God.' Remember how, in chapter 5, the possessed Legion addressed Jesus as the Son of the Most High God.

Recall how, in the early chapters of Mark's gospel, people kept speculating about who Jesus really was, and people kept getting it wrong. Remember how, in chapter 6, people were speculating that Jesus was John the baptizer raised to life, or Elijah, or one of the prophets of old.

Recall how, in the early chapters of Mark's gospel, Jesus was so keen not to let the rumour get out about who he really was. Remember how, in chapter 1, Jesus would not permit the demons to speak out because they knew him. Remember how, in chapter 1, Jesus commanded the healed leper to say nothing to anyone. Remember how, in chapter 5, Jesus commanded Jairus to say nothing about his daughter's restoration.

Jesus' Messiahship had been a well-kept secret, right up to that moment when Peter spoke out. 'You,' Peter said, 'you are the Messiah.'

Intuition

Suppose Jesus had addressed the question to you, 'But who do *you* say that I am?' What kind of answer would you give?

Suppose Jesus had addressed the question to you. How useful do you find the traditional answers of formal theology? How much do words like *Christ* or *Messiah* really express what you mean? How much do statements like *Son of God* or *the only begotten son of the father* really go to the heart of the matter for you?

Suppose Jesus had addressed the question to you. How useful do you find the traditional answers of the faith? How much do words like *Saviour* or *Redeemer* really express what you mean? How much do statements like *the propitiation for our sins* or *the supreme mediator between God and humankind* really go to the heart of the matter for you?

Suppose Jesus had addressed the question to you. How useful do you find the traditional images of the church? How much do words like *teacher, healer, prophet, priest, king* or *shepherd* really express what you mean?

Suppose Jesus had addressed the question to you. How useful do you find the contemporary images of modern theology? How much do phrases like *ground of being* or *ultimate reality* express what you mean?

Suppose Jesus had addressed the question to you. How useful do you find the contemporary images of human relationships? How much do phrases like *constant companion, true lover, sincere confidant,* or *most intimate friend* really go to the heart of the matter for you?

Suppose Jesus had addressed the question to you, 'But who do *you* say that I am?' What kind of answer would you give?

Feeling

For Peter the whole business must have been so unnerving. Try putting yourself in his shoes.

Ever since he had been called away from his fishing nets, Peter had felt himself drawn deeper and deeper into the mystery of Jesus' very being. Peter had listened to the stirring teaching and recognized the voice of authority. He had witnessed the stirring acts and recognized the unprecedented power, as lepers were cleansed, demoniacs released, storms stilled, and the dead raised. It must all have been so unnerving.

Ever since he had been called away from his fishing nets, Peter had struggled to give voice to his growing conviction. And now, at last, he could contain his conviction no longer. He spoke out and heard himself say, 'You are the Messiah.' It must all have been so unnerving.

No sooner had the words left his lips than Peter saw the smile leave Jesus' face. No sooner had Peter looked in Jesus' eyes to receive affirmation for his faith, than he heard the voice of rebuke. It must all have been so unnerving.

No sooner had Peter unfolded his vision of Messiahship, than Jesus stood the concept on its head. No sooner had Peter contemplated regal glory, than Jesus spoke of suffering, rejection and death. It must all have been so unnerving.

No sooner had Peter penetrated to the depths of the divine intention, than Jesus addressed him as Satan, and accused him of setting his mind not on divine things but on human things. It must all have been so unnerving.

For Peter the whole business must have been so unnerving. Try putting yourself in his shoes.

Thinking

So Jesus rebuked Peter for getting his thinking all wrong. 'Get behind me, Satan!' said Jesus to Peter. 'For you are setting your mind not on divine things but on human things.' Do you think Jesus was really being fair to Peter?

Look at the evidence. Peter had listened to Jesus' teaching that the kingdom of God had drawn near. And if God's reign was so clearly upon them, surely the Messianic age had dawned. Was not Peter reading the evidence correctly?

Look at the evidence. Peter had witnessed Jesus' acts of power. He had experienced the stilling of the storm. He had seen the healing of the leper. He had been there when Jairus' daughter was raised from the dead. And if God's reign was so clearly evident, surely the Messianic age had dawned. Was not Peter reading the evidence correctly?

Look at the authority. Peter had heard the words of scripture. He had listened to the Jewish hopes for the day of the Messiah. All the authorities pointed to God's triumphal splendour. Was not Peter understanding the authorities correctly?

Look at the contradiction. In one and the selfsame breath Jesus both accepted the title *Messiah* and set that title on its head. The discontinuity is profound. The paradox is stark. Was not Peter behaving quite rationally in rejecting such a sudden *volte-face*?

So Jesus rebuked Peter for getting his thinking all wrong. 'Get behind me, Satan!' said Jesus to Peter. 'For you are setting your mind not on divine things but on human things.' Do you think Jesus was really being fair to Peter?

21
Mark 9:2–9

²Six days later, Jesus took with him Peter and James and John, and led them up a high mountain apart, by themselves. And he was transfigured before them, ³and his clothes became dazzling white, such as no one on earth could bleach them. ⁴And there appeared to them Elijah with Moses, who were talking with Jesus. ⁵Then Peter said to Jesus, 'Rabbi, it is good for us to be here; let us make three dwellings, one for you, one for Moses, and one for Elijah.' ⁶He did not know what to say, for they were terrified. ⁷Then a cloud overshadowed them, and from the cloud there came a voice, 'This is my Son, the Beloved; listen to him!' ⁸Suddenly when they looked around, they saw no one with them any more, but only Jesus.

⁹As they were coming down the mountain, he ordered them to tell no one about what they had seen, until after the Son of Man had risen from the dead.

Context

The major watershed or turning point in Mark's gospel is provided by Peter's confession at Caesarea Philippi. Then Mark places the account of the transfiguration of Jesus immediately after Peter's confession. Here, then, is the seal of divine approval.

Sensing

The transfiguration is a narrative rich in sensory images. So come and explore.

Put on your climbing shoes and come climbing. Climb, climb, climb the high mountain. Feel the atmosphere change as you rise high above the pollution. Hear the sounds of traffic, chatter and work grow faint as you rise high above the noise. See the sights of people, houses and farms grow small, as you rise high above the world. Standing there, high on the mountain, you feel on top of the world and as if you have approached the gateway to heaven. Put on your climbing shoes and come climbing.

Put on your glasses and come looking. Look, look, look

carefully as Jesus stands there before you. See Jesus transfigured before your very eyes. See Jesus' clothes become dazzling white, whiter than any washing powder's wildest dream. See the sky open and Elijah and Moses appear. Standing there surrounded by such powerful sights, you feel as if you have approached the gateway to heaven. Put on your glasses and come looking.

Plug in your personal stereo and come listening. Listen, listen, listen carefully as Jesus stands there before you. Hear the divine voice speak from the clouds. Hear the affirmation and hear the command. 'This is my Son, the Beloved; listen to him!' Standing there surrounded by such powerful sounds, you feel as if you have approached the gateway to heaven. Plug in your personal stereo and come listening.

The transfiguration is a narrative rich in sensory images. So come and explore.

Intuition

Just occasionally in our spiritual life the curtains of heaven are pulled back and we are vouchsafed a vision of the glorious reality of God. I wonder what your experience has been?

Have you been out climbing and risen high above the mundane issues of daily life? Has the majesty of height opened your heart to the presence of God?

Have you been out walking at night when the sky is clear and when the stars shine bright? Has the magnitude of the night sky opened your heart to the presence of God?

Have you been out sailing on the still and open sea miles from all sight of land? Has the vastness of the waters opened your heart to the presence of God?

Have you been out visiting some prehistoric site where the forces of nature have shaped the landscape? Has the unrecorded passing of time opened your heart to the presence of God?

Have you been out looking into the face of a newborn child and recognized the archetype of humanity? Has the mystery of human life opened your heart to the presence of God?

Have you been out worshipping in the midst of the people of God where the Spirit is at work? Has the conviction of the Spirit's activity opened your heart to the presence of God?

Have you been out meditating alone before the blessed sacrament? Has the reality of the body of Christ opened your heart to the presence of God?

Just occasionally in our spiritual life the curtains of heaven are pulled back and we are vouchsafed a vision of the glorious reality of God. I wonder what your experiences have been?

Feeling

Just three special disciples stand at the heart of this narrative: Peter, James and John. I wonder what it felt like to be singled out in that way?

Look to the past and recall how those three special disciples, Peter, James and John, had been singled out once before. On that past occasion they had followed Jesus through the crowds to the home of Jairus, one of the leaders of the synagogue. On that past occasion they had been led through the house to the room where the dead girl lay. On that past occasion they, and they alone, had witnessed the dead restored to life. I wonder what kind of feelings that had engendered in Peter, James and John?

Look to the present occasion and see how these three special disciples, Peter, James and John, are singled out again. On this present occasion they follow Jesus right to the top of the mountain. On this present occasion they are led to stand in the presence of Elijah and Moses. On this present occasion they, and they alone, witness the transfiguration of Jesus as he stands in glory. I wonder what kind of feelings that engenders in Peter, James and John?

Look to a future occasion and see how these three special disciples, Peter, James and John, are singled out once more. On this future occasion they will follow Jesus through the Mount of Olives. On this future occasion they will be led to a place called Gethsemane. On this future occasion they, and they alone, will witness the agony which Jesus experiences in the garden before his arrest. I wonder what kind of feelings this will engender in Peter, James and John?

Just three special disciples stand at the heart of this narrative: Peter, James and John. I wonder what it felt like to be singled out in that way?

Thinking

If we are going to appreciate the theological significance of Mark's account of the transfiguration, we must begin to interrogate some of his detail.

Why, so uncharacteristically, does Mark begin the narrative

with such a precise location in time? Why *six days later*? Was this simply to bind this narrative to Peter's confession at Caesarea Philippi? Or is this a deliberate echo of the six days during which Moses waited before the Lord spoke out of the cloud (Exodus 24)?

Why does Mark locate the narrative so precisely *up a high mountain*? Was this simply to emphasize encounter with transcendence? Or is this a deliberate echo of God's decisive revelation to the people of the old Israel on Mount Sinai (Exodus 24)?

Why does Mark describe with such care the *dazzling* whiteness of Jesus' clothes? Was this simply to emphasize the supernatural nature of the occurrence? Or is there a deliberate echo of the way in which Moses had been transfigured by his encounter with God on the mountain (Exodus 34)?

Why does Mark identify so clearly the presence of *Elijah and Moses*? Was this simply to emphasize continuity with the old order? Or is there a deliberate allusion to Jesus being affirmed by the *Law* and the *Prophets*? And had not Malachi (chapter 4) promised that Elijah would come before the great and terrible day of the Lord?

Why does Mark refer so purposefully to the voice coming from *the cloud*? Was this simply to emphasize the mysterious nature of the revelation? Or is there a deliberate attempt to identify the voice as that of God alone, who spoke to Moses out of the self same cloud (Exodus 24)?

Why does Mark attribute to the divine voice words both so similar and so dissimilar to those cited at the moment of baptism? Is this carelessness or deliberate subtlety? At the baptism, when Jesus was *anointed* Messiah by the baptizer, God spoke to Jesus and to Jesus alone, 'You are my Son, the Beloved.' At the transfiguration, when Jesus' anointed Messiahship had been recognized and confessed by Peter, God spoke publicly, 'This is my Son, the Beloved.'

If we are going to appreciate the theological significance of Mark's account of the transfiguration, we must begin to interrogate some of this detail.

22

Mark 9:30–37

[30]They went on from there and passed through Galilee. He did not want anyone to know it; [31]for he was teaching his disciples, saying to them, 'The Son of Man is to be betrayed into human hands, and they will kill him, and three days after being killed, he will rise again.' [32]But they did not understand what he was saying and were afraid to ask him.

[33]Then they came to Capernaum; and when he was in the house he asked them, 'What were you arguing about on the way?' [34]But they were silent, for on the way they had argued with one another who was the greatest. [35]He sat down, called the twelve, and said to them, 'Whoever wants to be first must be last of all and servant of all.' [36]Then he took a little child and put it among them; and taking it in his arms, he said to them, [37]'Whoever welcomes one such child in my name welcomes me, and whoever welcomes me welcomes not me but the one who sent me.'

Context

According to Mark, after Peter's confession at Caesarea Philippi, Jesus made three clear predictions of the passion. Chapter 9 presents the second prediction: the other two are set out in 8:31 and 10:32. Each prediction is followed by disciples failing to grasp how things really are and what really matters.

Sensing

Cast your mind back and remember what it was like to be a six-year-old child. Picture your size and remember what it was like to be a pygmy in a land of giants. Remember how tall adults looked. Remember how steep were the treads on the stairs. Remember how you had to stretch to reach the cupboard. Remember how you had to struggle to sit on the stool. Remember how your arms were never quite long enough.

Cast your mind back and remember what it was like to be a six-year-old child. Remember how much you did not know. Recall how much you did not understand. Think how your vocabulary has grown. Think how your skills have expanded. Think how your perception of people has matured.

Cast your mind back and remember what it was like to be a six-year-old child. Remember the skills which you had not yet acquired. Think of life before you could drive a car or ride a bike. Think of life before you could buy alcohol or watch an adult movie. Think of life before you had a mortgage or accepted adult responsibilities.

Cast your mind back and remember what it was like to be treated as a six-year-old child by a world full of adults. Remember how adults did not notice you were there and trampled you underfoot. Remember how adults did not take your views into account and rode roughshod over your opinions. Remember how adults sent out the message that might really rules and that size really matters.

Cast your mind back and remember what it was like to be a six-year-old child. Picture yourself as a pygmy in a land of giants. Then remember that Jesus said, 'Whoever welcomes one such child in my name welcomes me.'

Intuition

Jesus took a little child in his arms and said to the disciples, 'Whoever welcomes one such child in my name welcomes me.' So where do you see that welcome today?

Do you see that welcome in schools, as dedicated teachers care for and shape young lives? Is Jesus truly welcomed there?

Do you see that welcome in children's hospital wards, as specialist nurses and doctors care for and heal young lives? Is Jesus truly welcomed there?

Do you see that welcome in the leaders of voluntary groups, like the Cubs and the Brownies, as the Brown Owl and Akela care for and shape young lives? Is Jesus truly welcomed there?

Do you see that welcome in counsellors and social workers, as they try to deal with the trauma and distress of young lives? Is Jesus truly welcomed there?

Do you see the welcome in the international care agencies, as child poverty, child abuse and child exploitation are brought on to the political agenda? Is Jesus truly welcomed there?

Do you see that welcome in the local church, as infants, children and adolescents are fully embraced as rightful members of the family of God? Is Jesus truly welcomed there?

Jesus took a young child in his arms and said to the disciples, 'Whoever welcomes one such child in my name welcomes me.' So where do you see that welcome today?

Feeling

It must have been difficult for those early disciples to come to terms with the ruthless way in which Jesus so consistently turned their expectations upside down. Can you imagine what it must have been like for them?

Put yourself in the disciples' place that day, as they pass through Galilee, as Jesus unfolded to them the stark plain facts. Put yourself in the disciples' place as Jesus predicted that 'The Son of Man is to be betrayed into human hands, and they will kill him, and three days after being killed, he will rise again.' Could anything have prepared the disciples for such reversal of their hopes for the Messiah, the promised one of God? Can you imagine their feelings of profound confusion, their feelings of disturbed equilibrium?

Put yourself in the disciples' place that day, as they were arguing on the way, and as they tried to establish their rightful ranking within the kingdom. Put yourself in the disciples' place as Jesus unwrapped to them the stark plain facts, as he asserted the principle of the kingdom that 'Whoever wants to be first must be last of all.' Could anything have prepared those disciples for such reversal of their understanding of life in the kingdom? Can you imagine their feelings of profound confusion, their feelings of disturbed equilibrium?

Put yourself in the disciples' place that day, as Jesus embraced a little child, as he unlocked to them the stark plain facts. Put yourself in the disciples' place as Jesus affirmed his own status in society by saying that 'Whoever welcomes one such child in my name welcomes me.' Could anything have prepared them for such reversal of majesty and power? Can you imagine their feelings of profound confusion, their feelings of disturbed equilibrium?

It must have been difficult for those early disciples to come to terms with the ruthless way in which Jesus so consistently turned their expectations upside down. Can you imagine what it must have been like for them?

Thinking

The three clear and precise predictions of the passion in Mark chapters 8, 9 and 10 raise an interesting question for New Testament scholars. Did Jesus really make predictions with this detail, or has the early church embroidered the prophecy with the wisdom of hindsight? Well, what do you think?

The case for later embroidery goes like this. First, the detail of the predictions is very accurate. Mark chapter 8, for example, notes four clear sequential points: the Son of Man will undergo great suffering, be rejected by the elders, chief priests and scribes, be killed, and after three days rise again. Mark chapter 10 goes into even greater detail and adds six further clear points: the Son of Man will be handed over to the chief priests and scribes, and they will condemn him to death; then they will hand him over to the Gentiles, who will mock him, spit upon him and flog him. Second, had the original disciples really been prepared for the passion, crucifixion and resurrection in such a careful and systematic way, it is unbelievable that they should have been so taken by surprise by the events when they happened. Mark attempts to address this problem by phrases like, 'But they did not understand what Jesus was saying and were afraid to ask him.' Such attempts, however, fail to carry conviction. Surely Jesus spoke plainly enough? Third, the formulae presented by Mark, especially in chapter 10, read like post-resurrection credal statements. They sound like the early church's way of condensing and communicating their faith in the death and resurrection of Jesus. So what do you think?

The case for authenticity goes like this. First, as the Son of God, Jesus has every right and every power to be in command of his own destiny. The passion, crucifixion and resurrection were all foreordained as part of the divine economy for the salvation of the fallen human race. It is quite appropriate that Jesus should have known and shared such insights and such detail with his closest followers. Second, the obtuseness of the disciples presents no real problem. This, too, was all part of the divine plan. After all, in spite of being so close to Jesus, these original disciples were no less part of the fallen human race. As Mark so clearly pointed out in chapter 8, their minds remain set on human things, not on divine things.

Third, the formulae presented by Mark, especially in chapter

10, show all the signs of carefully constructed prophetic utterances, designed to be concise and memorable. After all, the Old Testament test for a true prophet is whether or not the prophecy comes true. Well, what do you think?

The three clear and precise predictions of the passion in Mark chapters 8, 9 and 10 raise an interesting question for New Testament scholars.

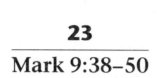

23
Mark 9:38–50

[38]John said to him, 'Teacher, we saw someone casting out demons in your name, and we tried to stop him, because he was not following us.' [39]But Jesus said, 'Do not stop him; for no one who does a deed of power in my name will be able soon afterward to speak evil of me. [40]Whoever is not against us is for us. [41]For truly I tell you, whoever gives you a cup of water to drink because you bear the name of Christ will by no means lose the reward.

[42]'If any of you put a stumbling block before one of these little ones who believe in me, it would be better for you if a great millstone were hung around your neck and you were thrown into the sea. [43]If your hand causes you to stumble, cut it off; it is better for you to enter life maimed than to have two hands and to go to hell, to the unquenchable fire. [45]And if your foot causes you to stumble, cut it off; it is better for you to enter life lame than to have two feet and to be thrown into hell. [47]And if your eye causes you to stumble, tear it out; it is better for you to enter the kingdom of God with one eye than to have two eyes and to be thrown into hell, [48]where their worm never dies, and the fire is never quenched.

[49]'For everyone will be salted with fire. [50]Salt is good; but if salt has lost its saltiness, how can you season it? Have salt in yourselves, and be at peace with one another.'

Context

This passage follows the second of the three predictions of the passion, which give structure to this part of Mark's gospel. After the first prediction, Mark tells how the disciples had failed to cast out an evil spirit (Mark 9:14–29). Now after the second prediction, Mark tells how the disciples witnessed others casting out demons in Jesus' name. After Jesus' death, the church must be prepared for difficulties and for surprises.

Sensing

There you are with Peter, James and John and all the other disciples. Pay attention to what has been happening since that momentous occasion when Peter said to Jesus, 'You are the Christ!' In particular, picture two contrasting occasions.

On the first occasion picture a distressed and distraught father. See the despair in the father's face. Hear the anxiety in the father's voice. Sense the desperation in the father's manner. Hear that father beg the disciples to cast out an unclean spirit from his son. See the son distressed and distraught. See the look of possession in the son's face. Sense the reality of possession in the son's manner.

On that first occasion picture the disciples standing there helpless and hopeless as the unclean spirit refuses to budge.

On the second occasion picture a jubilant and joyful father. See the gratitude in the father's face. Hear the exultation in the father's voice. Sense the excitement in the father's manner. Hear that father thank a group of strangers for casting out an unclean spirit in Jesus' name. See the son content and at peace. See the look of wholeness in the son's face. Sense the reality of healing in the son's manner.

On that second occasion picture the disciples standing there helpless and confused as a group of strangers work wonders in Jesus' name.

There you are with Peter, James and John and all the other disciples. Pay attention to what has been happening since that momentous occasion when Peter said to Jesus, 'You are the Christ!'

Intuition

Those early disciples found the power of Jesus at work where they least expected it. Open your hearts and speculate. Where have you glimpsed the power of Jesus at work in recent days?

Think about what you have experienced in your place of work. Think about the individuals whose lives have interacted with your life. Stop and think. In your place of work have you glimpsed the power of Jesus in unexpected ways or among unexpected people? Give thanks to God for the unexpected presence of Christ.

Think about what you have experienced among your family and friends. Think about the individuals whose lives have interacted with yours. Stop and think. Among your family and friends have you glimpsed the power of Jesus in unexpected ways or among unexpected people? Give thanks to God for the unexpected presence of Christ.

Think about what you have read in the newspapers, heard on the radio, or seen on the television. Think about the individuals whose lives have made an impact on your memory. Stop and think. In the happenings of the wide world, have you glimpsed the power of Jesus in unexpected ways and among unexpected people? Give thanks to God for the unexpected presence of Christ.

Those early disciples found the power of Jesus at work where they least expected it. Open your hearts and speculate. Where have you glimpsed the power of Jesus at work in recent days?

Feeling

Life in the kingdom of God is full of surprises. Put yourself in the shoes of those early disciples and explore how they felt in the face of such unpredictable goings-on.

Having followed Jesus so closely, having listened to Jesus so carefully, having been commissioned by Jesus so authoritatively, surely those early disciples had every right to expect to act decisively in Jesus' name. Share in their feeling of confidence.

Having laid such open claim to cast out demons in Jesus' name, having already such good experience of exercising this power, surely those early disciples had every right to expect this demon also to yield. Share in their feeling of anticipation.

Having encouraged the father, having welcomed the son, having confronted the demon, surely those early disciples had every right to expect the healing power of Jesus to flow at their command. Share in their feelings of surprise and confusion.

Having never seen those strangers following Jesus, having never seen those strangers listening to Jesus, having never seen those strangers commissioned by Jesus, surely those early

disciples had every right to expect Jesus to withdraw authoriza-
tion from their activities. Share in their feelings of indignation.

Having heard Jesus endorse such unlicensed exorcisms, having heard Jesus support such unfranchized healings, having heard
Jesus condone such uncontrolled ministry, surely those early
disciples had every right to be disturbed and perplexed. Share in
their feelings of surprise and confusion.

Life in the kingdom of God is full of surprises. Put yourself in
the shoes of those early disciples and explore how they felt in the
face of such unpredictable goings on.

Thinking

This account of the disciples trying to stop an unauthorized exorcist raises major questions about church order and discipline. Two
very different views exist. So what do you think?

The first view emphasizes the need for order and for control.
Without order and control just anyone could set up shop as
teacher, priest or healer in Jesus' name. And what guarantee
would there be of any real continuity between each and every
teacher, priest and healer and the authentic truth and power of
Christ bequeathed to the church? So what do you think?

The first view tests the truth of doctrine by distinguishing
carefully between orthodoxy and heresy. Preachers who deny
the accepted truths of the faith may have their licence to preach
withdrawn. The first view tests the validity of ministry by
distinguishing carefully between individuals who are self-
appointed and those who have been selected, trained and
authorized by accredited denominations. So what do you
think?

The second view emphasizes the need for greater openness
and flexibility. Without openness and flexibility no room is left
for the spontaneity of the Holy Spirit. And what guarantee would
there be that the gatekeepers of orthodoxy and ministry are
properly open to the promptings of the Holy Spirit. So what do
you think?

The second view points out that Jesus himself stood outside
the orthodox teaching and the authorized ministry of his own
generation. The second view points out that many major
developments in the life of the worldwide church of Christ have
sprung precisely from the Holy Spirit working outside the structures of the church. Examples are provided by the Reformation in

the fifteenth and sixteenth centuries and by the Pentecostal revival in the twentieth century. So what do you think?

This account of the disciples trying to stop an unauthorized exorcist raises major questions about church order and discipline. Two very different views exist. So what do you think?

24

Mark 10:2–16

²Some Pharisees came, and to test him they asked, 'Is it lawful for a man to divorce his wife?' ³He answered them, 'What did Moses command you?' ⁴They said, 'Moses allowed a man to write a certificate of dismissal and to divorce her.' ⁵But Jesus said to them, 'Because of your hardness of heart he wrote this commandment for you. ⁶But from the beginning of creation, "God made them male and female." ⁷"For this reason a man shall leave his father and mother and be joined to his wife, ⁸and the two shall become one flesh." So they are no longer two, but one flesh. ⁹Therefore what God has joined together, let no one separate.'

¹⁰Then in the house the disciples asked him again about this matter. ¹¹He said to them, 'Whoever divorces his wife and marries another commits adultery against her; ¹²and if she divorces her husband and marries another, she commits adultery.'

¹³People were bringing little children to him in order that he might touch them; and the disciples spoke sternly to them. ¹⁴But when Jesus saw this, he was indignant and said to them, 'Let the little children come to me; do not stop them; for it is to such as these that the kingdom of God belongs. ¹⁵Truly I tell you, whoever does not receive the kingdom of God as a little child will never enter it.' ¹⁶And he took them up in his arms, laid his hands on them, and blessed them.

Context

As Jesus makes his way from Galilee to Jerusalem, where he will be put to death, he continues to teach about life in the kingdom of God. In this passage Mark presents his understanding of marriage and of divorce within the kingdom of God. Biblical scholars are careful to note that *divorce* in the society of Jesus' day meant something rather different from divorce in today's society.

Sensing

Today you come as an honoured guest to the wedding. Open your eyes and describe all that you see. See the bride dressed in her long flowing gown, with white veil and white train. See the bridesmaids stand in attendance. See the groom dressed in his neatly pressed suit, with black top hat and black shoes. See the best man stand in attendance. Look into the eyes of the bride and the groom and see there the love and the commitment. See the rings exchanged. See the minister join their hands and bless them as man and wife.

Today you come as an honoured guest to the wedding. Open your eyes and describe all that you see. See the bride and the groom sign their name in the register as a permanent reminder of their intention. See the witnesses and the minister sign their names alongside the bride and groom as a permanent testimony of the sacred act. See the photographer seize every opportunity to create a permanent record of the holy occasion.

Today you come as an honoured guest to the wedding. Sniff the atmosphere and describe all that you smell. Smell the sweet fragrance of the flowers which so fittingly decorate the church. Smell the bride's bouquet. Smell the groom's buttonhole. Smell the promise of stability and permanence which hangs so heavily in the air.

Today you come as an honoured guest to the wedding. Prick up your ears and describe all that you hear. Hear the majestic wedding march as the bride walks down the aisle. Hear the joyful peal of the church bells. Hear the sweet singing in the choir. Hear the solemn vows so seriously taken by the bride and by the groom. Hear the awesome words of the minister as the couple are pronounced man and wife, 'What God has joined together, let no one separate.'

Today you come as an honoured guest to the wedding. Ponder over everything you have seen and everything you have heard.

Intuition

Life is rarely a bed of roses, even in the kingdom of God. Consider the pressures under which marriages are placed in today's world and ask how can the churches really help.

Go right back to secondary school and ask what preparation is given there for marriage and for family life. How can the ideals of Christian marriage be given a fair hearing alongside the values of secular society?

Go back to the opportunity which the church has to prepare couples for marriage. How can the local church be adequately and properly resourced to carry out such a crucial ministry?

Look at the examples of married life presented within the local congregation. How can such examples be openly, honestly and lovingly utilized to help the people of God face the reality of marriage in today's world?

Listen to the cries for help voiced by couples within your community. How can such couples be helped to face their difficulties and to appreciate each other's perspectives?

Look at the organizations in your area which exist to help people cope with marriage and family life. How can such organizations be properly resourced?

Look at the opportunities within the Christian community for programmes of marriage enrichment and the enhancement of family life. How well known are such opportunities within your own congregation?

Life is rarely a bed of roses, even in the kingdom of God. Consider the pressures under which marriages are placed in today's world and ask how can the churches really help.

Feeling

The question of divorce and the remarriage of divorcees is a matter which has vexed the church for years. Have a heart and ask whether the church should not exercise compassion and give people a second chance.

Consider, for example, Jennifer. She married, quite young, someone more experienced than herself. Right from the start her husband betrayed her trust and within a year or two had moved on to share his life with another partner. Who could deny Jennifer a second chance to establish a new life with someone more devoted to her well-being, and to begin that life with promises made in the presence of God?

Consider, for example, Jonathan. He too married, quite young, someone committed to her business career. Early on she admitted to an affair with a business colleague and asked Jonathan for a divorce. Who could deny Jonathan a second chance to establish a new life with someone more dedicated to family matters, and to begin that life with promises made in the presence of God?

Consider, for example, Richard. He married quite late, someone so very different from himself. It was neither's fault, but they were never really suited. Amicably they decided their ways should part. Who could deny Richard a second chance to establish a new life with someone better suited to his personality, and to begin that life with promises made in the presence of God?

Consider, for example, Rachel. She married someone less talented, less ambitious than herself. Quite frankly she became frustrated when her own career was held back by her husband's lack of drive. She moved out to reassume the life of a bachelor girl. Who could deny Rachel a second chance to establish a life with someone better suited to her ambition, and to begin that life with promises made in the presence of God?

The question of divorce and the remarriage of divorcees is a matter which has vexed the church for years. Have a heart and ask whether the church should not exercise compassion and give people a second chance.

Thinking

The New Testament scholar, anxious to discover what Jesus really said about divorce, has the problem of reconciling this account in Mark with a somewhat different account in Matthew 19:3–9. I wonder what you think about that?

In Mark, Pharisees ask Jesus the direct question, 'Is it lawful for a man to divorce his wife?' In Matthew, Pharisees ask Jesus about *grounds* on which divorce is lawful. Those who think that Matthew is more authentic argue that Pharisees would never have voiced the question as reported by Mark. Since the Deuteronomic law was so clear about the possibility of divorce, the only *real* question concerned the debate regarding the grounds on which divorce was to be permitted. So is Matthew nearer the truth?

In Mark, Jesus makes the uncompromising pronouncement, 'Whoever divorces his wife and marries another commits adultery against her.' In Matthew, Jesus makes the less uncompromising pronouncement, 'Whoever divorces his wife, except for unchastity, and marries another commits adultery.' Those who think that Matthew is more authentic argue that Jesus is properly engaging in the debate of his generation by adjudicating between the different grounds for divorce. So is Matthew nearer the truth?

In Mark, Jesus balances his statement about the man divorcing his wife with the parallel statement, 'And if she divorces her husband and marries another, she commits adultery.' In Matthew, Jesus makes no reference to the woman initiating divorce. Those who think that Matthew is more authentic argue that the right of a woman to divorce her husband (although established in Roman law) was unknown in Jewish law and in the context to which Jesus was speaking. So is Matthew nearer the truth?

Those who think that Mark is more authentic argue that generally Matthew used Mark as his major source. On this account, Matthew would have deliberately changed Mark's text in order to make it more accessible to his Jewish audience. So, after all, is Mark nearer the truth?

The New Testament scholar, anxious to discover what Jesus *really* said about divorce, has the problem of reconciling the two accounts in Matthew and Mark. I wonder what you think about that?

———————————➤-◉-◄———————————

25

Mark 10:17–31

¹⁷As he was setting out on a journey, a man ran up and knelt before him, and asked him, 'Good Teacher, what must I do to inherit eternal life?' ¹⁸Jesus said to him, 'Why do you call me good? No one is good but God alone. ¹⁹You know the commandments: "You shall not murder; You shall not commit adultery; You shall not steal; You shall not bear false witness; You shall not defraud; Honour your father and mother."' ²⁰He said to him, 'Teacher, I have kept all these since my youth.' ²¹Jesus, looking at him, loved him and said, 'You lack one thing; go, sell what you own, and give the money to the poor, and you will have treasure in heaven; then come, follow me.' ²²When he heard this, he was shocked and went away grieving, for he had many possessions.

²³Then Jesus looked around and said to his disciples, 'How hard it will be for those who have wealth to enter the kingdom of God!' ²⁴And the disciples were perplexed at these words. But Jesus said to them again, 'Children, how hard it is to enter the kingdom

of God! [25]It is easier for a camel to go through the eye of a needle than for someone who is rich to enter the kingdom of God.' [26]They were greatly astounded and said to one another, 'Then who can be saved?' [27]Jesus looked at them and said, 'For mortals it is impossible, but not for God; for God all things are possible.'

[28]Peter began to say to him, 'Look, we have left everything and followed you.' [29]Jesus said, 'Truly I tell you, there is no one who has left house or brothers or sisters or mother or father or children or fields, for my sake and for the sake of the good news, [30]who will not receive a hundredfold now in this age – houses, brothers and sisters, mothers and children, and fields with persecutions – and in the age to come eternal life. [31]But many who are first will be last, and the last will be first.'

Context

As Jesus makes his way from Galilee to Jerusalem, where he will be put to death, he continues to teach about life in the kingdom of God. In this passage Mark presents his understanding of riches in the kingdom of God.

Sensing

Sometimes possessions can get in the way of the kingdom of God.

Place a pound coin in the palm of your hand or picture a pound coin in your imagination. See the Queen's head on the face and feel the rough texture of the edges. Now begin to picture all that you can buy with that pound coin. Picture what you would most like to possess for a pound. Go on, spend it all at once. Do you sense that possessions like this can get in the way of your relationship with God?

Place a ten-pound note in the palm of your hand or picture a ten-pound note in your imagination. See the Queen's head on the face and feel the crisp paper between your fingers. Now begin to picture all that you can buy with that ten-pound note. Picture what you would most like to possess for ten pounds. Go on, spend it all at once. Do you sense that possessions like this can get in the way of your relationship with God?

Picture a cheque for a thousand pounds in your imagination. See your name written clearly on the top line and feel the crisp paper between your fingers. Now begin to picture all that you can buy with that cheque for a thousand pounds. Picture what you would most like to possess for a thousand pounds. Go on, spend it all at once. Do you sense that possessions like this can get in the way of your relationship with God?

Picture a cheque for one hundred thousand pounds in your imagination. See your name written clearly on the top line and feel the crisp paper between your fingers. Now begin to picture all that you can buy with that cheque for one hundred thousand pounds. Picture what you would most like to possess for one hundred thousand pounds. Go on, spend it all at once. Do you sense that possessions like this can get in the way of your relationship with God? Sometimes possessions can get in the way of the kingdom of God.

Intuition

Live dangerously for a few moments and imagine what it would be like to exchange your worldly possessions for treasure in heaven.

Live dangerously and give away your job to help the unemployed. Free yourself from the drudgery of the workplace to serve full time in the kingdom of God. But surely Jesus must be joking: who would benefit from behaviour like that?

Live dangerously and give away your car to help the immobile. Free yourself from polluting the atmosphere and burning up the world's oil resources. But surely Jesus must be joking: who would benefit from behaviour like that?

Live dangerously and give away your wardrobe to clothe the naked. Free yourself from the vanity of deciding what to wear each day. But surely Jesus must be joking: who would benefit from behaviour like that?

Live dangerously and give away the contents of your freezer and of your larder to feed the hungry. Free yourself from the anxiety of deciding what to eat each day. But surely Jesus must be joking: who would benefit from behaviour like that?

Live dangerously and give away your house to home the homeless. Free yourself from the stranglehold of mortgage repayments, water rates, council taxes and home insurance policies. But surely Jesus must be joking: who would benefit from behaviour like that?

Live dangerously for a few moments and imagine what it would be like to exchange your worldly possessions for treasure in heaven.

Feeling

The central character in this narrative is the young man who dared to ask a question. Try to see the story from his perspective.

Here is a young man who had set his heart on the most precious goal of all. This young man was seeking after eternal life. Share in his piety.

Here is a young man who had recognized in Jesus the most important religious teacher of them all. This young man knelt before Jesus: share in his adoration.

Here is a young man who openly placed his life's goal at Jesus' feet. This young man came seeking Jesus' guidance. Share in his supplication.

Here is a young man who had struggled to live the exemplary moral life. This young man had kept the commandments of God. Share in his obedience.

Here is a young man who is painfully aware that obedience alone was an inadequate foundation for the religious life. This young man was questing more. Share in his perception.

Here is a young man who could not stomach the advice Jesus offered to him. This young man was too attached to his past to embrace the new future which Jesus held out to him. This young man went away grieving. Share in his grief.

The central character in this narrative is the young man who dared to ask a question. Try to see the story from his perspective.

Thinking

Jesus' answer to the rich young man forces us constantly to critique the church's understanding of wealth. So how do you square Jesus' teaching with the wealth of the church?

Consider the fine buildings which the church possesses in the cities, towns and villages of our land. Consider the money spent on the upkeep of such fine architecture. How do you square this with Jesus' teaching on poverty? Or are such buildings essential witnesses to the stability and permanence of the faith?

Consider the precious gold and silver vessels and the precious jewels which the church possesses in the cities, towns and villages of our land. Consider the money spent on insuring such priceless objects or storing them in bank vaults. How do you square this with Jesus' teaching on poverty? Or are such possessions essential witnesses to the importance of religion in their benefactors' lives?

Consider the majestic robes and vestments which the church possesses in the cities, towns and villages of our land. Consider the time and skill invested in creating and maintaining such glorious objects. How do you square this with Jesus' teaching on poverty? Or are such vestments essential witnesses to the glory and majesty of worship?

Consider the huge wealth which the church has invested in land, in buildings and in the international money market. Consider the revenue generated by such investments. How do you square this with Jesus' teaching on poverty? Or are such financial infrastructures essential to safeguarding the mission of the church into the future?

Jesus' answer to the rich young man forces us constantly to critique the church's understanding of wealth. So how do you square Jesus' teaching with the wealth of the church?

26
Mark 10:35–45

³⁵James and John, the sons of Zebedee, came forward to him and said to him, 'Teacher, we want you to do for us whatever we ask of you.' ³⁶And he said to them, 'What is it you want me to do for you?' ³⁷And they said to him, 'Grant us to sit, one at your right hand and one at your left, in your glory.' ³⁸But Jesus said to them, 'You do not know what you are asking. Are you able to drink the cup that I drink, or be baptized with the baptism that I am baptized with?' ³⁹They replied, 'We are able.' Then Jesus said to them, 'The cup that I drink you will drink; and with the baptism with which I am baptized, you will be baptized; ⁴⁰but to sit at my right hand or at my left is not mine to grant, but it is for those for whom it has been prepared.'

⁴¹When the ten heard this, they began to be angry with James and John. ⁴²So Jesus called them and said to them, 'You know that among the Gentiles those whom they recognize as their rulers lord it over them, and their great ones are tyrants over them. ⁴³But it is not so among you; but whoever wishes to become great among you must be your servant, ⁴⁴and whoever wishes to be first among you must be slave of all. ⁴⁵For the Son of Man came not to be served but to serve, and to give his life a ransom for many.'

Context

Following Peter's confession at Caesarea Philippi, Mark presents three clear predictions of the passion. Each prediction is followed by clear evidence that the disciples failed to understand the true significance of what is to take place. This narrative regarding James and John follows the third prediction of the passion.

Sensing

Here are two very different pictures of what it means to follow in the path of Jesus as he sets his journey towards Jerusalem. Construct those pictures in your mind and set them side by side.

The first picture has as its centrepiece a reigning Eastern monarch. See the glorious throne. See the fine robes. See the regal crown. Hear the sounds of courtly music playing in the background. Sniff the smells of precious and costly perfumes filling the atmosphere. Touch the rich marble on the floor.

Then look to either side of that reigning Eastern monarch and see two further empty thrones. See the fine cushions on the chair. See the beautiful carved footstool. Hear the debate at court as the contenders for these thrones jostle for position. Either side of that reigning Eastern monarch stand two further empty thrones.

The second picture has as its centrepiece a hanging crucified Christ. See the rough wooden cross. See the bloodstained robes. See the crown of thorns. Hear the sounds of the rabble playing in the background. Sniff the smell of death hanging heavily in the air. Touch the parched grass on the ground.

Then look to either side of that hanging crucified Christ and see two further empty crosses. See the cruel sharp nails. See the rough-hewn ledge for the feet. Hear the debate as the executioners select their next victims. Either side of that hanging crucified Christ are two further empty crosses.

Here are two very different pictures of what it means to follow in the path of Jesus as he sets his journey towards Jerusalem.

Intuition

Here is a story about ambition. See how ambition has the power both to shape life and to destroy it.

Consider ambition in the schoolroom. Imagine Julian who has set his heart on the university chair. Admire his dedication to scholarship, to homework, to books and to study. Follow his course through the sixth form, through college and through graduate school. See his ambition realized through academic reward. And count the cost in terms of social isolation and emotional immaturity. See how ambition has the power both to shape life and to destroy it.

Again, consider ambition in the schoolroom. Imagine Justine who has set her heart on the Olympic games. Admire her dedication to fitness, to training, to competition and to personal development. Follow her course through school and through professional coaching. See her ambition realized through sporting success. And count the cost in terms of failed relationships and narrowness of vision. See how ambition has the power both to shape life and to destroy it.

Consider ambition in the business arena. Imagine Geoffrey who has set his heart on the chief executive's office. Admire his dedication as each strategic move brings him one step closer. See his ambition realized as a new nameplate is fitted to the chief executive's door. And count the cost in terms of colleagues' careers ruined. See how ambition has the power both to shape life and to destroy it.

Here is a story about ambition. Consider ambition in your own life. See how ambition has the power both to shape life and to destroy it. And then place that ambition in the hands of God that it may be shaped for the good of the kingdom.

Feeling

I wonder what your feelings would have been had you been there with those disciples, as Jesus set his journey towards Jerusalem? Listen as Jesus unfolds for the third time the fate that will befall him in Jerusalem. Listen as the detail is laid before you.

> The Son of Man will be handed over to the chief priests and the scribes, and they will condemn him to death; then they will hand him over to the Gentiles; they will mock him, and spit upon him, and flog him, and kill him; and after three days he will rise again.

Let the words sink in and feel the pain, the confusion, the incomprehension of the disciples.

Listen as James and John, the sons of Zebedee, unfold their plan for life in the kingdom of God. Listen as the detail is laid before you.

Teacher, we want you to do for us whatever we ask you. Grant us to sit, one at your right hand and one at your left, in your glory.

Let the words sink in and feel the ambition, the arrogance, the self-centredness of those two disciples.

Listen as the other disciples unfold their reaction to James and John's request. Listen as the detail is laid before you. Let the words sink in and feel that mixture of righteous indignation (for entrepreneurial ambition) and self-recrimination (for not having had the idea first).

Listen as Jesus unfolds yet again the fundamental paradox of the kingdom of God. Listen as the detail is laid before you.

You know that among the Gentiles those whom they recognize as their rulers lord it over them. But it is not so among you; but whoever wishes to become great among you must be your servant, and whoever wishes to be first among you must be slave of all.

Let the words sink in and face honestly your own personal reaction to knowing that this indeed is the kingdom of God to which you are now committed.

I wonder what your feelings would have been had you been there with those disciples, as Jesus set his journey towards Jerusalem?

Thinking

This narrative raises the fundamental theological question about the nature and propriety of petitionary prayer. So what do you think about the matter?

James and John came asking Jesus for something that was really very important to them (and something probably quite important for their family back home as well). Do you think that they should have had more reserve? Do you think that they should have kept quiet?

When James and John came asking Jesus for something that was really very important to them, Jesus took their request seriously and helped them to think through the implications of what they were asking. So what do you think about that as an example of divine fairness?

Surely there are times when you and I come asking Jesus for something that is really very important to us (and something probably quite important for our families back home as well). Do you think that we should have more reserve? Do you think that we should keep quiet?

Surely when you and I come asking Jesus for something that is really very important to us, Jesus takes our request seriously and helps us to think through the implications of what we are asking. So what do you think about that as a fair invitation to go on asking?

This narrative raises a fundamental theological question about the nature and propriety of petitional prayer. So what do you think about the matter?

━━━━━━━━━━━━━▷•◉•◁━━━━━━━━━━━━━

<h1 style="text-align:center;">27</h1>

<h1 style="text-align:center;">Mark 10:46–52</h1>

[46]They came to Jericho. As he and his disciples and a large crowd were leaving Jericho, Bartimaeus son of Timaeus, a blind beggar, was sitting by the roadside. [47]When he heard that it was Jesus of Nazareth, he began to shout out and say, 'Jesus, Son of David, have mercy on me!' [48]Many sternly ordered him to be quiet, but he cried out even more loudly, 'Son of David, have mercy on me!' [49]Jesus stood still and said, 'Call him here.' And they called the blind man, saying to him, 'Take heart; get up, he is calling you.' [50]So throwing off his cloak, he sprang up and came to Jesus. [51]Then Jesus said to him, 'What do you want me to do for you?' The blind man said to him, 'My teacher, let me see again.' [52]Jesus said to him, 'Go; your faith has made you well.' Immediately he regained his sight and followed him on the way.

Context

In the first part of Mark's gospel (1:16 to 8:22) Jesus is at pains to keep his Messiahship secret. The second major part of Mark's gospel (8:22 to 10:52) shows how Jesus' Messiahship became recognized. This transition begins when the eyes of a blind man are opened in two stages (8:22–26) and reaches its climax when a second blind man, Bartimaeus, openly addresses Jesus as 'Son of David' in the present narrative.

Sensing

Mark tells two stories about Jesus restoring sight to the blind. Listen to the details and compare the facts.

For the first healing come to Bethsaida, a long way from Jerusalem. See a group of people leading a blind man (still unnamed) to Jesus. Hear the group of people begging Jesus to touch the blind man in order to restore his sight.

For the first healing see Jesus lead the blind man out of the community away from the crowds and away from the public gaze. See Jesus use the ancient crafts of the healer. See him put saliva on the blind man's eyes and lay his hands on him.

For the healing hear the blind man tell Jesus, 'I can see people, but they look like trees walking.' See Jesus lay his hands on the blind man's eyes for the second time before his sight is properly restored. Hear Jesus tell the blind man to avoid public attention. Now the Messianic secret is growing uncertain.

For the second healing come to Jericho, only fifteen miles from Jerusalem. This time see the blind man (named as Bartimaeus) making his own way to Jesus, with other people holding him back. Hear the blind man cry out for his own healing, 'Jesus, Son of David, have mercy on me!'

For the second healing Jesus calls the blind man to stand in front of the crowd and in front of the public gaze. This time see Jesus forsake the ancient crafts of the healer. This time hear him pronounce with full authority, 'Go; your faith has made you well.'

For the second healing see how the blind man regained his sight immediately and followed Jesus on the way. This time Jesus made no attempt to bind the man to secrecy. Now, at last, the Messianic secret is out.

Mark tells two stories about Jesus restoring sight to the blind. Listen to the details and compare the facts.

Intuition

Bartimaeus' cry has re-echoed throughout the Christian centuries, 'Jesus, Son of David, have mercy on me!' Pause for a moment and make that petition your own.

In a moment of silence bring your own blind spots before

Jesus. Name the people whom you find it difficult to understand. Name the people whom you find it difficult to appreciate.

Name the people whom you find it difficult to tolerate. Then make Bartimaeus' prayer your own, 'Jesus, Son of David, have mercy on me!'

In a moment of silence bring your deaf ears before Jesus. Name the people to whom you find it difficult to listen. Name the people to whom you find it difficult to pay attention. Name the people whom you find it difficult to take seriously. Then make Bartimaeus' prayer your own, 'Jesus, Son of David, have mercy on me!'

In a moment of silence bring your lame limbs before Jesus. Name the people whom you find it difficult to help. Name the people whom you find it difficult to support. Name the people whom you find it difficult to serve. Then make Bartimaeus' prayer your own, 'Jesus, Son of David, have mercy on me!'

Bartimaeus' cry has re-echoed throughout the Christian centuries, 'Jesus, Son of David, have mercy on me!' Pause for a moment and make that petition your own.

Feeling

Here is a story which contrasts sight and insight. Stand where the blind man stood and experience life from his perspective.

Close your eyes tightly shut and picture how the world looked to Bartimaeus. Imagine the deprivation of knowing that there is a sunset and not being able to see it. Imagine the deprivation of knowing that there is a beautiful array of flowers and not being able to see them. Imagine the deprivation of knowing your family and friends and not being able to see them.

Close your eyes tightly shut and picture how the world looked to Bartimaeus. Imagine the disability of knowing there is a deep hole in the road and not being able to see it. Imagine the disability of knowing there is a snake in the field and not being able to see it. Imagine the disability of knowing there are jobs and not being able to secure them.

Close your eyes tight shut and picture how Bartimaeus construes his world. Imagine the sharpened sense of sound as Bartimaeus learns to distinguish people not by their faces but by their voices. Imagine the sharpened sense of smell as Bartimaeus learns how to distinguish places not by their appearance but by their aromas. Imagine the sharpened sense of touch as Bartimaeus learns to distinguish objects not by their visual qualities but by their tactile properties.

Close your eyes tight shut and picture how Bartimaeus construes his world. Imagine the well-developed ability to see to the heart of the matter which compensates for a lack of visual perception. Imagine the well-developed insight into the character of people which compensates for the lack of recognition of their physical attributes.

Close your eyes tight shut and remember that the blind Bartimaeus was the first person (apart from the privileged Peter) to see Jesus as the Messiah or the Son of David.

Here is a story which contrasts sight and insight. Stand where the blind man stood and experience life from his perspective.

Thinking

Think back over the second half of Mark's gospel and see if you can spot a pattern to what Mark is trying to say. Have your eyes been opened? Go right back to chapter 8 and think about the first blind man who was healed. Up to that point only the world of spirits and of demons had seen Jesus for who he really is. And now for the first time the eyes of the blind are opened, if somewhat haltingly.

Do you begin to see? No sooner had the eyes of the blind man been opened, than scales seem to fall from Peter's eyes as well. And now for the first time Peter began to see who Jesus really is, if somewhat haltingly. No sooner had the eyes of the blind man been opened, than Peter confessed Jesus as the Christ at Caesarea Philippi.

Do you begin to see? No sooner had the scales begun to fall from Peter's eyes than Jesus began to open the eyes of the disciples to the kind of Messiah he really is. In three clear predictions of the passion, the veil is drawn aside, although the disciples still fail to see the point.

Do you begin to see? No sooner had the veil been drawn aside in the third prediction of the passion, than the second blind man is seen. Blind as he is, he has seen the point. Without seeing Jesus, he sees who Jesus really is. For the first time the world of men and women see and confess 'Jesus, Son of David'. Do you begin to see? No sooner had the blind man seen who Jesus really is, than Jesus restores his sight.

And now seeing for the first time, the blind man follows Jesus on the way. Do you begin to see?

Think back over the second half of Mark's gospel and see if you spot a pattern in what Mark is trying to say. Have your eyes been opened?

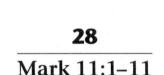

28
Mark 11:1–11

¹When they were approaching Jerusalem, at Bethphage and Bethany, near the Mount of Olives, he sent two of his disciples ²and said to them, 'Go into the village ahead of you, and immediately as you enter it, you will find tied there a colt that has never been ridden; untie it and bring it. ³If anyone says to you, "Why are you doing this?" just say this, "The Lord needs it and will send it back here immediately."' ⁴They went away and found a colt tied near a door, outside in the street. As they were untying it, ⁵some of the bystanders said to them, 'What are you doing, untying the colt?' ⁶They told them what Jesus had said; and they allowed them to take it. ⁷Then they brought the colt to Jesus and threw their cloaks on it; and he sat on it. ⁸Many people spread their cloaks on the road, and others spread leafy branches that they had cut in the fields. ⁹Then those who went ahead and those who followed were shouting,

'Hosanna!
Blessed is the one who comes in the name of the Lord!
¹⁰Blessed is the coming kingdom of our ancestor David!
Hosanna in the highest heaven!'
¹¹Then he entered Jerusalem and went into the temple; and when he had looked around at everything, as it was already late, he went out to Bethany with the twelve.

Context

In chapter 11 Mark begins the third and final part of his gospel. Now Jesus enters Jerusalem, which is to be the context for the trial and the crucifixion. The entry into Jerusalem occurs as dramatic enacted prophecy.

Sensing

Here is a story full of drama and action. Feel yourself drawn into the very heart of it.

Go outside and open your eyes. See a distant procession, a ragged motley crew, people coming in on the road from Bethphage and Bethany. See the central figure within the procession, a man riding an untamed colt, a beast of burden, an unpretentious and unprepossessing animal. Go outside and open your eyes.

Go outside and throw yourself into the action. Strip the coat off your back and spread it on the road before the path of the man riding an untamed colt. Reach up and tear the leafy branches from the trees and spread them on the road before the path of the man riding the colt. Go outside and throw yourself into the action.

Go outside and lift up your voice. Pick up the clear refrain of those all around you and shout for all you are worth:

Hosanna! Blessed is the one who comes in the name of the Lord! Blessed is the coming kingdom of our ancestor David!

Go outside and lift up your voice.

Go outside and become part of the procession. Let the procession carry you on through the city wall and into the city of Jerusalem, on through the city streets and into the temple. Go outside and become part of the procession.

Here is a story full of drama and action. Feel yourself drawn in to the very heart of it.

Intuition

There seems so much more to this simple story than ever meets the eye. Can you spot the connections and hear the resonances?

Is it pure chance that the whole account begins by naming the Mount of Olives as the location from which the action starts? Do you see here a connection with the prophecy of Zechariah (14:4) looking to the coming Messiah?

On that day his feet shall stand on the Mount of Olives.

Is it pure chance that the procession revolves around an untamed colt, a beast of burden? Do you see here a connection with another prophecy of Zechariah (9:9)?

Lo, your King comes to you:
>   triumphant and victorious is he,
> humble and riding on a donkey,
>   on a colt, the foal of a donkey.

Is it pure chance that the crowd stripped off their cloaks and cast them in Jesus' path? Do you see a connection with the enthronement rite of Jehu in 2 Kings (9:13)?

> Then hurriedly they all took their cloaks and spread them for him on the bare steps; and they blew the trumpet and proclaimed, 'Jehu is King.'

Is it pure chance that the crowd tore branches from the trees and cast them in Jesus' path? Do you see here a connection with the triumphal entry of Simon Maccabaeus into Jerusalem in 1 Maccabees (13:51)?

> The Jews entered Jerusalem with praise and palm branches, and with harps and cymbals and stringed instruments, and with hymns and songs, because a great enemy had been crushed and removed from Israel.

Is it pure chance that the crowd chanted from Psalm 118? Do you see here a connection with the way in which the selfsame psalm was used at the Feast of Dedication, which commemorated the re-cleansing of the temple by Judas Maccabaeus in 165 BC?

There seems so much more to this simple story than ever meets the eye. Can you spot the connections and hear the resonances?

Feeling

Here is a story of human dedication and of divine determination. Put yourself on the colt and experience what Jesus experienced.

Jesus knew that the conflict had been mounting right from those early days in Capernaum when he had healed the paralyzed man. Jesus knew that the conflict had been mounting right from those early days when he had accepted Levi's invitation to dinner. Jesus knew that the conflict had been mounting right from those early days when he had restored a withered hand on the Sabbath. Jesus knew right from those early days that there had been a conspiracy to destroy him (Mark 3:6). I wonder what it is like to live under such a shadow.

Jesus knew that the end was drawing closer from the moment of Peter's insightful confession at Caesarea Philippi. Jesus knew that the end was drawing closer from the moment of setting his journey towards Jerusalem. Jesus knew that the end was drawing closer from the moment of Bartimaeus' Messianic greeting in Jericho. Jesus knew right from those days that he would be condemned to death (Mark 10:33). I wonder what it is like to live under such a shadow?

Jesus knew that the end was inescapable from the moment he sat on the colt, the foal of a donkey. Jesus knew that the end was inescapable from the moment he accepted the cloaks and branches strewn in his way. Jesus knew that the end was inescapable from the moment he endorsed the Messianic palms of expectation. Jesus knew when he entered Jerusalem that he was going there to die. I wonder what it is like to live under such a shadow?

Here is a story of human dedication and of divine determination. Put yourself on the colt and experience what Jesus experienced.

Thinking

Mark's account of the entry into Jerusalem ends in a most puzzling way. What do you make of it?

According to Mark, Jesus' journey from Jericho, via the Mount of Olives, to Jerusalem had been full of determination, full of direction. Once in Jerusalem the determination and the direction persisted. Jesus went straight into the temple. But once in the temple the determination and the direction evaporates. The colt disappears. The crowds vanish. The Messianic fever subsides. Like a modern-day tourist Jesus looked around at everything and went away because it was already late. Mark's account of the entry into Jerusalem ends in a most puzzling way. What do you make of it?

According to Matthew, things happened in a very different kind of way. When Jesus entered Jerusalem the whole city was in turmoil, asking, 'Who is this?' According to Matthew, Jesus went straight to the temple and drove out all who were selling and buying. He rode into the temple not as a curious tourist, but as the one who cleansed it. What Mark presents as happening on the following day (the cleansing of the temple), Matthew presents as the proper climax to the triumphal entry. Mark's account of the entry into Jerusalem ends in a most puzzling way. What do you make of it?

What is so important for Mark, however, is the way in which he divides the events of chapter 11 so clearly into three consecutive days. Such divisions seem both deliberate and artificial. And this has led some commentators to conclude that Mark is really developing an early structure for a Holy Week liturgy. Mark's account of the entry into Jerusalem ends in a most puzzling of ways. What do you make of it?

29
Mark 12:28–34

²⁸One of the scribes came near and heard them disputing with one another, and seeing that he answered them well, he asked him, 'Which commandment is the first of all?' ²⁹Jesus answered, 'The first is, "Hear, O Israel: the Lord our God, the Lord is one; ³⁰you shall love the Lord your God with all your heart, and with all your soul, and with all your mind, and with all your strength." ³¹The second is this, "You shall love your neighbour as yourself." There is no other commandment greater than these.' ³²Then the scribe said to him, 'You are right, Teacher; you have truly said that "he is one, and besides him there is no other"; ³³and "to love him with all the heart, and with all the understanding, and with all the strength," and "to love one's neighbour as oneself," – this is much more important than all whole burnt offerings and sacrifices.' ³⁴When Jesus saw that he answered wisely, he said to him, 'You are not far from the kingdom of God.' After that no one dared to ask him any question.

Context

During the final days in Jerusalem before the trial and crucifixion, Mark shows Jesus being confronted by and skilfully circumventing four potentially controversial questions. The first question concerned the authority by which Jesus acted. The second question concerned paying taxes to the emperor. The third question concerned life after death. Now the fourth question concerns the law.

Sensing

Come away to the city of Jerusalem. Come to the temple of the Lord. Stand there and watch. Stand there and listen. The whole city is in turmoil. Two days ago Jesus came riding on a colt. Yesterday Jesus sent the tables of the money-changers flying. Today four very different-looking people come up to Jesus and spring four very surprising questions. Stand there and watch. Stand there and listen.

See the first of the questioners. See the characteristic dress of the chief priests. Hear the first of the questions. 'By what authority,' they ask Jesus, 'are you doing these things?' Then hear Jesus turn the tables on the questioners. See the confusion in the questioners' eyes. Stand there and watch. Stand there and listen.

See the second of the questioners. See the characteristic dress of the Pharisees. Hear the second of the questions. 'Is it lawful to pay taxes to the emperor or not?' Then hear Jesus turn the tables on the questioners. See the confusion in the questioners' eyes. Stand there and watch. Stand there and listen.

See the third of the questioners. See the characteristic dress of the Sadducees. Hear the third of the questions. 'In the resurrection whose wife will she be?' Then hear Jesus turn the tables on the questioners. See the confusion in their eyes. Stand there and watch. Stand there and listen.

See the fourth of the questioners. See the characteristic dress of the scribes. Hear the fourth of the questions. 'Which commandment is first of all?' Then hear Jesus turn the tables on the questioners. See the confusion in their eyes. Stand there and watch. Stand there and listen.

Come away to the city of Jerusalem. Come to the temple of the Lord. Stand there and watch. Stand there and listen. The whole city is in turmoil. Today four very different-looking people come up to Jesus and spring four very surprising questions. But after that, no one dared to ask Jesus any further questions. Stand there and watch; stand there and listen.

Intuition

At the heart of the great commandment is a tired, overworked four-letter word. The word is *love*. I wonder what that word means to you? Love is . . . love is what?

Love is doing the washing-up, whether it is our turn or not. Or does such behaviour simply teach others to be lazy and irresponsible?

Love is giving others whatever they ask. Or does such behaviour simply teach others to be spoilt and selfish?

Love is protecting others from harm and hurt. Or does such behaviour simply teach others to be careless and immature?

Love is always putting others first. Or does such behaviour simply undermine one's own true self-worth?

Love is preferring to give than to receive. Or does such behaviour simply deprive others of showing love to us?

Love is preferring to listen to the plaintive cries of others rather than to burden them with the deepest needs of our own souls. Or does such behaviour simply deprive us of the love we rightly need to receive?

Love is putting others first and ourselves last of all. Or does such behaviour simply inflate another's ego at the cost of our own?

At the heart of the great commandment is a tired, overworked four-letter word. The word is *love*. I wonder what that word means to you? Love is . . . love is what?

Feeling

According to Luke's gospel, when invited to illustrate the Christian commandment to love, Jesus told a simple tale, of a mugged and wounded traveller, so savagely attacked on the road between Jerusalem and Jericho. Does not your Christian heart go out in love to that mugged and wounded traveller?

When invited to illustrate the Christian commandment to love, Jesus told a tale of a despised and hated foreigner, who stopped to attend to the mugged and wounded traveller so savagely attacked on the road between Jerusalem and Jericho. Does not your Christian heart go out in love to that despised and hated foreigner?

When invited to illustrate the Christian commandment to love, Jesus told the tale of a dumb and laden donkey, who rescued and carried the mugged and wounded traveller so savagely attacked on the road between Jerusalem and Jericho. Does not your Christian heart go out in love to that dumb and laden donkey?

When invited to illustrate the Christian commandment to love, Jesus told a tale of a sincere and trusting innkeeper, who offered board and lodgings to the mugged and wounded traveller so savagely attacked on the road between Jerusalem and Jericho. Does not your Christian heart go out in love to that sincere and trusting innkeeper?

According to Luke's gospel, when invited to illustrate the Christian commandment to love, Jesus told a simple tale. Can you not sense your own life being woven into the fabric of that selfsame tale?

Thinking

Listen to Jesus' reply to the scribe and think through what Jesus is really trying to say. Do you hear one commandment, two commandments, or perhaps even three commandments? And which of these commandments, I wonder, do you find it most difficult to keep?

Perhaps there is just one commandment, and that commandment is to love. Listen to Jesus' reply to the scribe and think through what Jesus is really trying to say.

Or perhaps there are really two rather different commandments. The first commandment is to love the Lord your God with all your heart, and with all your soul, and with all your mind, and with all your strength. The second commandment is to love your neighbour as yourself. Listen to Jesus' reply to the scribe and think through what Jesus is really trying to say.

Or perhaps there are really three rather different commandments. The first commandment is to love the Lord your God. The second commandment is to love your neighbour. The third commandment is to love yourself. Listen to Jesus' reply to the scribe and think through what Jesus is really trying to say.

Perhaps the first letter of John makes a very true and valid point when the author argues that those who do not love a brother (or a sister or a neighbour) whom they have seen, cannot love God whom they have not seen. In other words, love of neighbour becomes the prerequisite of the love of God.

Perhaps the commandment to love your neighbour as yourself is making the rather similar point that those who do not love themselves (whom they have the opportunity to know very well) cannot truly love the neighbour (whom they have the opportunity to know less well). In other words, love of self becomes the prerequisite of the love of neighbour.

Listen to Jesus' reply to the scribe and think through what Jesus is really trying to say. Do you hear one commandment, two commandments, or perhaps even three commandments? And which of these commandments, I wonder, do you find it most difficult to keep?

Mark 12:38–44

38As he taught, he said, 'Beware of the scribes, who like to walk around in long robes, and to be greeted with respect in the marketplaces, 39and to have the best seats in the synagogues and places of honour at banquets! 40They devour widows' houses and for the sake of appearance say long prayers. They will receive the greater condemnation.'

41He sat down opposite the treasury, and watched the crowd putting money into the treasury. Many rich people put in large sums. 42A poor widow came and put in two small copper coins, which are worth a penny. 43Then he called his disciples and said to them, 'Truly I tell you, this poor widow has put in more than all those who are contributing to the treasury. 44For all of them have contributed out of their abundance; but she out of her poverty has put in everything she had, all she had to live on.'

Context

The last verses of chapter 12 draw to a close Jesus' teaching ministry in Jerusalem, before the apocalyptic discourse of chapter 13 and the opening of the passion narrative in chapter 14. Here Mark contrasts the scribes who devour widows' houses and the widow who gives everything she has.

Sensing

Here is a story of contrasts, a story of wealth and a story of poverty. Picture those contrasts.

Sit down alongside Jesus, right at the heart of the city of Jerusalem, right opposite the temple treasury. Sit down alongside Jesus and watch, watch the people walk by.

Let your eyes rest on the people of wealth. Let your eyes rest on the successful and the rich. See the fine robes sweep down to the pavement. See the fine sandals covering the feet. See the fine jewellery glisten in the sun. Let your eyes rest on the people of wealth in ancient Jerusalem.

Let your eyes rest on the people of poverty. Let your eyes rest on the destitute and the poor. See their tattered robes, their bare

feet, their hungry look. Let your eyes rest on the people of poverty
in ancient Jerusalem. Sit down alongside Jesus, right at the heart
of the city of London, right opposite St Paul's Cathedral. Sit down
alongside Jesus and watch, watch the people walk by.

Let your eyes rest on the people of wealth. Let your eyes rest on
the successful and the rich. See the well-cut suits and the well-
tailored outfits. See the up-market footwear and the graceful shoes.
See the gold watch and the diamond brooch glisten in the sun. Let
your eyes rest on the people of wealth in contemporary London.

Let your eyes rest on the people of poverty. Let your eyes rest
on the destitute and the poor. See their ill-fitting and shabby
clothes. See their down-at-heel and badly-scuffed shoes. See their
hungry and ill-fed faces. Let your eyes rest on the people of
poverty in contemporary London.

Here is a story of contrasts, a story of wealth and a story of
poverty. Picture those contrasts.

Intuition

Here is a story of contrasts, a story of a large gift which costs so
little and a story of a small gift which costs so much. So what does
this story suggest to you about stewardship in today's church,
stewardship of money and stewardship of time? Where is the
balance between quantity and cost?

Consider the generous corporate sponsor, the generous
business person, the generous property owner, who is able to offer
a substantial donation or to undertake a significant covenant
without feeling the pinch or running the risk of hardship. Surely
their generosity is no less acceptable to God simply because the
donor could afford the gift?

On the other hand, consider the pressure under which some
less well-off church members may place themselves to sustain a
high level of tithing. Surely God remains reasonable in the
demands on our pockets?

Consider the people whose pattern of life enables them to
offer significant time commitments to the local church, in caring
for the fabric or carrying out pastoral work, without feeling over-
stretched or short-changing their personal or family life. Surely
their dedication is no less acceptable to God simply because they
can afford the time?

On the other hand, consider the pressure under which some
very busy church members place themselves to sustain a high

level of commitment and participation. Surely God remains reasonable in the demands on our time?

Here is a story of contrasts, a story of a large gift which costs so little and a story of a small gift which costs so much. So what does this story suggest to you about stewardship in today's church?

Feeling

The real heroine of this story is the widow. Put yourself in her widow's robes and see the narrative from her perspective, imprisoned as she is behind almost impenetrable stereotypes.

Experience the heroine's frustration being cast always in the stereotype of the widow woman. Dig behind that stereotype and find there the fresh memory of the young girl in love, the fresh memory of the young bride proudly clasping the arm of her husband, the fresh memory of the young mother gently nursing her first born. Dig behind the stereotype of the widow woman and release the true richness of her experience as wife and as mother.

Experience the heroine's frustration being cast always in the stereotype of the poor woman. Dig behind that stereotype and find there the fresh memory of the well-furnished house, the fresh memory of the well-stocked larder, the fresh memory of the well-loved home. Dig behind the stereotype of the poor woman and release the true wealth of her experience as housekeeper and as home-maker.

Experience the heroine's frustration being cast always in the stereotype of the woman who gives away everything that she has. Dig behind that stereotype and find there the fresh memory of a well-managed home economy, the fresh memory of a well-ordered stewardship of resources, the fresh memory of a generous and responsible response to the needs of others. Dig behind the stereotype of the woman who gives away everything that she has and release the true worth of her experience as home economist and as public benefactor.

The real heroine of this story is the widow. Put yourself in her widow's robes and see the narrative from her perspective, imprisoned as she is behind almost impenetrable stereotypes.

Thinking

This narrative raises profound questions of fairness and of justice. So what is your verdict?

Take the example of those rich people who can donate large

sums to the temple treasury. Then set alongside those rich people the poor widow whose whole livelihood is summed up in two small coins. What do you make of such stark inequalities? Is that the way God intended things to be?

Take the example of the top-paid executives of the major multi-national corporations. Then set alongside those top-paid executives the poorly-paid labour force of the selfsame corporations. What do you make of such stark inequalities? Is that the way God intended things to be?

Take the example of relatively well-paid skilled workers making electronic components within the developed world. Then set alongside these relatively well-paid skilled workers equally skilled workers doing the selfsame job for a fraction of the pay within the developing world. What do you make of such stark inequalities? Is that the way God intended things to be?

Take the example of those rich nations who can set aside large budgets for world development aid. Then set alongside those rich nations the poorest nations of the world whose whole economy is summed up in exploited exports. What do you make of such stark inequalities? Is that the way God intended things to be?

This narrative raises profound questions of fairness and of justice. So what is your verdict?

31
Mark 13:1–8

[1]As he came out of the temple, one of his disciples said to him, 'Look, Teacher, what large stones and what large buildings!' [2]Then Jesus asked him, 'Do you see these great buildings? Not one stone will be left here upon another; all will be thrown down.'

[3]When he was sitting on the Mount of Olives opposite the temple, Peter, James, John, and Andrew asked him privately, [4]'Tell us, when will this be, and what will be the sign that all these things are about to be accomplished?' [5]Then Jesus began to say to them, 'Beware that no one leads you astray. [6]Many will come in my name and say, "I am he!" and they will lead many astray. [7]When you hear of wars and rumors of wars, do not be alarmed; this must

take place, but the end is still to come. [8]For nation will rise against nation, and kingdom against kingdom; there will be earthquakes in various places; there will be famines. This is but the beginning of the birth pangs.'

Context

Chapter 13 stands apart from the rest of Mark's gospel both in style and content. Coming between the climax of Jesus' ministry in Jerusalem (chapter 12) and the beginning of the passion narrative (chapter 14), chapter 13 faces questions about the future. It is often known as the apocalyptic discourse.

Sensing

Prick up your ears and listen with care as Jesus teaches about the end of the age. 'Do not be led astray,' says Jesus. 'Do not misread the signs.'

Prick up your ears and listen with care as Jesus teaches about the end of the ages. Switch on the television and see the sights of wars. Pick up the newspaper and read the accounts of wars. Tune in the radio and hear the commentators speculate about the intensification of wars. But do not be led astray. Do not misread the signs. All these things are part of the present world, not signs of the world to come.

Prick up your ears and listen with care as Jesus teaches about the end of the ages. Switch on the television and see the sights of earthquakes and natural disasters. Pick up the newspaper and read the accounts of earthquakes and natural disasters. Tune in the radio and hear the commentators speculate about the intensification of earthquakes and natural disasters. But do not be led astray. Do not misread the signs. All these things are part of the present world, not signs of the world to come.

Prick up your ears and listen with care as Jesus teaches about the end of the ages. Switch on the television and see the sights of famines and starvation. Pick up the newspaper and read the accounts of famines and starvation. Tune in the radio and hear the commentators speculate about the intensification of famines and starvation. But do not be led astray. Do not misread the signs. All these things are part of the present world, not signs of the world to come.

Prick up your ears and listen with care as Jesus teaches about the end of the ages. 'Do not be led astray,' says Jesus. 'Do not mis-read the signs.'

Intuition

Here is a story of four disciples who wanted Jesus to give them the key to the future, and Jesus warned them not to be misled. Many people in today's world are still looking for the same key. I wonder whether they too are in danger of being misled?

Consider the people who read their horoscopes day by day. Day by day they are warned by the stars of the dangers to avoid. Day by day they are advised by the stars of the opportunities to be grasped. Day by day they feel that the outcome of their actions has been pre-shaped by the stars. I wonder whether they are being misled?

Consider the people who treat their bible like a prophetic *vade-mecum*. Day by day they are warned by holy text of the dangers to avoid. Day by day they are advised by holy text of the divine promises to be seized. Day by day they feel that the outcome of their actions has been pre-shaped by the divine will. I wonder whether they are being misled?

Consider the people who visit fortune-tellers to hear their future unfold. They are warned by the crystal ball of the dangers to avoid. They are advised by the crystal ball of the opportunities to be grasped. They feel that the outcome of their actions has been pre-shaped by the crystal ball. I wonder whether they are being misled?

Here is a story of four disciples who wanted Jesus to give them the key to the future. And Jesus refused their request.

Feeling

Jesus said to the disciples, 'There will be wars, earthquakes and famines.' Here is a story not about the end of the world, but about the world in which Christian men and women continue to live out their lives. What is Jesus asking of your life in such a world today?

Jesus said to the disciples, 'There will be wars.' This is not a story about the end of the world, but about the world in which we are called to live. We know that in far-away places (and in places not so far away) men and women are waging war. We know that human life is being lost. We know that human suffering is being endured. So what is Jesus asking of your life in such a world as this?

Jesus said to the disciples, 'There will be earthquakes.' This is not a story about the end of the world, but about the world in which we are called to live. We know that in far-away places (and in places not so far away) earthquakes and natural disasters are taking their toll. We know that human life is being lost. We know that human suffering is being endured. So what is Jesus asking of your life in such a world as this?

Jesus said to the disciples, 'There will be famines.' This is not a story about the end of the world, but about the world in which we are called to live. We know that in far-away places (and even on the streets of our own towns) famine and hunger are taking their tolls. We know that human life is being lost. We know that human suffering is being endured. So what is Jesus asking of your life in such a world as this?

Jesus said to the disciples, 'There will be wars, earthquakes and famines.' What can we do to help the victims whose lives are torn apart in a world such as this?

Thinking

Jesus made it clear to the disciples that the purpose of his passion and death was not to put an end to wars and conflicts, to earthquakes and natural disasters, to famines and hunger. What do you make of a mighty saviour who thinks like that?

Jesus made it clear to his disciples that wars and conflicts would continue. But surely those are nothing other than the result of a fundamental flaw built in to the fabric of the human heart? Surely a mighty saviour could over-rule the fundamental flaw built in to the fabric of the human heart? Jesus said that wars and conflicts would continue. What do you make of a mighty saviour who thinks like that?

Jesus made it clear to his disciples that earthquakes and natural disasters would continue. But surely earthquakes and natural disasters are nothing other than the result of a fundamental flaw built in to the fabric of the universe? Surely a mighty saviour could over-rule the fundamental flaw built in to the fabric of the universe? Jesus said that earthquakes and natural disasters would continue. What do you make of a mighty saviour who thinks like that?

Jesus made it clear to his disciples that famines and hunger would continue. But surely famines and hunger are nothing other than the combined result of fundamental flaws built in to the fabric of the human heart and built in to the fabric of the universe? Surely a mighty saviour could overrule the combined result of fundamental flaws built in to the fabric of the human heart and in to the fabric of the universe? Jesus said that hunger and famine would continue. What do you make of a mighty saviour who thinks like that?

Jesus made it clear to his disciples that wars and conflicts, earthquakes and natural disasters, famine and hunger would continue. Jesus also made it clear to his disciples that a world like this was a world worth dying for. What do you make of a mighty saviour who thinks like that?

➤➤━❍━◄◄

32
Mark 13:24–37

²⁴'But in those days, after that suffering,
   the sun will be darkened,
      and the moon will not give its light,
   ²⁵and the stars will be falling from heaven,
      and the powers in the heavens will be shaken.
²⁶Then they will see "the Son of Man coming in clouds" with great power and glory. ²⁷Then he will send out the angels, and gather his elect from the four winds, from the ends of the earth to the ends of heaven.

²⁸'From the fig tree learn its lesson: as soon as its branch becomes tender and puts forth its leaves, you know that summer is near. ²⁹So also, when you see these things taking place, you know that he is near, at the very gates. ³⁰Truly I tell you, this generation will not pass away until all these things have taken place. ³¹Heaven and earth will pass away, but my words will not pass away.

³²'But about that day or hour no one knows, neither the angels in heaven, nor the Son, but only the Father. ³³Beware, keep alert; for you do not know when the time will come. ³⁴It is like a man going on a journey, when he leaves home and puts his slaves in charge, each with his work, and commands the doorkeeper to be on the watch. ³⁵Therefore, keep awake – for you do not know

when the master of the house will come, in the evening, or at midnight, or at cockcrow, or at dawn, [36]or else he may find you asleep when he comes suddenly. [37]And what I say to you I say to all: Keep awake.'

Context

Chapter 13, often known as the apocalyptic discourse, is usually seen to contain five distinct sections: introduction to the discourse (1–4), the miseries preceding the last days (5–13), the last days (14–23), the end (24–27), and a supplement of independent sayings (25–37). This passage combines the last two sections.

Sensing

Jesus said, 'It is like when the master goes away on a journey.'

Picture the scene there in first-century Palestine. See the small family business, the well-kept vineyard, the wine press, the casks of last year's vintage. See the walls around the vineyard and the gateway to the outer world.

Picture the scene. See the master of the vineyard settle his affairs, pack his bags, make preparations for a journey. Hear the master of the vineyard give instructions to his men on how to carry on the business.

Picture the scene. See the workmen stand by the gate as the master collects his bags, says his farewells and takes his leave. See the puzzlement in their faces when they discover that no one knows when the master will return.

Picture the scene. Every day, at evening time, the doorkeeper peers down the long, long road searching for the master's return. Every day, at midnight, the doorkeeper peers down the long, long road seeking for the master's return. Every day, at cock-crow, the doorkeeper peers down the long, long road seeking for the master's return. Every day, at dawn, the doorkeeper peers down the long, long road seeking for the master's return.

Picture the scene there in first-century Palestine. Day in and day out, life in the vineyard goes on. Day in and day out, the men live and work in constant expectation of the master's imminent return. See how looking for the master's return shapes their daily lives.

Jesus said, 'Keep awake, for you do not know when the master of the house will come.'

Intuition

Jesus' command to his disciples was to be alert, to keep awake, to be on watch, while the master is away. So how does that command translate into the lives of Christian disciples today?

While the master is away, what have you observed happening to the social welfare of the people? How are the needy being cared for? How are the hungry being fed? How are the homeless being housed? How are the unemployed being supported? Have Christian men and women been properly alert to what is taking place? Jesus said, 'Be awake, keep on watch!'

While the master is away, what have you observed happening to the health care of the people? How are the sick being cared for? How is the health of the young being promoted?

How is the health of the elderly being sustained? How are the terminally ill being prepared for death? Have Christian men and women been properly alert to what is taking place? Jesus said, 'Be awake, keep on watch!'

While the master is away, what have you observed happening to the education of the people? How is provision being made for pre-school education? How are schools being resourced? How are teachers being trained? What core values are being promoted through the educational system? Have Christian men and women been properly alert to what is taking place? Jesus said, 'Be awake, keep on watch!'

Jesus' command to his disciples was to be alert, to keep awake, to be on watch, while the master is away. So how does that command translate into the lives of Christian disciples today?

Feeling

Things must have felt somewhat different to those original disciples, who saw the master set out on his journey. Put yourself in their company and enter into the five stages of their religious experience.

In stage one, those original disciples were living their lives, day in and day out, in the immediate presence of their Lord. Share in their experience of living in the Lord's presence.

In stage two, those original disciples were living their lives through the trauma of the crucifixion and death of their Lord. Share in their experience of trauma, bereavement and loss.

In stage three, those original disciples were living their lives through the excitement of the empty tomb and resurrection experiences of their Lord. Share in their experience of excitement, unpredictability and amazement.

In stage four, those original disciples were living their lives through the spreading news of the ascension of their Lord. Share in their bewilderment as they experience the mixed feeling of triumphant vindication and future uncertainty.

In stage five, those original disciples were living their lives, day in and day out, both in the presence of their ascended Lord and in the absence of their physical Lord. Share in their profound experience of standing on the edge of a new age.

In stage five, those original disciples were looking back to the past, when the Lord stood among them. Share in their experience of remembering the past as they stand on the edge of a new age.

In stage five, those original disciples were looking forward to the future when the Lord would stand among them once more. Share in their experience of anticipating the future as they stand on the edge of a new age.

Things must have felt somewhat different to those original disciples, who saw the master set out on his journey. Put yourself in their company and enter into the five stages of their religious experience.

Thinking

The thirteenth chapter of Mark's gospel is clearly so very different from the rest of the gospel narrative. So what do you make of this apocalyptic discourse? Do you hear the voice of Jesus revealing secrets about the end of the world? Or do you hear the puzzlement of the early church reconciling Jewish expectations from the Messianic age with the experienced reality of life in the Christian community?

In verses 5–8, the gospel writer promises wars, earthquakes and famines, but warns the reader not to read too much into such occurrences. The timescale is longer than that. So do you hear the voice of Jesus, or the puzzlement of the early church?

In verses 9–13, the gospel writer promises persecutions, beatings and trials, but warns the reader not to read too much into such occurrences. The gospel must first be preached to all nations. So do you hear the voice of Jesus, or the puzzlement of the early church?

In verses 14–23, the gospel writer draws on the rich imagery of the Jewish tradition to heighten the sufferings of the last days. He advises those who can to flee to the mountains. The detail and anticipation is there, but the timescale is absent. So do you hear the voice of Jesus, or the puzzlement of the early church?

In verses 24–27, the gospel writer draws on other rich strands of the Jewish tradition to profile the close of the ages. The sun will be darkened and the stars will be falling from heaven. Again the detail and the anticipation is there, but the timescale is absent. So do you hear the voice of Jesus, or the puzzlement of the early church?

In verses 28–31, the gospel writer suddenly and for the first time asserts a timescale. This generation will not pass away until all these things have taken place. So do you hear the voice of Jesus, or the puzzlement of the early church?

In verses 32–37, the gospel writer introduces a new and original note of uncertainty. But about that day or hour no one knows, neither the angels in heaven, nor the Son, but only the Father. So do you hear the voice of Jesus, or the puzzlement of the early church?

The thirteenth chapter of Mark's gospel is clearly different. So what do you make of the apocalyptic discourse? Do you hear the voice of Jesus revealing secrets about the end of the world? Or do you hear the puzzlement of the early church reconciling Jewish expectations for the Messianic age and the experienced reality of life in the Christian community?

33
Mark 15:1–39

[1] As soon as it was morning, the chief priests held a consultation with the elders and scribes and the whole council. They bound Jesus, led him away, and handed him over to Pilate. [2] Pilate asked him, 'Are you the King of the Jews?' He answered him, 'You say so.' [3] Then the chief priests accused him of many things. [4] Pilate asked him again, 'Have you no answer? See how many charges they bring against you.' [5] But Jesus made no further reply, so that Pilate was amazed.

⁶Now at the festival he used to release a prisoner for them, anyone for whom they asked. ⁷Now a man called Barabbas was in prison with the rebels who had committed murder during the insurrection. ⁸So the crowd came and began to ask Pilate to do for them according to his custom. ⁹Then he answered them, 'Do you want me to release for you the King of the Jews?' ¹⁰For he realized that it was out of jealousy that the chief priests had handed him over. ¹¹But the chief priests stirred up the crowd to have him release Barabbas for them instead. ¹²Pilate spoke to them again, 'Then what do you wish me to do with the man you call the King of the Jews?' ¹³They shouted back, 'Crucify him!' ¹⁴Pilate asked them, 'Why, what evil has he done?' But they shouted all the more, 'Crucify him!' ¹⁵So Pilate, wishing to satisfy the crowd, released Barabbas for them; and after flogging Jesus, he handed him over to be crucified.

¹⁶Then the soldiers led him into the courtyard of the palace (that is, the governor's headquarters); and they called together the whole cohort. ¹⁷And they clothed him in a purple cloak; and after twisting some thorns into a crown, they put it on him. ¹⁸And they began saluting him, 'Hail, King of the Jews!' ¹⁹They struck his head with a reed, spat upon him, and knelt down in homage to him. ²⁰After mocking him, they stripped him of the purple cloak and put his own clothes on him. Then they led him out to crucify him.

²¹They compelled a passer-by, who was coming in from the country, to carry his cross; it was Simon of Cyrene, the father of Alexander and Rufus. ²²Then they brought Jesus to the place called Golgotha (which means the place of a skull). ²³And they offered him wine mixed with myrrh; but he did not take it. ²⁴And they crucified him, and divided his clothes among them, casting lots to decide what each should take.

²⁵It was nine o'clock in the morning when they crucified him. ²⁶The inscription of the charge against him read, 'The King of the Jews.' ²⁷And with him they crucified two bandits, one on his right and one on his left. ²⁹Those who passed by derided him, shaking their heads and saying, 'Aha! You who would destroy the temple and build it in three days, ³⁰save yourself, and come down from the cross!' ³¹In the same way the chief priests, along with the scribes, were also mocking him among themselves and saying, 'He saved others; he cannot save himself. ³²Let the Messiah, the King of Israel, come down from the cross now, so that we may see and believe.' Those who were crucified with him also taunted him.

^{33} When it was noon, darkness came over the whole land until three in the afternoon. ^{34}At three o'clock Jesus cried out with a loud voice, 'Eloi, Eloi, lema sabachthani?' which means, 'My God, my God, why have you forsaken me?' ^{35}When some of the bystanders heard it, they said, 'Listen, he is calling for Elijah.' ^{36}And someone ran, filled a sponge with sour wine, put it on a stick, and gave it to him to drink, saying, 'Wait, let us see whether Elijah will come to take him down.' ^{37}Then Jesus gave a loud cry and breathed his last. ^{38}And the curtain of the temple was torn in two, from top to bottom. ^{39}Now when the centurion, who stood facing him, saw that in this way he breathed his last, he said, 'Truly this man was God's Son!'

Context

The whole of chapters 14 and 15 of Mark's gospel present what is generally known as the *passion narrative*, covering the last two days before the Passover through to the burial. The present passage begins with the trial before Pilate.

Sensing

Like Peter, you have been watching from a distance. Come closer and listen more carefully. See the elders and the scribes bind Jesus and hand him over to Pilate. Hear how Pilate throws their accusation in Jesus' face, 'Are *you* the King of the Jews?' Sense Pilate's contempt for the Jewish leaders.

Like Peter, you have been watching from a distance. Come closer and listen more carefully. See the elders and the scribes present their charges to Pilate. Hear how Pilate gives Jesus the right of response, 'See how many charges they bring against you. Have you no answer?' Sense Pilate's amazement at Jesus' silence.

Like Peter, you have been watching from a distance. Come closer and listen more carefully. See the chief priests incite the crowds to campaign for the release of Barabbas. Hear how Pilate offers to release Jesus instead, 'Do you want me to release to you the King of the Jews?' Sense Pilate's knack for tormenting his subjects.

Like Peter, you have been watching from a distance. Come closer and listen more carefully. See the elders and the scribes incite the crowds to campaign for Jesus to be crucified. Hear Pilate challenge their condemnation, 'Why, what evil has he done?' Sense Pilate's disregard for the case brought against Jesus.

Like Peter, you have been watching from a distance. Come closer and listen more carefully. See the Roman soldiers standing ready to lead Jesus away to the cross. Hear Pilate speak the command to carry out the execution, 'Crucify that man.' Sense Pilate's relief that the trouble is over.

Like Peter, you have been watching from a distance. Come closer and listen more carefully.

Intuition

Here is a narrative about crowd psychology. Consider how the crowd campaigned for the liberation of Barabbas, a committed murderer, how the crowd challenged the authority of the judicial system and secured Barabbas' release, how the voice of the crowd becomes the source of good and the channel for liberation.

Now in today's world, recall how the voice of the crowd continues to shout for the liberation of political prisoners, how the voice of the crowd continues to challenge governments and the ruling powers, how the voice of the crowd continues to be the source of good and the channel for liberation.

Here is a narrative about crowd psychology. Consider how the crowd campaigned for the condemnation of Jesus, God's anointed one, how the crowd corrupted the authority of the judicial system and secured Jesus' crucifixion, how the voice of the crowd becomes a source of evil and the channel for oppression.

Now in today's world, recall how the voice of the crowd continues to shout for the blood of the innocent, how the voice of the crowd continues to corrupt governments and the ruling powers, how the voice of the crowd continues to be the source of evil and the channel for oppression.

Here is a narrative about crowd psychology. Consider how little responsibility each individual in the crowd took for the release of Barabbas, how little responsibility each individual in the crowd took for the crucifixion of Jesus, how the moral autonomy of the individual is eroded by the power of the crowd.

Now in today's world, review just how much your own personal sense of responsibility is eroded by the crowd, just how much your own moral autonomy is undermined by the crowd.

Are you ever there shouting 'Liberate' or 'Crucify' without quite knowing why?

Here is a narrative about crowd psychology.

Feeling

Pause for a moment and try to see how the whole thing looked through Pilate's eyes. After all, Pilate was not even in Judea by choice. He held the office of procurator between AD 26 and 36, probably on the ladder of promotion. What did Pilate care for the Jews or for their faith?

Pause for a moment and try to see how the whole thing looked through Pilate's eyes. Certainly, Pilate was not in Jerusalem by choice. The procurator's normal place of residence was Caesarea, but it was prudent for the procurator to be in Jerusalem at Passover. What did Pilate care for the Jews or for their faith?

Pause for a moment and try to see how the whole thing looked through Pilate's eyes. Under Roman occupation the Jews were permitted to keep the festivals of their faith. But Passover was a volatile time, celebrating (as it does) liberation in the past and looking forward to liberation in the future. What did Pilate care for the Jews or for their faith?

Pause for a moment and try to see how the whole thing looked through Pilate's eyes. Here at the Passover the Jewish leaders warned him of a man claiming to be king. He needed to check out that accusation and satisfy himself that no real threat was being posed to Caesar. What did Pilate care for the Jews or for their faith?

Pause for a moment and try to see how the whole thing looked through Pilate's eyes. The man whom they accused stood weak and helpless before him. He carried no weapon. He was supported by no army. He clearly posed no significant political threat. What did Pilate care for the Jews or for their faith?

Pause for a moment and try to see how the whole thing looked through Pilate's eyes. The Jewish leaders were clearly adamant that Jesus was guilty of death. The Jewish people were clearly baying for Jesus' blood. He gave in to the clear pressure to pass sentence. After all, it would be foolish to risk a popular uprising at the festival of the Passover. What did Pilate care for Jesus or for the faith to be founded on his death and resurrection?

Thinking

When you think closely about the text, the trial before Pilate establishes three themes concerning the crucifixion, very central for the early church. Do you see why these themes are so important to the early church?

When you think closely about the text, the trial before Pilate establishes the *grounds* on which Jesus was crucified. The accusation is clear. Jesus was crucified not for any identifiable wrongdoing, but because he carried the title 'King of the Jews'. Jesus was crucified precisely because he was anointed as the Messiah. Do you see why this theme was so important to the early church?

When you think closely about the text, the trial before Pilate establishes that Jesus was judged to be totally innocent by the Roman procurator. Not only did Pilate seek to release Jesus, he made the open and public statement, 'Why, what evil has he done?' Jesus was crucified in spite of being declared innocent by the Roman authorities. Do you see why this theme was so important to the early church?

When you think closely about the text, the trial before Pilate establishes that the crucifixion was brought about entirely by the Jewish leaders. It was the elders and the scribes who bound Jesus and handed him over to Pilate. It was the elders and the scribes who pressed the charges before Pilate. It was the chief priests who stirred up the crowd to cry for the release of Barabbas and for the crucifixion of Jesus. It was the whole Jewish council which had held consultation. Do you see why this theme was so important to the early church?

When you think closely about the text, the trial before Pilate establishes three themes concerning the crucifixion, very central for the early church. Do you see why these themes are so important to the early church?

34
Mark 16:1–8

¹When the sabbath was over, Mary Magdalene, and Mary the mother of James, and Salome bought spices, so that they might go and anoint him. ²And very early on the first day of the week, when the sun had risen, they went to the tomb. ³They had been saying to one another, 'Who will roll away the stone for us from the entrance to the tomb?' ⁴When they looked up, they saw that the stone, which was very large, had already been rolled back. ⁵As they entered the tomb, they saw a young man, dressed in a white robe, sitting on the right side; and they were alarmed. ⁶But he said to them, 'Do not be alarmed; you are looking for Jesus of Nazareth, who was crucified. He has been raised; he is not here. Look, there is the place they laid him. ⁷But go, tell his disciples and Peter that he is going ahead of you to Galilee; there you will see him, just as he told you.' ⁸So they went out and fled from the tomb, for terror and amazement had seized them; and they said nothing to anyone, for they were afraid.

Context

After devoting two whole chapters to a well-developed and detailed account of the passion narrative, Mark's gospel (as we know it) devotes just eight verses to the resurrection. The verses which follow (9–20) are generally regarded as an appendix added some years later by another hand.

Sensing

Mark's account of the resurrection must speak for itself. So pay attention to the detail of the narrative.

See there on the first Easter Sunday three women: Mary Magdalene, Mary the mother of James, and Salome. See the sadness of mourning in their dress. Hear the sadness of grieving in their slow step. Smell the sadness of death in the spices which they bring.

See there on the first Easter Sunday morning three women: Mary Magdalene, Mary the mother of James, and Salome. See them approach the tomb. Hear them saying to one another, 'Who will roll away the stone for us from the entrance to the tomb?' Sense their surprise that the stone has gone.

See there on the first Easter Sunday three women: Mary Magdalene, Mary the mother of James, and Salome. See them enter the tomb. Hear the young man dressed in the white robe saying to them, 'Jesus of Nazareth, who was crucified, has been raised.' Sense their confusion.

See there on the first Easter Sunday three women: Mary Magdalene, Mary the mother of James, and Salome. See them look round the tomb. Hear the young man dressed in the white robe saying to them, 'He is not here. Look, there is the place where they laid him.' Sense their anxiety.

See there on the first Easter Sunday three women: Mary Magdalene, Mary the mother of James, and Salome. See them scurrying away from the tomb. See the terror of confusion in their faces. Hear the terror of incomprehension in their quickening step. Smell the terror of the unknown in the atmosphere. And they said nothing to anyone, for they were afraid.

Mark's account of the resurrection must speak for itself. So pay attention to the detail of the narrative.

Intuition

Above all else, Mark's account of the resurrection is a narrative of surprises. The women came to the tomb expecting to find it securely sealed. Instead they found it right open. What a surprise! Now, I wonder what Christian men and women are expecting today when they come to explore the story of the tomb? Are they expecting to find it all buttoned up, or are they expecting to find it left open for discussion and interpretation? How willing are they to come face to face with the risen Christ of surprises?

Above all else, Mark's account of the resurrection is a narrative of surprises. The women came to the tomb expecting to find a dead body. Instead they found a messenger of life. What a surprise! Now, I wonder what Christian men and women are looking for today when they study the resurrection narratives? Are they looking for an old body resuscitated? Or are they looking for a new experience of the resurrection life? How willing are they to come face to face with the risen Christ of surprises?

Above all else, Mark's account of the resurrection is a narrative of surprises. The women listened to the messenger of life expecting to learn where their Lord was to be found. Instead the messenger of life pointed to the spot where he had last been seen. What a surprise! Now, I wonder what Christian men and women are questing today when they go seeking the risen Christ? Are they questing irrefutable evidence of the risen Christ? Or are they content with the rumours of the lives the risen Christ has touched? How willing are they to come face to face with the risen Christ of surprises?

Above all else, Mark's account of the resurrection is a narrative of surprises. We come to the story expecting the women to go away rejoicing and spreading the good news. Instead the women went away trembling with fear and said nothing to anyone. What a surprise! Now, I wonder what Christian men and women are doing today about making known the good news of the resurrection? Are they trembling in silence? Or are they proclaiming in confidence? How willing are they to come face to face with the risen Christ of surprises?

Above all else, Mark's account of the resurrection is a narrative of surprises.

Feeling

Pick up your jar of ointment for anointing the dead and set out in the early morning light to tread the sorrowful path to the tomb. Feel with those women their certain sense of death and finality. Share with those women their certainty that life terminates finally and fully in the grave. Know what it is like to live without the good news of the resurrection.

Pick up your jar of ointment for anointing the dead and arrive at the open and empty tomb in the early morning. Feel with those women as their certainty begins to crumble. Share with those women their uncertainty regarding what has happened to the body. Know what it is like to have lost the dead and not yet to have found the promise of the living.

Pick up your jar of ointment for anointing the dead and look round the empty tomb in the early morning light. Feel with those women as their certainty crumbles. Share with those women their uncertainty as they listen to the young man's message of the resurrection. Know what it is like to be confronted with the message of life that is too extraordinary to believe.

Pick up your jar of ointment for anointing the dead and flee away from the empty tomb in the early morning light. Feel with those women their certain sense of disruption and discontinuity.

Share with those women their certainty that the status of death has been changed finally and fully. Know what it is like to live with the good news of the resurrection without yet having encountered the risen Lord.

Pick up your jar of ointment for anointing the dead and smash it forever against the empty tomb. Having heard the good news of the resurrection, travel with those women to meet with the risen Lord.

Thinking

Mark's gospel ends in the most extraordinary of ways. Listen to the final cadence:

> So they went out and fled from the tomb, for terror and amazement had seized them; and they said nothing to anyone, for they were afraid.

So how would you account for an ending like that?

The persecution theory suggests that Mark had intended to write more, but was prevented from doing so. According to this theory, it was the persecution of the early church which provided the very motivation for Mark to write in the first place. Mark was determined to put it all down on paper before it was too late. But the persecutors came and took him away just as the women were fleeing from the tomb. But can you believe that an interrupted ending would end so well?

The carelessness theory suggests that Mark had in fact written more, but his ending has now been lost. According to this theory, the last page of the manuscript was mislaid on the copyist's desk. But can you believe that this could have happened so early on, even before one full ending survived, or that Mark and his closest friends would never have noticed the loss?

The intentionality theory suggests that Mark had indeed intended to finish right here. According to this theory, Mark, the master craftsman of the gospel narrative, knew precisely what he was about. The good news of Jesus Christ, with which his whole gospel is concerned, is not based on the narrative of the empty tomb at all, but on the presence of the living Christ living within the Christian community, for whom Mark was writing. Can you believe that Mark was such a skilful and subtle writer?

Mark's gospel ends in the most extraordinary of ways. Listen to the final cadence:

> So they went out and fled from the tomb, for terror and amazement had seized them; and they said nothing to anyone, for they were afraid.

So how would you account for an ending like that?

35
John 1:6–8, 19–28

⁶There was a man sent from God, whose name was John. ⁷He came as a witness to testify to the light, so that all might believe through him. ⁸He himself was not the light, but he came to testify to the light.

¹⁹This is the testimony given by John when the Jews sent priests and Levites from Jerusalem to ask him, 'Who are you?' ²⁰He confessed and did not deny it, but confessed, 'I am not the Messiah.' ²¹And they asked him, 'What then? Are you Elijah?' He said, 'I am not.' 'Are you the prophet?' He answered, 'No.' ²²Then they said to him, 'Who are you? Let us have an answer for those who sent us. What do you say about yourself?' ²³He said,

'I am the voice of one crying out in the wilderness,
"Make straight the way of the Lord," '
as the prophet Isaiah said.

²⁴Now they had been sent from the Pharisees. ²⁵They asked him, 'Why then are you baptizing if you are neither the Messiah, nor Elijah, nor the prophet?' ²⁶John answered them, 'I baptize with water. Among you stands one whom you do not know, ²⁷the one who is coming after me; I am not worthy to untie the thong of his sandal.' ²⁸This took place in Bethany across the Jordan where John was baptizing.

Context

At the beginning of John's gospel the author clarifies the role of John the Baptist. He appears as a witness and forerunner to the Messiah, who comes to bring life and light to the world. John the Baptist's humility is highlighted as the story prepares for Jesus' revelation through his baptism.

Sensing

Take a look at John the Baptist. You would pick him for an honest witness to the truth. He looks a blunt down-to-earth person who would be true to his testimony.

Stand there with John the Baptist and be a witness to the truth. Listen as he is cross-examined by the religious experts from Jerusalem. In their eyes Jerusalem should be the place for religious learning, not the wilderness. Hear them fire questions at this witness, 'Who are you?' 'What are you?' 'Why are you acting as you are?'

Stand there with John the Baptist and be a witness to the truth. Hear John trying to make them understand the role he has to play in this divine drama. The task of the witness is to prepare the way for the one who holds all truth.

When they ask, 'Who are you?', listen as John tells them, 'I am not the Messiah.' There must be no doubt about that. There is room for only one Messiah, one revelation from the one who is the light of truth. Hear it again, 'I am not the Messiah.'

When they ask, 'Are you the prophet?', listen as John bluntly tells them, 'No!' There must be no doubt about that. To claim to be *the* prophet is to go beyond the task in hand. Witnesses point to others' words and deeds, not to their own.

When they ask, 'What are you?', listen as John firmly describes his role, 'I am the voice who commands preparation for the way of the Lord.' That is my task, that is why I act as I do. Baptism with water is my action of preparation. Baptism with water will reveal the One to whom I bear witness.

Watch John the Baptist point to a pair of sandals. The servant is privileged to undo the master's sandal. This man is so humble he does not even claim that right. Humility, not pride, befits the witness. Our only pride is in Jesus to whom we, with John, bear witness.

Intuition

The true light, which enlightens everyone, was coming into the world. This Advent what does 'light' suggest to you? Advent is a time of lighting candles. Advent is a time of contrasting light with darkness. Advent is a time for choosing between darkness and light.

You can choose to live in darkness. In the darkness of confusion people spend the night in front of the gambling machine, pouring the food money down the throat of the monster. Occasionally it has indigestion and spills its load, and the darkness seems to turn to gold. But when will the truth dawn; when will the hungry be fed with the bread of life?

You can choose to live in the darkness. In the darkness people hide their deeds of violence, thinking that no one will see. They feed their drug habit or their thirst for revenge by the blood of their victims. But when will they see the light that the saviour has come, and choose to accept the power of love?

You can choose to live in the darkness. In the darkness people shut themselves away from the cries of the needy and stay imprisoned from the inside against the invitations of involvement. They ignore the mission of love and live entombed in isolation. But when will they open the door to let the light of hope shine on them and release their hearts in love?

You can choose to live in the light. Bursting forth with energy you can greet the coming Messiah on his mission of love. His light will guide your 'Yes' and 'No' to life's choices. You can choose to live with others in the co-operative venture of life, sharing joys and sorrows, and forming true community.

You can choose to live in the light. Hold high the Christ candle. Bear witness that God has come to share the life of humanity so that humanity can share the creative life of God. In the light there is truth. In the light there is joy. In the light there is love.

What are your choices this Advent?

Feeling

We value the virtue of humility when we see it in others. Humility is the quality you show when you are in touch with yourself, are able to handle comparison with others, and feel right about your role in life.

Step into the place of John the Baptist and feel for this man who speaks and acts with true humility.

Step into his place when he responds to the questions of the religious leaders of the day. Feel for him as he pushes back any feelings of frustration and anger at the tone of their examination. They put him on the spot but he answers them with assurance and without bitterness. He turns down any claims to key positions. He knows who he is. That is a sign of true humility.

Step into his place as he calmly explains why he is calling people to baptism in water. Feel for him as he proclaims a new start and calls others to make a new beginning. He shows confidence in his role and has a clear sense of purpose in his life. That is a sign of true humility.

Step into his place as he points out the gap between his role and that of the coming Messiah. There can be no false comparisons. There can be no basking in reflected glory. There can be no pride in being the king-maker. Feel for him as he declares, 'I am not worthy to untie the thongs of his sandals.' That is a sign of true humility.

Step into his place as he steadfastly carries on with his ministry of baptism when the religious leaders have departed. He feels comfortable about his role in life, and what he has to do to fulfil God's plan. He is well aware that actions are required as well as words. Feel for him as he carries out his vocation. That is a sign of true humility.

Step into his place and share his humility. Only the humble shall touch the earth to enter the stable to behold the Christ-child. That is a sign of true humility.

Thinking

We must be clear in our thinking about the distinct roles of the Messiah and John the Baptist. The records of the New Testament portray John the Baptist as a powerful figure who attracted a major following. The Acts of the Apostles (19:4) shows us that at least at Ephesus, but probably more widely, there were still followers of John the Baptist in the period of the expansion of the early church. The prologue to John's gospel (1:1–18) addresses this issue and clarifies the distinct roles of John and Jesus. The author makes certain that it is the Baptist himself who declares he is not the Messiah. There must be no confusion in the minds of his readers, nor in ours. John the Baptist has his place, and it is an important place, but it is not the primary place. That belongs to the Word made flesh, to the true light that comes from the full radiance of the Godhead.

We must be clear in our thinking about the scripture references highlighting the roles of the Messiah and John the Baptist. In Wisdom 9:9–12 and in Proverbs 8:22–36 Wisdom is pictured as dwelling with God, sharing in the acts of creation, coming to the earth to bring gifts to humankind. In the prologue the Messiah assumes the role of Wisdom. In contrast John the Baptist is seen as the knowledgeable witness to Jesus, God's Wisdom. John declares that he is not the expected Elijah of Malachi 3:23, or the prophet of Deuteronomy 18:15, but the fulfilment of the prophecy found in Isaiah 40:3. The gospel author knows that his readers will be familiar with these references and that he must make abundantly clear which roles Jesus and John the Baptist fulfil.

We must be clear in our thinking about our response to this evidence. We must know in whom we believe, whom we can trust, and whom we will worship. Such clarity of thought is still necessary as we approach the Christmas festival. Too many Christmas cards concentrate on the shepherds, or the angels, or the farmhouse in the snow, or 'Father Christmas', and overshadow the Christ-child. Even the Christmas tree can dazzle our eyes with its lights so that we miss the one true light, the Word made flesh, God's Wisdom revealed, Jesus the Messiah, the Christ. It is he for whom John the Baptist prepares. It is he for whom we must prepare this Advent by our knowledge of the truth.

36
John 1:1-14

[1]In the beginning was the Word, and the Word was with God, and the Word was God. [2]He was in the beginning with God. [3]All things came into being through him, and without him not one thing came into being. What has come into being [4]in him was life, and the life was the light of all people. [5]The light shines in the darkness, and the darkness did not overcome it.

[6]There was a man sent from God, whose name was John. [7]He came as a witness to testify to the light, so that all might believe through him. [8]He himself was not the light, but he came to testify to the light. [9]The true light, which enlightens everyone, was coming into the world.

[10]He was in the world, and the world came into being through him; yet the world did not know him. [11]He came to what was his own, and his own people did not accept him. [12]But to all who received him, who believed in his name, he gave power to become children of God, [13]who were born, not of blood or of the will of the flesh or of the will of man, but of God.

[14]And the Word became flesh and lived among us, and we have seen his glory, the glory as of a father's only son, full of grace and truth.

Context

The prologue to John's gospel introduces its main themes: that the creative Word and Wisdom of God has been revealed in Jesus Christ; that his coming has brought life and light to a world in darkness; that he was rejected by some but received by others who by faith become true children of God.

Sensing

Light the candle in the darkness. Watch the way the flame flickers into life. See the light penetrate further and further into the shadows, pushing back the sense of fear and confusion. The light fills the whole space. Now you can see clearly and the shadows no longer make you feel afraid.

Light the candle in the darkness. Approach the candle flame and feel its warmth. Hold your hands out to cradle the flame. See how it dances before you in pure delight. Feel how its reflected glow illuminates your face. Receive its messages of hope and joy. Darkness cannot overcome this light. Nothing can take away this hope. Nothing can replace this inner joy.

Light the candle in the darkness. Draw near with faith and adoration. Sense your heartbeat responding to the good news of the light of Christ. Fix your eyes in wonder on the light which tells you that Jesus has brought life to you in all its fullness.

Light the candle in the darkness. Touch the candle of your baptism. Let it tell you again that you are a child of God, born of God's Spirit; and that you are sharing the life of Christ. Touch the candle of your baptism. Then you were welcomed to the community that received Christ and believed in his name. Now you live as part of that community. Fulfil your baptism and walk in the light of Christ.

Light the candle in the darkness. Place it in the window of your house. Listen to the shouts of all those who pass by and behold it in wonder and delight. Watch the fingers point to the candle, your witness to the light of Christ. Your candle tells your neighbours that Jesus is the true light who enlightens everyone who takes notice of his coming.

Light the candle in the darkness. Hold it high for those in trouble and despair to see. Guide their steps on the right paths. By the light of the candle tend their wounds and wash their feet.

Hold the candle carefully in the darkness. Walk into the future with courage, knowing that the power of Christ will sustain you. Christ is life and light for all his children.

Intuition

In an age when the media predominate and we are bombarded on all sides with words of propaganda, how do you hear the word of God?

Have you heard the word of God spoken in creation? The whole created order exists by the command of God and as such speaks for God. Its creativity tells us of the One who gives life to all that lives. Let the words of the environmentalists reveal God's wisdom and God's power to bring to fruition God's planning. Have you heard God's word spoken in creation?

Have you heard the word of God spoken through God's witnesses? God's word comes through the voice of the prophets. The divine creative activity needs an interpreter who illuminates its meaning and the ways of goodness and light. The long line of prophets reaches its climax in John the Baptist. The line needs to be continued in the interpreters of the word today. There are many voices and we need discernment. Have you heard God's word spoken through the prophets of every age?

Have you heard the word of God spoken through the Word made flesh, in the words and actions of Jesus Christ? Only the mind of God can reveal the truth about God. As Christ dwells with the Father, so we must dwell in the word of God if we are to be able to apply the teaching of Christ to be our light and our life. God's Word is made flesh in Jesus Christ. Have you heard God's Word revealed in Scripture?

The Word of God reveals the grace of God and the truth of God. God's word is a sentence of generosity. It tells of the overflowing gifts of forgiveness and of eternal life. God's word reveals the truth about the nature of God and the purpose of God for all of humanity and all of creation. Have you heard God's truth revealed in Christ?

Despite the noise of propaganda, have you heard the word of God for your own situation? Let it speak to you of a new creation, of a new humanity, of a new person, of a new life lived in accordance with the word of God. Have you heard God's word spoken to you?

Feeling

There is a depth of pathos in this prologue: 'He came to what was his own, and his own people did not accept him' (verse 11). The feelings of sadness at such rejection are obvious.

We can empathize with God's feelings as the divine attempts to communicate with humanity are rejected by so many who have all the advantages of life. It seems that having much they see little point in responding to God's initiatives. Share the sadness in the heart of God at such rejection.

We can empathize with God's feelings when so many shut their eyes and refuse to see the light of Christ leading them in a true direction for living. They seem dazzled by the brightness of modern life, or on the other hand are blinded by the darkness of tragedy, and refuse to see the light of God in their midst. Share the sadness in the heart of God at such rejection.

We can empathize with those who feel rejected by those close to them when as new disciples they accept the light of Christ. For some the acceptance of Christ leads to rejection by those dearest to them. Share the sadness in the heart of Christians at such rejection.

We can empathize with those who feel that their children, younger or older, have rejected the faith they hold dear. Some parents and grandparents have tried to keep the light of faith burning, but the new generation has spurned the truth, and trivialized the gospel. Share the sadness in the heart of the older generation at such rejection.

Yet there is also a depth of joy in this prologue: 'But to all those who received him, who believed in his name, he gave power to become children of God' (verse 12). The feelings of joy at such acceptance are obvious.

We can empathize with those who feel overjoyed at finding the Christ, the light of the world and life for eternity. With joyous faith they have believed in his name and become children of God. Share the gladness in the heart of God and among Christians at such acceptance.

Thinking

Note how this prologue to John's gospel is written in poetic prose form. You can trace its shape and its style. Some have called it a hymn of reverence to the Word made flesh.

The purpose of this hymn is threefold: to tell us about the nature of God; to tell us about humanity and how it acts; and to tell us about God's relationship to humanity. Careful study will be rewarded with enlightenment.

The first stanza of the hymn (verses 1–5) tells us about the nature of God. God's creating 'wisdom' causes the world to come into being. There are echoes of the Genesis story here. In creation the Word of God acts as divine agent. God designed this universe to have life and to reflect the divine light. Verses 6–9 should be seen as a parenthesis about John the Baptist acting as witness to that light.

The second stanza (verses 10–12) tells us about the humanity that God has created. Humanity was brought into being as a people who could relate to God and know God. They were to be God's own people, but they failed to recognize God when God's Son shared that humanity. Only some received the ambassador of life, and it was those people who could claim to be true children of God. Verse 13 should be seen as a parenthesis about the way that such children were related to God.

The third stanza (verse 14) tells us of the fact that God has become fully human so that those who recognize him can accept him as God the Father's only Son, and through him experience divine grace and truth.

Such a hymn requires study to draw out the parallel with the concept of divine wisdom contained in the Wisdom Literature of the Hebrew scriptures. It requires prayer to reflect on the mysterious union within the Godhead, and on the mystery of Christ's being as both fully divine and fully human. Such study and prayer inspire our hymn of worship to God.

37
John 1:43–51

[43]The next day Jesus decided to go to Galilee. He found Philip and said to him, 'Follow me.' [44]Now Philip was from Bethsaida, the city of Andrew and Peter. [45]Philip found Nathanael and said to him, 'We have found him about whom Moses in the law and also the prophets wrote, Jesus son of Joseph from Nazareth.' [46]Nathanael said to him, 'Can anything good come out of Nazareth?' Philip said to him, 'Come and see.' [47]When Jesus saw Nathanael coming toward him, he said of him, 'Here is truly an Israelite in whom there is no deceit!' [48]Nathanael asked him, 'Where did you get to know me?' Jesus answered, 'I saw you under the fig tree before Philip called you.' [49]Nathanael replied, 'Rabbi, you are the Son of God! You are the King of Israel!' [50]Jesus answered, 'Do you believe because I told you that I saw you under the fig tree? You will see greater things than these.' [51]And he said to him, 'Very truly, I tell you, you will see heaven opened and the angels of God ascending and descending upon the Son of Man.'

Context

The revelation of who Jesus is passes from disciple to disciple. The circle of those who recognize Jesus widens. In explaining how people came to know Jesus, the author of the gospel shows that it occurs first within families and then between friends. This was the likely pattern in the Christian community for which he wrote.

Sensing

Note the way that disciples of Jesus come to know him. Take yourself back to Galilee and see the way that Jesus chooses the team to lead his new community.

Listen to Jesus' command to Philip, 'Follow me!' Hear the clear challenge in his voice. Philip came from the same place as Andrew and Peter. They would understand one another and share the same experiences. Watch Philip become a member of this new team of followers of Jesus.

Listen to the witness of Philip to his friend Nathanael, 'We have found the one of whom Moses and the prophets wrote. He is Jesus, son of Joseph, from Nazareth.' Hear the note of excitement at the discovery. Philip and Nathanael had gone to the synagogue together. They had studied the law and pondered the prophets' meaning. Now it all came together in a man from the hill town of Nazareth, and his name was Jesus.

Listen to the scorning question that Nathanael asked his friend Philip, 'Can anything good come out of Nazareth?' Hear the note of disbelief that a small hill town could produce the long-expected one of Israel. Important people come from important places. Nothing important happens in Galilee; this is a backwater.

Listen to the invitation of Philip to his friend Nathanael, 'Come and see.' Hear the tone of certainty that a meeting with Jesus will transform his life. Decisions about Jesus cannot be made at a distance. Secondhand stories cannot replace firsthand experience. Disciples have to meet the Master.

Listen to the tribute that Jesus paid to his potential disciple Nathanael, 'Here is truly an Israelite in whom there is no deceit!' Hear the tone of appreciation that there were such genuine people among those who claimed to know God. Honesty would be a good quality in a disciple. As Nathanael had been tempted to dismiss a man from Nazareth, it would be wrong to dismiss all religious people as deceiving themselves and others.

Listen to the confession of faith that Nathanael made to Jesus, 'You are the Son of God! You are the King of Israel!' Watch another disciple join the team.

Intuition

Here is an example of how knowledge of Jesus spread among the first disciples. Can you apply the story to the ways we might share our faith about Jesus with others in our day?

The author of the gospel tells us that the first example of evangelism was within the family. Andrew was attracted to Jesus because of the witness of John the Baptist that Jesus was the Lamb of God. Convinced that Jesus was the Messiah he went off to find his brother Simon. Can you see in Andrew an example of evangelism within the family? By Andrew's efforts Peter was claimed as a disciple by Christ who called him 'the Rock'. Andrew issued the invitation: 'Come and see.' If Andrew had kept his find to himself, Simon Peter would not have met Jesus. What a tragedy that would have been! Can you apply this story to the way you share your faith in Jesus with the other members of your family?

The author of the gospel shows that the second example of evangelism was between neighbours in the same community. Philip came from the same town as Andrew and Peter. Can you see in Philip an example of evangelism within a community? Among your associates there may well be those who will readily respond to the call of the Master. Can you apply this story to the way you present Christ to people from your community who will hear the call and respond to the voice of Jesus?

The author of the gospel shows that the third example of evangelism was between close friends. Philip found his friend Nathanael and told him all about his new-found knowledge of Jesus. Can you see in Nathanael an example of evangelism between friends? Can you give your friends an invitation to 'come and see' for themselves? They may, like Nathanael, at first dismiss the idea that Jesus is God, but later become convinced that Jesus is the Christ. Can you apply this story to the way that you might bring your friends to meet the Master?

Can you see how this story might help us fulfil our responsibilities for evangelism?

Feeling

Here is a story about relationships based on honesty and enquiry. Share the feelings of Philip, Nathanael and Jesus.

Share the feelings of Philip. He had the most exciting encounter with God in his life. His heart was pounding when he was invited to follow Jesus. Was he worthy of such a key role in the kingdom? Did he have what it takes to be a leader? Was he right to throw in his lot with this relative stranger? Could he work with others from the same town? Enter into the relationship and share the feelings of Philip.

Share the feelings of Nathanael. He had great reservations about big claims by people from small places. He wondered if he could trust the new enthusiasm of his old friend Philip. He always preferred to ask searching questions than to give ready answers. He valued honesty above all virtues. How could he trust his friend's judgement? How could he trust the insight of this new prophet? Could he bear to live with those who might see into his inner heart? Enter into the relationship and share the feelings of Nathanael.

Share the feelings of Jesus. He did not have long to make up his mind about whom it would be best to call into his team of disciples. Could he trust them to be reliable? Could he trust those, like Philip, who asked few questions before they agreed to follow him? Could he trust those, like Nathanael, who wanted answers before they were willing to follow him? Could such diverse characters be welded together to form a strong team? Enter into the relationship and share the feelings of Jesus.

Unpack your own feelings as you listen to this gospel. Does it make you frightened with its challenges? Does it give you encouragement that others have followed their hunches and become disciples, with or without too many questions? Do you feel worthy of such a high calling? Enter into the relationship with Jesus and share honestly your feelings about yourself.

Thinking

The conversation between Jesus and the disciple Nathanael has provoked a lot of debate about who Nathanael might be.

The name Nathanael does not appear in the list of the twelve disciples in the gospels of Mark (3:16–19), or Matthew (10:1–4), or Luke (6:12–16). There the name linked with Philip is

Bartholomew. Yet by making comparisons in this way we may be missing the point that the author of John's gospel wishes to make. The opening scene in the gospel drama introduces key elements about who Jesus is, and these are explored more fully in the chapters to come.

Nathanael is the last in a series of witnesses as to who Jesus is. First there is John the Baptist, the forerunner of Jesus. Then there is the Holy Spirit at the baptism of Jesus. Then come disciples like Andrew and his friend who stay with Jesus and learn from this rabbi. Andrew shares his discovery with his brother Simon, given the name 'Rock' as a foundation stone of the future church. Then Philip provides an example of those disciples found by Christ and given a direct call. He becomes a missionary as he shares his knowledge of Jesus with his friend Nathanael.

The way that the author of the gospel tells the story sounds like a parallel to the way that different groups of people responded to the message about Jesus in the early church. We may then ask whether Nathanael represents the Johannine communities for which this fourth gospel was written. Nathanael means 'the gift of God'. He was a student of the Torah if we follow scholars' interpretation of the puzzling reference to sitting under the fig tree, the place of study for those steeped in the law of Moses. That would tie in with Jesus' acknowledgement of Nathanael as a 'true Israelite', one who would not be deceived about the Messiah when he appeared. Nathanael may well represent all those disciples who, through study of scripture, discover that this rabbi is indeed the Son of God and the hoped-for leader of the new Israel. Nathanael exemplifies the proper outcome of all gospel writing that 'you may come to believe that Jesus is the Messiah, the Son of God, and that through believing you may have life in his name' (John 20:31).

John 2:1–11

¹On the third day there was a wedding in Cana of Galilee, and the mother of Jesus was there. ²Jesus and his disciples had also been invited to the wedding. ³When the wine gave out, the mother of Jesus said to him, 'They have no wine.' ⁴And Jesus said to her, 'Woman, what concern is that to you and to me? My hour has not yet come.' ⁵His mother said to the servants, 'Do whatever he tells you.' ⁶Now standing there were six stone water jars for the Jewish rites of purification, each holding twenty or thirty gallons. ⁷Jesus said to them, 'Fill the jars with water.' And they filled them up to the brim. ⁸He said to them, 'Now draw some out, and take it to the chief steward.' So they took it. ⁹When the steward tasted the water that had become wine, and did not know where it came from (though the servants who had drawn the water knew), the steward called the bridegroom ¹⁰and said to him, 'Everyone serves the good wine first, and then the inferior wine after the guests have become drunk. But you have kept the good wine until now.' ¹¹Jesus did this, the first of his signs, in Cana of Galilee, and revealed his glory; and his disciples believed in him.

Context

At the opening of John's gospel a series of people bear witness to who Jesus is. The author then confirms this witness by recording the actions of Jesus. These are signs of his nature and power. The first sign is given at a wedding at Cana, the next village to Nazareth. The transformation of ritual water into gospel wine reveals Jesus' glory and gives rise to belief in those with perception.

Sensing

Mingle with the wedding guests and taste the wine. There is joy in every cup. On this happy occasion all the guests rejoice with the family.

Look across the room to Mary from Nazareth, one of the bride's aunts or cousins. She is there to support her family. Watch as she makes sure all the guests have enough food and drink to share the rejoicing at this new beginning. This is a celebration to mark a wedding. Listen to the laughter of family unity and of the hope of new life.

Look across the room to Mary from Nazareth. Watch the smile on her face turn to a frown. She realizes that the supply of wine is not enough for all those who have responded to the wedding invitation. Even her son Jesus has brought along his new friends. Strain your ears to hear Mary's embarrassed admission to Jesus; 'They have no wine.' A feast is a time for plenty; listen to this cry of shortage.

Look across the room to Jesus from Nazareth. He is a member of the family circle. Watch him ponder what to do. Should he leave the party and go along to the village shop to buy more wine? Strain your ears to hear Jesus' curt reply: 'Woman, this is not the time and occasion for me to reveal my power.'

Look across the room to Mary from Nazareth. Watch her beginning to organize the servants. Her faith in her son is so strong that she believes that his actions will speak louder than words. She is showing her trust that Jesus will turn the old waters of Judaism into the new wine of the gospel.

Look across the room at Jesus. Watch him step forward. He is responding to her faith and to the needs of the people. They need a new taste of wine. They need a new sense of life – a mature, satisfying, enjoyable life, a life as rich as wine.

Behold, the stewards offer you another glass of wine. Taste it, it is the best you have ever enjoyed. Drink a toast to life. Drink a toast to Jesus.

Intuition

Read the signs of the wedding feast. You will be excited by John's gospel and the way signs are used in it. The first sign is an event which happens in the life of most families, a time of wedding celebrations. Read the signs of the wedding feast.

A wedding feast is a time of unity and fellowship. It is a gathering of two families and their friends. Over the feast they become one, just as the bride and groom are united as one. The wedding feast fulfils our dream for the unity of all people through the love of God. Here is a sign that all the families of the world will be united into the one family of God.

A wedding feast is a time for sharing hope for the future. The speeches tell of hopes for new beginnings, for a new start in life, for a new generation yet to be born. At the wedding feast the toast for happiness is not just for the couple, but for their family, and for wider society. Here there is a new Adam and a new Eve, a sign of new creation for humanity.

A wedding feast is a time of gratitude for all the gifts of God the creator and provider. Without the creator there is no life. Without the creator there is no food. Without the creator there is no wine to gladden the hearts of the guests. A wedding feast is a sign of human dependence on God and of humanity's thanksgiving for the generosity of God. Grace is said for the gift of love and the gift of bread and wine.

A wedding feast is a time of commitment and faith. The couple pledge their trust in each other and their commitment to the bonds of love and mutuality. A wedding feast is a time for a new faith to be affirmed by all the family and guests that God's love will be sufficient for the future of the couple and themselves. Here is a sign that new life, new faith, new love abound.

Feeling

It must have been hard for Mary on the day of the family wedding at Cana. As a close member of the family she would share its responsibilities for the entertainment of the guests. Feel for her as she watches the wine run dry.

Feel Mary's mixture of pride and embarrassment at the number of guests who have answered the invitation and the shortage of wine that was the result. The support of so many family and friends at a marriage is wonderful, but it causes problems. Feel for Mary as the guests keep coming and she realizes that the supply of wine will run out.

Feel Mary's hopes rise as Jesus and his new friends all arrive. Feel her pride at seeing her special firstborn being surrounded by such strong support. Feel her confidence that with Jesus present all will be well. He is a caring, loving person who seeks the happiness of all. Surely she can trust Jesus to transform the occasion.

Feel Mary's profound dismay as she listens to Jesus' reply to her request for help. Why does he mention time and occasion as an excuse for ignoring the problem? He has always been so helpful in the past, why not now?

Feel Mary's faithful persistence as she brushes aside the reply and puts out a challenge: 'Do as he tells you.' Her faith is in the servants as well as in the Master. This is the time for both faith and action.

Feel Mary's relief as she sees the servants pouring the wine out of the massive water jars at the command of Jesus. Share her sense of satisfaction that she has been the means of this renewed celebration.

Feel Mary's joy as she hears the guests express their amazement at how good the wine is. Share her joy as she sees people trusting her son as she has done. Her heart leaps for joy at this new birth of faith. The contrast with the old is striking. With joy all hail a new richness in life.

Thinking

On the face of it this story does not add up. What wedding party would need 120 to 180 gallons of wine to quench a second thirst? But when you do some research, the clues the author gives reveal in dramatic fashion the transforming ways of the gospel message.

Consider carefully the first clue: 'On the third day'. Initially this phrase seems irrelevant. On the third day from what starting point? Deeper thinking helps us understand that 'On the third day' is the clue to the resurrection and the transformation that it brought. This story reveals how the resurrected Christ has transformed the whole of life.

Consider carefully the second clue: 'My hour has not yet come.' The words might be better expressed in the form of a question: 'Is not this the turning point of time?' The phrase is used in John's gospel as a 'clue' phrase about the occasions when Jesus is revealed as the source and the instigator of divine activity. The author says that, if you have eyes to see, God's great power is at work in this action of Jesus. He gives the same clue about the actions of Christ on the cross: 'The hour has come for the Son of Man to be glorified' (John 12:23).

Carefully consider the third clue: 'Now standing there were six stone water jars for the Jewish rites of purification.' This story is about the contrast between the way of salvation in the old religion and the way of salvation through the death and resurrection of Jesus. Ritual water becomes gospel wine. There is a new way to find forgiveness and new life, and it is Jesus who acts to bring about this transformation.

Consider carefully the fourth clue: 'You have kept the good wine until now.' Despite God being active in the 'old' wine of the people of Israel, God's full riches are now poured out in the superior wine of the death of Christ. Here we see echoes of the eucharistic feast celebrated in the communities to which the gospel was addressed. They would understand the clues. With careful consideration we can too. In the new wine of the Eucharist Christ reveals his glory and we believe in him.

39
John 2:13–22

¹³The Passover of the Jews was near, and Jesus went up to Jerusalem. ¹⁴In the temple he found people selling cattle, sheep, and doves, and the money changers seated at their tables. ¹⁵Making a whip of cords, he drove all of them out of the temple, both the sheep and the cattle. He also poured out the coins of the money changers and overturned their tables. ¹⁶He told those who were selling the doves, 'Take these things out of here! Stop making my Father's house a marketplace!' ¹⁷His disciples remembered that it was written, 'Zeal for your house will consume me.' ¹⁸The Jews then said to him, 'What sign can you show us for doing this?' ¹⁹Jesus answered them, 'Destroy this temple, and in three days I will raise it up.' ²⁰The Jews then said, 'This temple has been under construction for forty-six years, and will you raise it up in three days?' ²¹But he was speaking of the temple of his body. ²²After he was raised from the dead, his disciples remembered that he had said this; and they believed the scripture and the word that Jesus had spoken.

Context

For the Jewish people the temple was the pinnacle of their response in worship to God. In the temple God was manifested to seeking humanity. In John's gospel the story of the cleansing of the temple is brought forward to the early days of Jesus' ministry to show how his resurrection body would supersede the temple as the place of revelation and worship.

Sensing

Stand at the entrance to the glorious temple building and observe the preparations for the daily sacrifices. Look over there. People are buying a pair of turtle doves to sacrifice in thanksgiving for the birth of a child. And over there another group are buying a calf as a thank-offering for a successful business venture. Down by the steps see another family buying a lamb as a sin-offering to seek forgiveness for cheating a neighbour in a land deal. Smell the smoke of the sacrificial fires.

Stand at the entrance to the glorious temple building and observe the pilgrims coming to worship carrying their donations in their local currency. Watch as they approach the dealers who will change such 'tainted' money into the sacred coinage used in the temple. Listen to the haggling and the shouting: 'You swindler! You robber! That's not a fair rate of exchange.'

Stand at the entrance to the glorious temple building. Look, there is the prophet from Nazareth arriving with his disciples. Watch as he makes a whip out of cords and drives the stock for sacrifice right out of the temple courtyard. Listen to the bleating of the sheep and the bellowing of the cattle, and to the bleats and the bellowing of their owners.

Stand at the entrance of the glorious temple building and watch Jesus return to the colonnades. Watch as he flips over the tables of the traders and money changers and throws the bags of coins down on the marble floor. Listen to their protests as their wealth drains away.

Stand in the centre of the glorious temple building and listen as the firm voice of this prophet drowns out the noise of protest. Hear his command: 'Stop making my Father's house a market-place.'

Stand in the centre of the glorious temple building and listen to the firm voice of this prophet. Hear his challenge: 'Destroy this temple and in three days I will raise it up.'

Behold this glorious building, you will see it destroyed by soldiers. Behold Christ's resurrected body, you will see it rise in glory. It will be for you the revelation of God's glory and power for ever.

Intuition

This account of the cleansing of the temple brings into focus the ways people think are best to honour their God.

Consider the traders in cattle, sheep and doves. They wanted to provide a vehicle for sacrifice as a means of worship. Surely God should be honoured by the offering of what we consider of greatest value in our lives. How can we express our love and worship to God? Should we cease to eat meat or refrain from pleasures as a sign of our devotion to God? What sacrifices do you make as a sign of your dedication and worship?

Consider the money changers. They wanted to provide a vehicle for the offering of 'pure' money to God. How can we express our love and devotion to God through our wealth? Should we not use our money as a way of offering God service? What contributions are you making to the mission and service of the church? What money have you put aside for the support of the poor? We may condemn the money changers, but our money is part of our response to the gospel.

Consider Christ's challenge about worship in the marketplace. Most people are called to be involved in one way or another with the 'marketplace' of commerce and trade. How do you worship God in the midst of the marketplace? Do you turn your back on it, or do you use it as the place in which to serve God? The early Christian communities were very involved in trade and made converts as part of their commerce. How will you witness to God in the marketplace?

Consider Christ's challenge about the destruction of the temple. Most Christians have set apart buildings as places to honour God and provide a space for worship. How do you regard places for worship? The Puritans destroyed centuries of art in an attempt to cleanse churches for pure worship. How can you sanctify your 'temple' for worship?

When we consider the implications of this story it is full of challenges to the way we worship today.

Feeling

This story is about zeal, and we can relate to that. There is evidence of a lot of feeling and passion in this account of what happened in the temple. It has prompted a zealous debate about values and actions.

Share the feelings of those who came to express the place God had in their hearts. Some worshippers came to the temple full of joy and thanksgiving. Some came to the temple full of guilt, worry and confusion about how to live their lives. Pilgrims travelled miles to present themselves and their causes to God in the temple. Stand with them and put all your heart into your worship. Express your depth of feelings to God. Join in the hymns; drop to your knees in supplication. Offer your shouts of adoration and praise. Lift up your heart in thankful amazement at Christ's sacrifice for our sins. Sing to the Lamb who was slain for us!

Share the feelings of those who were outraged at the way their worship was despoiled by the dishonesty of the traders. So often we find our feelings at worship upset by the actions of those who worship alongside us. When we want to express ourselves with zeal, we find others trying to suppress our feelings, and trying to limit our cries of faith and joy. Be in touch with your feelings. Can you forgive but still show them that you are hurting?

Share the feelings of Jesus as he acts with zeal to honour God in the way that worship is offered. Share his zeal for a total focus on God's love and goodness. Share his zeal for right dealings as well as right praise. Share his zeal that the offering of his body in sacrifice will lead people to see God in action for the salvation of all humanity. Let your worship be fired with zeal by this story.

Thinking

The placement of this story about the cleansing of the temple so early in Jesus' ministry raises a number of questions. Why does the author of John's gospel break with the tradition of the other gospel writers in placing the story at the beginning rather than the end of Jesus' ministry? Why does the author link the destruction of the temple to the death and resurrection of Jesus? Does the author intend us to draw the conclusion that Jesus wanted his disciples to cease participation in Jewish ritual and focus on the Eucharist as the means of sacrificial worship? Careful study of the way John's gospel is written will help us address these three questions.

John's gospel focuses on the theological themes that explain who Jesus is. The author constructs the story with this in mind, aiming to convince his hearers that they should believe in Jesus as the Messiah, the Son of God. To achieve this he must show that the Messiah acts with divine authority on behalf of God. The story of the cleansing of the temple makes this obvious. It is one of the key 'signs' which help us interpret what follows.

When you consider the gospel in its sequence you can see the author's purpose in placing this story so early in the ministry of

Jesus. To better understand the full story of Jesus we need clues about the purpose of his ministry. Jesus came to reveal God and the type of life that would be a worthy offering to God. Just as ritual water had to be transformed into gospel wine, so ritual sacrifice had to be transformed into eucharistic thanksgiving by Christ's death and resurrection. To understand both 'signs', faith would need to be developed by understanding. The story of how Nicodemus found faith is the third part of this transformation trilogy.

By the time the fourth gospel was written the temple had been destroyed and Christian communities as well as Jewish communities had to come to grips with that fact. This story points Christians to a new direction for worship. The old Passover was superseded by the new Passover of Christ's death and the victory of the resurrection. Early in the gospel such a fact needed to be clearly stated. The old ways must go to make way for the new. Easter is the new focus for our devotion. Therefore let us prepare to keep the feast.

40
John 3:1–17

¹Now there was a Pharisee named Nicodemus, a leader of the Jews. ²He came to Jesus by night and said to him, 'Rabbi, we know that you are a teacher who has come from God; for no one can do these signs that you do apart from the presence of God.' ³Jesus answered him, 'Very truly, I tell you, no one can see the kingdom of God without being born from above.' ⁴Nicodemus said to him, 'How can anyone be born after having grown old? Can one enter a second time into the mother's womb and be born?' ⁵Jesus answered, 'Very truly, I tell you, no one can enter the kingdom of God without being born of water and Spirit. ⁶What is born of the flesh is flesh, and what is born of the Spirit is spirit. ⁷Do not be astonished that I said to you, "You must be born from above." ⁸The wind blows where it chooses, and you hear the sound of it, but you do not know where it comes from or where it goes. So it is with everyone who is born of the Spirit.' ⁹Nicodemus said to

him, 'How can these things be?' [10]Jesus answered him, 'Are you a teacher of Israel, and yet you do not understand these things?

[11]'Very truly, I tell you, we speak of what we know and testify to what we have seen; yet you do not receive our testimony. [12]If I have told you about earthly things and you do not believe, how can you believe if I tell you about heavenly things? [13]No one has ascended into heaven except the one who descended from heaven, the Son of Man. [14]And just as Moses lifted up the serpent in the wilderness, so must the Son of Man be lifted up, [15]that whoever believes in him may have eternal life.

[16]'For God so loved the world that he gave his only Son, so that everyone who believes in him may not perish but may have eternal life.

[17]'Indeed, God did not send the Son into the world to condemn the world, but in order that the world might be saved through him.'

Context

In the opening chapters of John's gospel water is transformed into wine; the presence of God is transferred from the temple to Christ's resurrected body; and in these verses an old teacher is transformed into a new-born disciple. God's purpose of transformation is revealed. Out of divine love Christ is born into the world. Divine love desires that each person is reborn to eternal life in the Spirit. At the heart of the Trinity there is love and recreating energy.

Sensing

Witness the meeting between two learned teachers. Be there in the night as the lamps are lit. See the two men silhouetted against the light. Nicodemus is standing with his back to the darkness. Jesus is standing with the light illuminating his face. Listen to the dialogue flowing backwards and forwards between these two learned teachers.

See the cultured face of Nicodemus. Watch his assured stance as a man of experience. Listen as he proclaims what is obvious about Jesus from the actions he has performed: 'You are a teacher who has come from God.'

See the challenging face of Jesus. Watch his assured stance as a man of action. Listen as he calls for a greater response to his teaching than just listening: 'No one can see the kingdom of God with-out being born anew.'

See the puzzled face of Nicodemus. Watch as he shifts from one foot to another as a man without all the answers. What does being born anew mean? Listen as he blurts out: 'How can anyone be born after having grown old?'

See the open face of Jesus. Watch as he puts his hand on Nicodemus' shoulder as a man of understanding. Listen to his explanation: 'What is born of the flesh is flesh, and what is born of the Spirit is spirit.'

See the relieved face of Nicodemus. Watch as he looks up into Jesus' eyes. Listen as he puts his trusting question to the Master: 'How can these things be?'

See the loving face of Jesus. Watch as he looks into Nicodemus' eyes. Listen as he assures him of God's purpose for his life:

> God so loved the world that he gave his only Son, so that everyone who believes in him may not perish, but have eternal life.

See the joyful face of Nicodemus. He has grasped the truth, about Jesus, about God's plan, about the appropriate response he must make. Sense the wind stirring through the door. Nicodemus turns to the light. A new life has been born.

Intuition

Those with a preference for intuition are good at seeing the double meanings in the one statement.

So make the connection between the wind and the Spirit. You are aware that the wind is blowing when you see its effects on the environment. The trees move into life; the flags flutter with joy; the daffodils dance in the fields. When the wind stirs creation into life, it is a signal that the wind is real.

So make the connection between the Spirit and the wind. You are aware that the Spirit moves when you see its effects in people, and when faith bursts into assurance; when the darkness of evil is transformed into the light of goodness and truth; when the cries of distress become the prayers of comfort. When the Spirit stirs people into new life, it is a signal that the Spirit is real.

So make the connection between the serpent and the cross. From Numbers 21:9 you are aware that when Moses held up the token sign of the serpent on a pole, those who were poisoned by the snakebite were healed and saved. From the threat of death came the transformation to life.

So make the connection between the cross and the serpent. From the story of the cross and the resurrection you are aware that when Christ allowed himself to be lifted on the cross those poisoned by sin found healing and forgiveness. From the death of Christ came the transformation to life.

So make the connection between the one who ascends and the one who descends. You are aware that out of the Father's love the saviour was sent to bring life to the world. The incarnation was his descent. So the ascension is the signal that Christ, carrying the cares of the world in his heart for ever, returned to the heart of God.

So make the connection between the Spirit and your life. Be aware of the signs of the Spirit's activity. Make the connection between the cross and your salvation. Be aware of the signs that you have accepted your forgiveness. Make the connection between Christ and the Trinity. Be aware of the signs that you have responded to the call to love.

Feeling

The story of Nicodemus is a story about relationships. Put yourself into Nicodemus' place and see how it feels.

Identify with Nicodemus as he experiences the relationship with Jesus. As a teacher yourself, you recognize a teacher who comes from God. Experience the depth of awe, mystery and enquiry involved in such a meeting. Feel the anxiety as you step out of the shadows of darkness into the light of his presence. In the light all will be revealed. Feel the awe as you face this charismatic figure who does such powerful actions. Feel the mystery as you dialogue with one who speaks in 'double-talk'. Feel the enquiry rising in you as you ask: 'How can these things be?' Feel the sense of worship as you approach Jesus, the Son of Man, and the only Son of God.

Identify with Nicodemus as he experiences the relationship with the Spirit. As a teacher yourself, you have learnt that the word for 'wind' and 'Spirit' are the same. Both are powerful; both are a mystery; both stir creation. Feel the deep emotion of approaching such a sign of the activity of God. Feel the creativity of the Spirit stirring your inner being with the pangs of new birth.

Feel the exuberance of the Spirit as, like oxygen in your lungs, it gives power for prayer and praise. Feel the energy of the Spirit inspiring you to fresh deeds of love. Feel the sense of worship as you approach the Spirit's holiness and truth.

Identify with Nicodemus as he experiences the relationship with God the Father. As a teacher yourself, you have learnt that God is One and God exists before the creation. Feel the depth of reverence and gratitude to the One who has caused your creation. Feel the depth of affection for the One who has declared that you are loved. Feel the depth of wonder that the love within the God-head is so strong that it reaches out to all to bring them salvation and eternal life. Feel the sense of worship as you approach God, the lover and parent of all.

Thinking

The author of John's gospel portrays Nicodemus both as an individual and as a representative of the listening community.

Nicodemus is the man who has seen the signs that Jesus performed and has acknowledged that Jesus is a teacher come from God. He is also every enquirer who must move from knowledge ('We know' in verse 2) to involvement with the deep mystery of the Spirit ('You [plural] must be born from above' in verse 7). Every member of the listening community can identify with Nicodemus.

The story suggests that the community which listened to this gospel was in a missionary situation. In their area the members of the local synagogue were ready, like Nicodemus, to recognize Jesus as a prophet or teacher, but had no experience of the unity between the Father and the Son, nor of the Spirit. The author does not set out to explain the Trinitarian form of the Godhead, but rather points to the experience of the Christian community. As Christ was sent, so every member of the community is called upon to share in the missionary situation.

The community is fully conscious of the Spirit's effect on their lives. It is as powerful and different as the experience of birth. To understand this new faith requires a willingness to use 'spiritual' rather than 'physical' language. It involves seeing the parallels between Moses' ministry of salvation and Jesus' ministry of salvation through the cross. Every member of the community is called upon to interpret these truths.

The Spirit and the Saviour are both seen as part of the divine imperative of love. Here is the Trinity in action. The purpose of that action is that every member of the community who believes should not perish, but have eternal life.

Hearing the story of Nicodemus, every member of the community affirms the experience of new life. Using the Spirit's power to share the purpose of God with others, every member is equipped for the missionary task. Knowledge must lead to action. Worship must lead to witness and service. That is Trinitarian logic to be accepted by every member of the community.

41

John 6:1–21

¹After this Jesus went to the other side of the Sea of Galilee, also called the Sea of Tiberias. ²A large crowd kept following him, because they saw the signs that he was doing for the sick. ³Jesus went up the mountain and sat down there with his disciples. ⁴Now the Passover, the festival of the Jews, was near. ⁵When he looked up and saw a large crowd coming toward him, Jesus said to Philip, 'Where are we to buy bread for these people to eat?' ⁶He said this to test him, for he himself knew what he was going to do. ⁷Philip answered him, 'Six months' wages would not buy enough bread for each of them to get a little.' ⁸One of his disciples, Andrew, Simon Peter's brother, said to him, ⁹'There is a boy here who has five barley loaves and two fish. But what are they among so many people?' ¹⁰Jesus said, 'Make the people sit down.' Now there was a great deal of grass in the place; so they sat down, about five thousand in all. ¹¹Then Jesus took the loaves, and when he had given thanks, he distributed them to those who were seated; so also the fish, as much as they wanted. ¹²When they were satisfied, he told his disciples, 'Gather up the fragments left over, so that nothing may be lost.' ¹³So they gathered them up, and from the fragments of the five barley loaves, left by those who had eaten, they filled twelve baskets. ¹⁴When the people saw the sign that he had done, they began to say, 'This is indeed the prophet who is to come into the world.'

[15]When Jesus realized that they were about to come and take him by force to make him king, he withdrew again to the mountain by himself.

[16]When evening came, his disciples went down to the sea, [17]got into a boat, and started across the sea to Capernaum. It was now dark, and Jesus had not yet come to them. [18]The sea became rough because a strong wind was blowing. [19]When they had rowed about three or four miles, they saw Jesus walking on the sea and coming near the boat, and they were terrified. [20]But he said to them, 'It is I; do not be afraid.' [21]Then they wanted to take him into the boat, and immediately the boat reached the land toward which they were going.

Context

The sixth chapter of John's gospel highlights the significance of bread. Jesus is experienced as the bread of life, the provider of spiritual sustenance. In this passage we hear of the feeding of the five thousand and the response of the crowd as they try to make Jesus their king. Later in the midst of the storm Jesus provides peace.

Sensing

Sit on the grass and stretch forth your hands to receive some bread and fish. Smell the wholesome food as it is offered to you. Count the crowd. There must be five thousand. Everyone has enough. This is wonderful. Catch the question from those sitting beside you on the grass: 'Where has all this food come from?'

Sit on the grass and share the barley loaf with your family. See the adults break it in pieces and feed the little ones. Smell the fresh green grass all around you. This is Passover time. Spring is in the air. See the new signs of life in the gambolling lambs and the shooting blades of barley. Catch the question from those sitting beside you on the grass: 'Is this a new Passover?'

Sit on the grass and taste the bread on your tongue. Here is the sweetness of life. Feel your stomach's pleasure. Here is food for the hungry. Here is sustenance for the pilgrim. Here is bread from heaven. Catch the question from those sitting beside you on the grass: 'Is this Jesus the new Moses?'

Sit on the grass and collect the bread and the pieces of fish left over. Place the surplus in the basket held by the disciples as they gather up the fragments. There is more than enough to go around. There is more than enough to satisfy all this great crowd. Here is another sign of God's generosity. Catch the response of those sitting beside you on the grass: 'This is the sort of plenty we need in life. Jesus is responsible for this. Let us make him king!'

Stand on the grassy bank and join in the shouting from the crowd: 'No more work! Free lunches for all! God will provide! Catch the response of those sitting beside you on the grass: 'Here is our daily bread! This is our king!'

Stand on the grassy bank and focus on the figure of Jesus. Watch his response. You can't believe your eyes; Jesus is walking away.

Intuition

There is bread on the table and food to share. The hearts of the people are glad. Grace is said. Family prayers conclude the meal: 'Your kingdom come; your will be done. Give us today our daily bread.' Thanks be to God.

There is bread on the table and food to spare. There is laughter, singing and dancing. The table groans with food. Some is spilt on the floor. Another five families could be fed. No one gathers it up. This is a criminal waste. Lord, have mercy.

There is bread on the table, enough but none to spare. Neighbours have shared their food between all who hunger. They have gathered everyone in and sat them down. With care and grace there is just enough for all. Thanks be to God.

There is no bread on the table and no food to share. All the villagers are scratching at the barren earth. There is no harvest for there was no seed. War, mismanagement, greed and corruption have robbed the poor of the potential for food. Starvation is rife. Dead children have no hunger. Lord, have mercy.

There is no bread on the table and no food to share. The table is covered in dust. The house is empty for the occupants have fled far afield as refugees. Now they live in a tent set in a dust bowl. They scramble for food as the aid truck arrives. The scraps of the nations are thrown from the back of the vehicle. Hands stretch forth to fight for the crust of life. There is a little bread, but no dignity. Thanks be to God. Lord, have mercy.

There is no bread and no table. The newspaper on the floor of the alleyway holds the leftover meal for the street-kids. There is not enough to satisfy hunger. This is no way for teenagers to discover life. There is just enough food to keep them alive but not enough love to help them live. Thanks be to God. Lord, have mercy.

Royal bread from heaven – where?

Feeling

Feel the satisfaction of having enough food and enjoyable company. It is a great feeling. It gives rise to thanksgiving and a sense of contentment. The joy of being alive springs forth, especially in the warmth of knowing that all around you others are satisfied too. As evening comes, rest in contentment. It has been a good day.

Feel the satisfaction of seeing good organization at work. It is a great feeling. It gives rise to feelings of admiration and enthusiasm. Watching a leader at work who knows what to do and why, is always satisfying. You are sure that every crisis will be solved, and every need met. It has been an admirable day.

Feel the satisfaction of supporting a popular leader who has the vote of all the people. It is a great feeling. It gives rise to feelings of comradeship and community pride. Experience the glow of seeing all the people heap praise on the leader and place all their hopes for the future in his or her hands. There is unity and common purpose. It has been a proud day.

Feel the sense of dissatisfaction as the leader refuses to accept the honour. It gives rise to feelings of betrayal and desertion. Feel the foreboding as all hopes for the future are suspended. Feel the depth of despair after all the elation. Hope is sinking at the end of the day.

Feel the sense of dissatisfaction as things go wrong. It gives rise to feelings of fear and terror. You have struggled to fix things for yourself but the hard work has not achieved your goal. Feel the sense of anger that God has deserted you. The storm is rising at the end of the day.

Feel the sense of peace in the midst of the storm. It gives rise to feelings of assurance. When you could not cope, Christ heard your cries. Feel your fears subside with his reassurance: 'I am here, be not afraid.' There is peace at the end of the day.

Feel the sense of rest on reaching your goal. Experience the joy of your homecoming and a welcoming embrace. There is rest at the end of the day.

Thinking

Study of the Hebrew scriptures helps us gain deeper understanding of the meaning behind this gospel passage.

Examine carefully the reference to the Passover in verse 4. Those with a knowledge of the Hebrew scriptures will recall how Exodus chapter 12 records that the Passover marks the work of God in bringing salvation to the Hebrews in Egypt. This gospel makes the point that it is through the new Passover of Christ's crucifixion that believers will receive salvation. At this Passover Jesus gives them bread. At the next Passover at Jerusalem (John 31:1) Jesus will give them his body on the cross. At the Passover unleavened bread is eaten, and the lamb is slain.

Examine carefully the reference to the large crowd in search of food in verse 5. Those with a knowledge of the Hebrew scriptures will recall the crowd in the wilderness in Exodus chapter 16. They complained that they had no food. God saw their plight and fed them with 'the bread that the Lord has given you to eat' (Exodus 16:15). This gospel makes the point that Jesus is the new Moses who brings God's bread to the hungry.

Examine carefully the reference to the five barley loaves in verse 9. Those with a knowledge of the Hebrew scriptures will recall that Elisha fed one hundred people with twenty barley loaves in 2 Kings 4:43. This gospel makes the point that Jesus is able to do greater signs than the prophet Elisha. In his time also there was plenty of food left over as the sign of the overwhelming generosity of God.

Examine carefully the reference to 'king' in verse 15. Those with a knowledge of the Hebrew scriptures will recall the hope that a great king like David would return to rule over God's people. As David was anointed by God (2 Samuel 5:3), so God would raise up a new king (Isaiah 32:1) to take his place and bring prosperity and justice to God's people.

The author of this gospel proclaims the truth to his knowledgeable listeners. Jesus is the new Moses providing true bread from heaven for God's people. Jesus is the new prophet, greater than Elisha in providing for God's people. Jesus is the new king, greater than David in bringing justice and peace to the new Israel.

42
John 6:24–35

[24]So when the crowd saw that neither Jesus nor his disciples were there, they themselves got into the boats and went to Capernaum looking for Jesus.

[25]When they found him on the other side of the sea, they said to him, 'Rabbi, when did you come here?' [26]Jesus answered them, 'Very truly, I tell you, you are looking for me, not because you saw signs, but because you ate your fill of the loaves. [27]Do not work for the food that perishes, but for the food that endures for eternal life, which the Son of Man will give you. For it is on him that God the Father has set his seal.' [28]Then they said to him, 'What must we do to perform the works of God?' [29]Jesus answered them, 'This is the work of God, that you believe in him whom he has sent.' [30]So they said to him, 'What sign are you going to give us then, so that we may see it and believe you? What work are you performing? [31]Our ancestors ate the manna in the wilderness; as it is written, "He gave them bread from heaven to eat." ' [32]Then Jesus said to them, 'Very truly, I tell you, it was not Moses who gave you the bread from heaven, but it is my Father who gives you the true bread from heaven. [33]For the bread of God is that which comes down from heaven and gives life to the world.' [34]They said to him, 'Sir, give us this bread always.'

[35]Jesus said to them, 'I am the bread of life. Whoever comes to me will never be hungry, and whoever believes in me will never be thirsty.'

Context

The dialogue between Jesus and the crowd in this gospel passage is a series of questions and responses. The crowd's quest for the answer to their longing for a sign from God is met by Jesus' challenge as to whether they believe in him as the one who feeds them with the bread of eternal life.

Sensing

Stand on the shore of the lake at Capernaum as the crowd surges around Jesus. Smell the fish in the bottom of the boats in which you have crossed the lake. Here is the place of plentiful food. Capernaum is the bread and fish basket of Galilee. Listen as the questions and answers between the crowd and Jesus lap backwards and forwards like the waves on the lake shore.

Catch the question from the crowd: 'Rabbi, when did you come here? We could not find you on the other side of the lake. You slipped away just when we thought you would solve all the problems of hunger. Rabbi, when did you come here?'

Hear the response from Jesus: 'Admit the truth. You were looking for me because you had lots to eat. Work for the food that lasts for ever. The Son of Man will give you that food; God's favour rests on him.'

Catch the question from the crowd: 'Rabbi, what must we do to do the work of God? If having food, enough and to spare, takes work by us as well as you, what is it that we have to do?'

Hear the response from Jesus: 'It is quite simple. It is always a matter of trust. Believe in him whom God has sent.'

Catch the question from the crowd: 'Rabbi, of course we will believe when we have seen the evidence of God's power at work. Rabbi, what sign are you going to give us?'

Hear the response from Jesus: 'My Father gives you the true bread from heaven, and this bread gives life to the world. God is the provider. You have been fed. God is my Father and I act on God's behalf. Recognize the signs.'

Catch the plea from the crowd: 'Lord, give us this bread always. We no longer call you Rabbi, but Lord. We do not want just one meal, we want food that lasts for ever.'

Hear the promise of Jesus: 'I am the bread of life. Whoever comes to me will never be hungry. Whoever believes in me will never be thirsty.'

Stand on the shore of the lake at Capernaum, the bread and fish basket of Galilee. Smell the new bread. Smell the fresh fish. Hear the Word of God. In Capernaum we find lasting food.

Intuition

'Workers wanted!' is an encouraging sign for many people. It is a sign of confidence in the economy; that hands are needed and people are valued. 'Workers wanted!' People long to be employed in a worthwhile occupation that brings them the physical necessities of life and the spiritual satisfaction of using their God-given talents. What springs to mind when you hear the word 'work' in this passage?

What springs to mind when you hear the words, 'Do not work for the food that perishes'? How many people find satisfaction in work that is so boring that it is simply done to buy basic provisions? Surely there should be more to life than drudgery. How many people want to work for the good of our community and to enhance the accumulating knowledge of the world? Surely many want to work for long-term goals. Is Jesus right to say, 'There is more to life than bread?'

What springs to mind when you hear the words: 'What must we do to perform the works of God?' Christian people who have dedicated their lives to fulfil God's purpose want to know what to do and how to do it. What guidance do they need to identify the work God wants done to meet the physical needs of the poor, the lonely, the depressed and the sick? What guidance do they need to identify the work God wants done to meet the spiritual needs of the faithless, the confused and the searchers?

What springs to mind when you hear the words: 'This is the work of God, that you believe in him whom he has sent?' Workers want someone to trust, to show them what to do and how to do it. Christian workers believe that Jesus revealed the actions which fulfilled God's purpose. How can Christian workers be sustained by the life which Jesus poured out for the world? How can Christian workers find such faith in Jesus Christ that they dwell in him as they believe he dwells in them?

Workers wanted! Your application will be welcomed!

Feeling

When Jesus said, 'I am the bread of life', that must have been a wonderful moment for the people in the crowd. Step into their shoes and share in their reactions.

Feel the sense of deep satisfaction that your physical needs will be recognized and met. Here is no airy-fairy religion; no pie in the sky when you die. Feel the joy of having a faith that takes the physical seriously, that feeds the hungry, tends the sick, provides work for the unemployed. Feel the deep sense of satisfaction that Christianity is about flesh and blood, food and wine, housing and aged care. Feel the joy in hearing: 'I am the bread of physical life'.

Feel the deep sense of satisfaction that your spiritual needs will be recognized and met. Jesus promises to be the bread of life. Feel the joy of entering into the relationship with God, and receiving an answer to your prayers. Experience a union with God in the deep mystery of worship. Feel courage and hope flowing from God, and rejoice in a spiritual life fed and nurtured in Jesus. Feel the joy in hearing: 'I am the bread of spiritual life.'

Feel the deep sense of satisfaction that your hopes of eternal life will be recognized and met. Share the common struggle to satisfy physical and spiritual needs, and also the hope of growing to perfection. The hunger in this life continues. Each day we need daily bread. We also look for the hope of bread for tomorrow to be satisfied. Feel the joy in hearing that Jesus' promise is not only for today but for ever: 'I am the bread of eternal life.'

Feel the sense of deep satisfaction that your faith in Jesus will be recognized and rewarded. Be in touch with your relationship with Jesus. Through faith you trust in him. Through faith you feed on him. Through faith you drink from the eternal fountain of life. O what joy to hear his promise: '*I am* the bread of life.'

Thinking

This meditation draws on the insights of the Wisdom Literature in which a proposition is often progressed using a question and answer format to make the truth known.

Consider the questions posed: Who is Jesus? How do we recognize him? How do we understand his words?

The response to the question, 'Who is Jesus?' is first expressed in a negative saying. Jesus is not a miracle worker providing only for the physical needs of people. In verse 27 the contrast is drawn between 'food that perishes' and 'food that endures'. Jesus is not a miracle producer of earthly food and drink. Jesus is the provider of spiritual food. What do you think this means for Christian witness and mission?

The response to the question, 'Who is this Jesus?' is then expressed in a positive revelation. Jesus is the 'bread of life' (verse 35). Jesus is the source of all provision for every human need, material and spiritual. It is the Son of Man who gives us the food that endures (verse 28). What do you think this means for Christian witness and mission?

The response to the question, 'How do we recognize him?' is

that this is a matter of faith (verse 29). Without true belief there can be no insight as to what to do to fulfil God's purpose. To believe in Jesus is to know that he has the seal of God's approval (verse 27), and that he is more than a second Moses. Jesus is the gift of God who has come down from heaven to give life to the world (verses 32–33). What do you think this means for Christian witness and mission?

The response to the question, 'How do we understand Jesus' words?' is that this requires wisdom. Only thoughtful meditation can make the connection between the physical and the spiritual. In Proverbs 9:1–6 Wisdom issues the invitation: 'Come, eat my bread.' Jesus, the Wisdom of God, so nourishes our thinking that we can discern the truth and understand its meaning as embodied in a person who feeds us with all the necessities of life. What do you think this means for Christian witness and mission?

———————>⊳·◉·⊲<———————

43

John 6:35, 41–51

[35]Jesus said to them, 'I am the bread of life. Whoever comes to me will never be hungry, and whoever believes in me will never be thirsty.'

[41]Then the Jews began to complain about him because he said, 'I am the bread that came down from heaven.' [42]They were saying, 'Is not this Jesus, the son of Joseph, whose father and mother we know? How can he now say, "I have come down from heaven"?' [43]Jesus answered them, 'Do not complain among yourselves. [44]No one can come to me unless drawn by the Father who sent me; and I will raise that person up on the last day. [45]It is written in the prophets, "And they shall all be taught by God." Everyone who has heard and learned from the Father comes to me. [46]Not that anyone has seen the Father except the one who is from God; he has seen the Father. [47]Very truly, I tell you, whoever believes has eternal life. [48]I am the bread of life. [49]Your ancestors ate the manna in the wilderness, and they died. [50]This is the bread that comes down from heaven, so that one may eat of it and not

die. [51]I am the living bread that came down from heaven. Whoever eats of this bread will live forever; and the bread that I will
give for the life of the world is my flesh.'

Context

Reflection on Jesus' claim to be the bread of life continues in this
gospel passage. Here the focus turns to eternal life. The bread from
heaven feeds the faithful not only in this life, but also in the life
after death. Jesus promises that whoever believes in him has
eternal life.

Sensing

Sit in the circle of Christian followers in the upper room of the
leader's house in Ephesus. Listen as the sixth chapter of the gospel
is read. See the bread of the Eucharist lying on the table. Hear the
contributions of the community as they sit around the table to
discuss the gospel reading.

Listen as one of the younger disciples, John, recounts his clash
with the Jews from the local synagogue. 'They say that Jesus cannot be from God because we know his human family. Did not
Mary come here from Jerusalem after the first persecution killed
her son James? Was not her husband's name Joseph from
Nazareth, though he was dead long before she came to Ephesus?
In the opinion of the synagogue Jesus was human; they admit he
may have been a prophet but certainly not from heaven.'

Listen as one of the older disciples, James, counters that opinion. 'The Jews may say that he was only human but we know
about the resurrection of Jesus. The first disciples shared their
experience of that with us. They had no doubt that Jesus came
from God once they had seen the resurrection of Christ. We have
their word on that.'

Listen as the reader of the gospel interprets its message. 'The
words of the prophets we read in the synagogue pointed to Jesus.
They foresaw a time when God would teach us directly. That is
what Jesus did. He alone has seen the Father and told us about it.
He promised that we too would share his resurrected life. We have
his word on that.'

Listen as the president of the assembly points to the bread of
the Eucharist. 'Remember, this is the bread of resurrection. This is
the bread of eternal life. We believe that in Christ our dead are

raised up and share eternity with Jesus. This bread is his flesh given for the life of the world.'

Gather at the table as the discussion fades away. The president gives thanks over the bread and concludes: 'Whoever eats of this bread will live forever.' Now stretch forth your hands. Eat the bread and taste the gift of eternal life.

Intuition

The promise of eternal life is most welcome when we are faced with our own death or the death of others.

Consider how the promise sounds in the hospice room. Life has been so rich and full for the patient. Now it is fast ebbing away. How does the promise of eternal life sound to this patient fixed to the pain-killing line? The promise floats back into the consciousness: 'Whoever believes has eternal life.'

Consider how the promise sounds in the family bedroom where the long-loved parent is surrounded by many generations. Life has been full of caring and rich in loving. Now it is fast ebbing away. How does the promise of eternal life sound to the family fixed to the deathbed by the ties of love? The words of the gospel float back into the memory. 'No one can come to me unless drawn by the Father who sent me; and I will raise that person up on the last day.'

Consider how the promise sounds in the funeral chapel as the coffin rests on the stand, surrounded with flowers and love. Life has been short, but full of bravery and courage in the face of illness. Pain is no more but tears still fall. How does the promise sound to the circle of the mourners, bound together by the bonds of grief? The words of the preacher echo back from the walls. 'Very truly, I tell you, whoever believes has eternal life.'

Consider how the promise sounds in the parish church as the family keeps the anniversary of the death of their loved one. They come forward to receive Communion and the priest offers them the bread. How does the promise of eternal life sound to the mourning family bound to the risen Christ by loyalty and faith? At the altar rail the words of the priest resound in their ears: 'This is the bread of eternal life.'

Consider the words of the writer: 'Now faith is the assurance of things hoped for, the conviction of things not seen' (Hebrews 11:1). How do they sound for you?

Feeling

Feelings of security about the future because you believe in Christ are one thing. Some people cannot accept faith that easily. Put yourself in the place of the doubter and share the doubter's feelings.

Share the feelings of those, like the Jews in the gospel passage, who complain that Jesus' claims are outrageous. These doubters find it hard to see beyond the obvious. Jesus was human, with a human ancestry. That is what they saw. That is all they can accept. Share the feelings of those who dismiss anything out of the ordinary and who cannot handle the demands of faith. Share the certainty of doubt. What is, is what will be; nothing more, nothing less. Share the feelings of the certain doubter.

Share the feelings of those, like many in our own day, who say that one life is what is given to each of us. Feel the sense of reality in the doubter. Feel for them as they try to live life now to the full in the sure belief that there is nothing more to have. Every moment is precious; every relationship valued. What is, is all there is and must be treasured. Share the feelings of the realist.

Share the feelings of those, like the many in our own day, who say that our children are our future. Feel the sense of hope in the doubter. Feel for them as they try to pass on the best advice and the noblest example of living to the next generation. Every child is precious; every new birth is valued. Share the feelings of those who invest themselves in children.

Share the feelings of those, like the many in our own day, who hold on to faith in the midst of doubt. Feel for them as they risk ridicule for hoping beyond hope, for trusting beyond sight, for betting the future on God. Christ is precious; new birth is valued; hope springs eternal. Share the feelings of the faithful who despite the odds invest themselves in the promise of eternal life.

When you hear Jesus saying, 'I tell you, whoever believes has eternal life,' share the feelings of the doubters; share the feelings of the faithful; share the feelings within yourself.

Thinking

In this gospel passage you can detect the arguments in the early church communities about the nature of Christ's being. Deep questions lie beneath the text: How is Jesus able to claim divine knowledge if he is a human child? How do you find faith in Jesus?

Is faith a divine gift or a human response? Is the revelation of Jesus about God superior to that given to Moses and the religion of the old Israel?

Deep answers lie within the text. The author sets out to respond to such questions in a series of reflections on the saying, 'I am the bread of life.' This is the first in a series of seven such 'I am' sayings that are found in John's gospel. They make the claim that Jesus reveals the divine nature and the divine gift for humanity.

Deep answers lie within the text. 'I am the bread of life' focuses on God as provider, not only for mortal life but also for eternal life. The bread we receive comes from God. Christ comes from heaven out of the generosity and love of God.

Deep answers lie within the text. 'I am the living bread who came down from heaven.' Jesus is able to reveal God because he is fully divine as well as fully human. Verse 51 acknowledges his divinity. Verse 42 acknowledges his humanity.

Deep answers lie within the text. Faith is a matter of divine action and human response. No one finds faith in Jesus unless drawn by the Father (verse 44). And yet each one has to believe in order to find eternal life (verse 47). The believer recognizes the divine initiative and the human responsibility.

Deep answers lie within the text. The resurrection shows that Jesus is superior to Moses and the old way of approaching God. Those who ate of the bread from Moses died (verse 49). Those who feed on Christ share his resurrection (verse 51). His bread is both a sign of his sacrificial death and a sign of his resurrection life. Eternal life encompasses both dying to live and living to die. This is the logic of faith.

44

John 6:51–58

[51]'I am the living bread that came down from heaven. Whoever eats of this bread will live forever; and the bread that I will give for the life of the world is my flesh.'

[52]The Jews then disputed among themselves, saying, 'How can this man give us his flesh to eat?' [53]So Jesus said to them, 'Very truly, I tell you, unless you eat the flesh of the Son of Man and drink his blood, you have no life in you. [54]Those who eat my flesh and drink my blood have eternal life, and I will raise them up on the last day; [55]for my flesh is true food and my blood is true drink. [56]Those who eat my flesh and drink my blood abide in me, and I in them. [57]Just as the living Father sent me, and I live because of the Father, so whoever eats me will live because of me. [58]This is the bread that came down from heaven, not like that which your ancestors ate, and they died. But the one who eats this bread will live forever.'

Context
John's gospel continues to reflect on the significance of Jesus as the bread of life. In this passage the focus is on the words 'flesh and blood', and the constant demand to 'eat' as the means of abiding in Jesus and gaining eternal life.

Sensing
Stand in front of the table of the Eucharist. See the white cloth and the sparkling silver. Gaze at the bread and wine set before you. Feel the sense of anticipation and awe. Hear the words of celebration: 'Lift up your hearts.'

Gaze at the bread and wine on the altar. Feel the sense of anticipation and awe. See the priest bend over them in prayer. Hear the words of transformation: 'Send your Holy Spirit that these gifts of bread and wine may be for us the body and blood of Christ.'

Gaze at the bread and wine on the altar. Feel the sense of anticipation and awe. See the priest raise the paten and the

cup for all to see. Hear the words of invitation: 'Take and eat this
. . . Drink this in remembrance of me.'

Gaze at the bread and wine on the altar. See the people bend
low in cautious faith. Feel your lips tremble as you pray: 'Grant us
therefore, gracious Lord, so to eat the body of your dear Son, Jesus
Christ, and to drink his blood, that we may dwell in him and he
in us.'

Taste the bread from off the altar. Feel your hands tremble as
you make them a throne. See the priest bend low and put the
bread into your hands. Hear the words of sacrifice: 'The body of
our Lord Jesus Christ, broken for you.'

Taste the wine from off the altar. Feel your lips tremble as you
long for life. See the priest bend low and hold the cup to your lips.
Hear the words of salvation: 'The blood of our Lord Jesus Christ,
shed for you.'

Return to your place and kneel in adoration. Feel your ears tingle as you remember the sayings in the gospel: 'And the Word was
made flesh and dwelt among us. Unless you eat the flesh of the
Son of Man and drink his blood, you have no life in you. My flesh
is true food and my blood is true drink.'

Stand in front of the table of the Eucharist. Marvel at God's
provisions.

Intuition

We use the words 'flesh and blood' to speak of real physical life.
Our bodies are made of flesh and blood. Flesh and blood represent
the basic substances of which we are created. There is nothing
ethereal about flesh and blood.

So consider how in everyday speech we use 'flesh and blood' to
describe the very stuff of human existence. We refer to our mortal
bodies as flesh and blood, knowing they are real because we can
touch and feel them. When we say that we are made of flesh and
blood we make clear that we share the same attributes that all
human beings possess.

So consider how in everyday speech we use 'flesh and blood' to
describe the rough and tumble of human life. We refer to the reality of pain and mortality in contrast to any idea that our bodies
can escape into another type of existence.

So consider how in everyday speech we use 'flesh and blood' to
describe the common bonds of human relationships. We are making clear that we are kith and kin, born of a common gene pool,

and that those of our own flesh and blood share our family circle.

Now consider the connection between those meanings and the saying in this gospel passage: 'Those who eat my flesh and drink my blood abide in me, and I in them.' It refers to the belief that the Word was made flesh; that Jesus came down from heaven to earth; and that he fully shared our human nature.

Now consider the connection between those meanings and the saying in this gospel passage: 'Those who eat my flesh and drink my blood abide in me, and I in them.' It refers to the pain and death that Jesus suffered on the cross as he poured out his life for us.

Now consider the connection between those meanings and the saying in this gospel passage: 'Those who eat my flesh and drink my blood abide in me, and I in them.' It refers to the way that Christians through Baptism and Eucharist become the body, the family of Christ. We are now his flesh and blood for others. That is the joy and the responsibility of 'abiding in him for ever'.

Feeling

People have positive and negative feelings about food and drink.

Share the feelings of enjoyment at having food to eat and drink to quench your thirst. When you last looked in the mirror and saw yourself, how did you feel? Food builds up our bodies and keeps us looking healthy and strong. Drink gives us satisfaction and a sense of well-being. Share the experience of those who feel good at having enough to eat and drink.

Share the feelings of enjoyment at participating in a meal where we all eat and drink together. When you last looked across the table and saw family and friends sharing the meal, how did you feel? Participating in a meal builds up our fellowship and keeps us strongly bound to one another. Share the experience of those who feel good about eating with others at the same table.

Share the feelings of enjoyment at taking part in the meal at the Eucharist. When you last received bread and wine at the altar, how did you feel? Holy Communion restores our sense of well-being and gives us strength for the pilgrim journey. It unites us with Christ and the church community. Share the experience of those who feel good about receiving Communion at Christ's table.

Share the feelings of revulsion when food and drink is repulsive; when we think that it will do us harm. When you last ate something that you found hard to stomach, how did you feel? Food that causes sickness is harmful and drains away our strength. Share the experience of those who feel bad at having to eat and drink rotten food.

Share the feelings of revulsion when we focus on the way we are depriving other creatures of life by consuming them. When you last ate something that you felt should not have died to feed you, how did you feel? Food for human consumption should not be prepared inhumanely. Share the experience of those who feel bad about causing suffering that they might eat.

Share the feelings of revulsion in those who take Christ's words literally: 'Unless you eat the flesh of the Son of Man and drink his blood, you have no life in you.' These words are enough to stop them coming to receive Holy Communion. Would they not feel better focusing on this saying: 'It is the Spirit that gives life; the flesh is useless' (verse 63)?

Thinking

Scholars have quoted verse 53 to argue that Jesus gave a command to his disciples to distribute the sacrament in both kinds, bread *and* wine. They contend that the custom of using bread only for the people is purely practical convenience. Surely both kinds should be distributed. What do you think?

Scholars have pointed out that verses 52 to 59 indicate that thinking people, both in the Jewish synagogue and in the Christian community for which John wrote, refused to participate in a religion that spoke of drinking blood because this was the essence of a life. But the idea of eating the flesh is countered by recognition of the Spirit in verse 63. Surely the two statements should be read together. What do you think?

Scholars have taken verse 53 to be a reference to Christ's body as the sacrificial lamb that must be 'eaten' if the worshipper is to participate in the salvation of God. The Hebrews ate the Passover lamb to participate in the saving work of God. So must the Christian 'eat and drink' Christ's sacrifice to share in his life? What do you think?

Scholars have shown from verses 58 and 54 the contrast between the old religion, focused on gaining strength for this life, for 'our ancestors ate, and they died' (verse 58), and the new faith in Jesus, based on gaining strength for eternal life (verse 54). Does the resurrection transform the agenda? What do you think?

Scholars have seen in this passage confirmation of the unity between the Father and the Son. The source of life is the Father who gives life to the incarnate Son, who in turn gives life to those who 'eat' (verse 57). In the Wisdom Literature (Sirach 24:21) to 'eat' is to participate in the life of something: 'Those who eat of me will hunger no more.' Is Jesus the new wisdom that gives life to the faithful? What do you think?

45

John 6:56-69

⁵⁶'Those who eat my flesh and drink my blood abide in me, and I in them. ⁵⁷Just as the living Father sent me, and I live because of the Father, so whoever eats me will live because of me. ⁵⁸This is the bread that came down from heaven, not like that which your ancestors ate, and they died. But the one who eats this bread will live forever.' ⁵⁹He said these things while he was teaching in the synagogue at Capernaum.

⁶⁰When many of his disciples heard it, they said, 'This teaching is difficult; who can accept it?' ⁶¹But Jesus, being aware that his disciples were complaining about it, said to them, 'Does this offend you? ⁶²Then what if you were to see the Son of Man ascending to where he was before? ⁶³It is the spirit that gives life; the flesh is useless. The words that I have spoken to you are spirit and life. ⁶⁴But among you there are some who do not believe.' For Jesus knew from the first who were the ones that did not believe, and who was the one that would betray him. ⁶⁵And he said, 'For this reason I have told you that no one can come to me unless it is granted by the Father.'

⁶⁶Because of this many of his disciples turned back and no longer went about with him. ⁶⁷So Jesus asked the twelve, 'Do you also wish to go away?' ⁶⁸Simon Peter answered him, 'Lord, to whom can we go? You have the words of eternal life. ⁶⁹We have come to believe and know that you are the Holy One of God.'

Context

In this final section from the sixth chapter of John's gospel the emphasis is on the acceptance or rejection of Jesus as the one who brings eternal life to those who believe. It contrasts the desertion of many of Jesus' first disciples with Peter's confession of loyalty and faith.

Sensing

Join the disciples in the synagogue at Capernaum. There Jesus, the rabbi, has claimed to be a greater teacher than Moses, giving his followers not bread from heaven but his own flesh to eat. The reaction of the leading scholars has been fractious. One held one opinion, another the contrary. Listen to the sharp dispute. See how tempers are rising.

Join the disciples in the synagogue at Capernaum. There Jesus, the Son of Man, has claimed to be more powerful for salvation than the Passover sacrifice. He has spoken of eating his flesh and drinking his blood. The reaction of many of the religious people has been shock and horror. Blood is the essence of life. It is always drained away and offered to God as too holy to handle. Listen to the cries of alarm. See how anxiety is rising.

Join the disciples in the synagogue at Capernaum. There Jesus, sent from the Father, has claimed to be the giver of eternal life. He has said that whoever eats of him will live for ever. The reaction of some religious people is disbelief. What power has a human being to offer eternal life to other human beings? Listen to the cries of strong disbelief. See how doubts are rising.

Join the disciples as they speak privately to Jesus. Listen as they bring the complaints out into the open: 'This teaching is difficult, who can accept it?' Watch their faces as they look for words of encouragement from Jesus. They want the truth. See how desire for reality is rising.

Join the disciples as they speak privately to Jesus. Listen as Jesus makes exclusive claims about himself to his disciples: 'No one can come to me unless it is granted by the Father.' Watch the faces of some disciples as they decide this is too much to stomach. They want to leave. See how thoughts of desertion are rising.

Join the disciples as they speak privately to Jesus. Listen as Peter expresses his faith despite the doubts and the realism: 'We have come to believe and know that you are the Holy One from God.' See how faith is rising.

Intuition

The question of why some people believe and others do not has always puzzled Christians. Consider these examples. Can you offer a resolution to this puzzle from your experience?

There are those who will not believe in anything which they cannot touch and see. They are fundamentalists with fixed positions. They will not believe in eternal life because it cannot be scientifically proved from the human condition.

There are those who will not believe in anything which contains a divine element. Unless it has a human explanation it beggars belief. They are sceptics with inclination for doubt. Such people cannot believe that Jesus was more than a teacher with good advice for moral conduct.

There are those who will not believe in historical persons unless they can cross-question their reliability for themselves. They are those who must live in the present. They will not rely on the testimony of others. Only their own experience is believable. They will not believe in Jesus unless he reappears to them personally now.

There are those who do believe in spiritual matters. They recognize a world of the spirit which is not to be limited to physical factors. They are naturally religious. They believe in eternal life as the spiritual extension of human existence.

There are those who do accept the testimony of others in addition to their own experience. They are the trusting ones who accept tradition. They believe that there are ample witnesses that Jesus came down from heaven to give life to the world.

There are those who do accept that Jesus speaks the words of eternal life as the Holy One of God. They readily share Peter's sense of sure knowledge and faith. They are the faithful ones we all admire, and often long to be.

All these sorts of people are found in the church and in the world. Some find faith and some reject it all as nonsense. Why this is so is a puzzle. This gospel bears witness that belief is a matter of divine initiative and matched by human response. Some believe and others will not. Why? Can you offer a resolution to this puzzle from your experience?

Feeling

Step into the sandals of the fisherman, the disciple Peter. Feel for him as he responds to the challenge of faith.

Step into Peter's sandals and feel his discomfort at the hostile opposition of some Jews in the synagogue when they heard Jesus' words. The arguments are raging and the insults are flying. Some cannot believe in a God who left the heavens. Others cannot believe in a life beyond this life. Feel Peter's discomfort that Jesus is met with such opposition from the thinkers of the day and the leading religious people.

Step into Peter's sandals and feel his dismay at the complaining attitude of some of those who would claim to be followers of Jesus. The complaints come thick and fast about the difficulty of language in Jesus' sayings, about the mystery of his person, about the knowledge of the scriptural background necessary for interpretation. Feel Peter's dismay as disciples complain that everything has been pushed to the limits and made too complicated to continue discipleship.

Step into Peter's sandals and feel his alarm at the blunt, uncompromising statement made by Jesus about some of Peter's fellow disciples. The realism is devastating: 'Among you there are some who do not believe.' That might be true but it is hard to lose friends. Feel Peter's alarm as his companions and fellow disciples turn their backs on Jesus and leave the group.

Step into Peter's sandals and feel his anxiety as Jesus asks him about his own attitude: 'Do you also wish to go away?' The hostility, the desertion, are all about him. How will they influence his decision? Can he find faith in a faithless society? Feel for Peter's anxiety as the question of his response is put so clearly to him.

Step into Peter's sandals and feel his courage as he answers Jesus. He has committed himself thus far. Where else can he go but with Jesus? Jesus has the words that make sense of life, that give hope for eternity. Feel Peter's courage as in faith he declares: 'You are the Holy One of God!'

Step back into your own shoes. Feel for yourself as you face the same challenges to faith.

Thinking

A phrase such as 'This teaching is difficult' often precedes a resolution of the misunderstanding. Examine three statements in these verses carefully.

Examine the reference to the ascension: 'What if you see the Son of Man ascending to where he was before?' The Son of Man, the humanity of Jesus, must be taken back within the nature of the Godhead. The first hearers of the gospel knew that this doctrine was part of the faith of the Christian community. The logic is that the physical body of Jesus was no longer tangible. So there must be a new meaning to the words 'eat' and 'flesh and blood'. With an understanding of the ascension, this teaching is less difficult.

Examine the reference to the Spirit: 'It is the Spirit that gives life; the flesh is useless.' At the ascension the Son of God bestowed his Spirit on the disciples to be his new presence for his followers. The first hearers of the gospel knew that the doctrine of the Holy Spirit was part of the faith of the Christian community. The logic is that the Spirit of Christ is the means of being in touch with the ascended Christ. Simply a physical interpretation of his words will not do. This is indicated by the saying, 'The flesh is useless.' We must experience the Spirit of Christ to be able to feed from his words. With an understanding of the Spirit, this teaching is less difficult.

Examine the reference to the combination of word, spirit and life: 'The words that I have spoken to you are spirit and life.' The Wisdom of God, as expressed in the Son, who knows the Father's nature and will, is received by the indwelling Spirit, and this combination produces new life in the believer. The first hearers of the gospel knew that the doctrine of Wisdom was part of the faith of the Christian community. The logic is that those who have received the Spirit are able to interpret the words of Christ and in doing so find life in all its abundance. With an understanding of Wisdom as a unity of word, spirit and life, this teaching is less difficult.

John 10:11–18

[11]'I am the good shepherd. The good shepherd lays down his life for the sheep. [12]The hired hand, who is not the shepherd and does not own the sheep, sees the wolf coming and leaves the sheep and runs away - and the wolf snatches them and scatters them. [13]The hired hand runs away because a hired hand does not care for the sheep. [14]I am the good shepherd. I know my own and my own know me, [15]just as the Father knows me and I know the Father. And I lay down my life for the sheep. [16]I have other sheep that do not belong to this fold. I must bring them also, and they will listen to my voice. So there will be one flock, one shepherd. [17]For this reason the Father loves me, because I lay down my life in order to take it up again. [18]No one takes it from me, but I lay it down of my own accord. I have power to lay it down, and I have power to take it up again. I have received this command from my Father.'

Context

This passage contains one of the seven 'I am' sayings found in John's gospel. It is based on an illustration from the rural scene of caring for sheep. The concept of the Messiah being a shepherd can be traced back to King David, the shepherd leader of the first united kingdom.

Sensing

For shepherds, keeping watch over their flocks by night, danger lurks on every side. Hear the wolf baying as it smells the tender flesh of the lambs. Listen to the bleating sheep; listen to the howling wolves. Who can best protect the sheep and lambs from harm?

Observe the hired hand. Hear his heavy breathing as he senses the presence of the wolves. See him all alert as the snarls of the wolves reach his ears. Look at his dagger tucked into his belt. Hear him count the wolves in the pack – one, two, three, four. Listen as he hurls abuse at them.

Observe the hired hand. See the moonbeam reflecting on the shining coins, his wages for a night's work. Hear him count the wolves in the pack – one, two, three, four. Hear him count the coins in his palm – one, two, three. Listen to his abuse as he reckons the dangers far exceed the wages.

Observe the hired hand. See him point to his escape route by keeping the sheep between himself and the wolves to protect him from harm. Listen as he abuses the sheep: 'Curse you! The sacrifice of a few stragglers is better than losing my life.'

Observe the dedicated shepherd in another fold. Hear his soft voice calling as the night enfolds the frightened lambs. See him take up his club as the wolves grow closer. Hear him count the sheep and call them all by name. He values them more than his own safety. Hear him shout out the challenge to the wolves: 'Depart and be gone! No one shall take my sheep from me.' See him put his body on the line.

Observe the dedicated shepherd. The attack has taken place. The sheep are safely in the fold. Listen as the roar of the wolves dies away. See the shepherd lying, covered in blood, across the entrance. His injuries are mortal.

Observe the dedicated shepherd. See how the owner of the sheep has come down to lift his body away. There is salvation for the sheep. There is resurrection for the dedicated shepherd.

From your observation, which one can claim to be the good shepherd?

Intuition

Consider the voice of the Good Shepherd: 'I have other sheep who do not belong to this fold. I must bring them also. There will be one flock, one shepherd.' But is unity a concept we value more in the ideal than in the reality?

Consider the life of a group of people whom you know well. They work in unity as long as all members put effort into it and feel they get something out of it. People unite in common endeavour as long as they receive personal satisfaction.

Consider the life of a sports club you know well. People work in unity for as long as everyone is seen as making a full and equal contribution. The complaints and divisions soon arise when some people believe that they are carrying too much of the burden.

Consider the life of a family whom you know well. It works in unity as long as there are common goals, bonds of affection and unity is seen to be mutually beneficial. But what keeps it together when individual interests diverge and the younger members are old enough to want to make their own decisions?

Consider the life of a prayer group which you know well. It works in unity as long as people feel inspired by each other's prayers and personalities. But what keeps it together when theological positions diverge and members have differing reactions to the outcome of the prayers?

Consider the life of the local churches you know well. They have probably formed a council or conference of churches. This seems to work in unity as long as their discussions and actions stay on surface issues. But what keeps it together when entrenched attitudes to sacraments and worship cannot be reconciled, and members want to take differing actions for justice?

Consider your own actions towards the unity of the church you know well. How have you brought groups together to make one flock? How have you moved towards others on the pathway to unity?

Consider the voice of the good shepherd: 'There shall be one shepherd and one flock.' Do we value the reality of unity as much as the ideal?

Feeling

What joy there is to hear Jesus say: 'I am the good shepherd. I know my own, and my own know me.'

Feel the joy of being fully accepted by Jesus, the good shepherd. The sheep feel secure when they are in relationship to the one who guides them to food, secures their safety, and keeps them from harm and evil. It feels good to be one of the flock, accepted by Jesus.

Feel the joy of being forgiven by Jesus, the good shepherd. The sheep feel a sense of belonging again once they are restored to the flock after wilfully straying away on their own. The good shepherd has searched for the lost ones and found them. It feels good to be forgiven and restored by Jesus.

Feel the joy of being saved by Jesus, the good shepherd. The sheep feel a sense of deep gratitude at seeing the shepherd overpower the attacking evil, be it wolf or brigand. The good shepherd lays down his life for the sheep. It feels good to be saved from evil by Jesus.

Feel the joy of putting your whole trust in Jesus, the good

shepherd. The sheep give their total trust to the one whose voice they know. They stay close to the shepherd and follow the shepherd's directions as they go in and out of the fold. It feels good to put our whole trust in Jesus.

Feel the joy of being owned through baptism by Christ, the good shepherd. The sheep are marked with the ownership logo of the shepherd. It is a sign of belonging both to the master and to the flock. It feels good through baptism to claim our relationship with Jesus.

Feel the joy of your knowledge of Jesus, the good shepherd. The sheep learn how to know the master's voice, and to find the best food to sustain their life, eating as the shepherd directs. It feels good to share in the word and sacrament of Jesus.

Feel the joy of your relationship to the good shepherd and to the one flock.

Thinking

Consider the three statements Jesus makes about laying down his life on the cross and how he takes his life up again in resurrection:

'I will lay [my life] down of my own accord.'
'I have power to take it up again.'
'I have received this command from my Father.' (verse 18)

Those three statements are a key to our understanding of Christ's crucifixion and resurrection.

The three statements explain that the crucifixion was a voluntary action taken freely by Jesus. The crucifixion was not a defeat of God by human endeavours but an action of willing sacrifice taken by the saviour. It was an act of giving by the good shepherd: 'I lay down my life for the sheep.'

The three statements explain that the crucifixion was accepted by the followers of Jesus in the light of the resurrection that followed it. Both actions must be seen together. Life could be laid down because God had power to take it up again. Jesus can offer his life up on the cross in faith that God will raise it up in resurrection. Thus in the light of the resurrection the sacrifice of the crucifixion makes sense.

The three statements explain that the death and resurrection of Christ were part of the divine plan to bring salvation to the world:

God so loved the world that he gave his only Son, so that everyone who believes in him may not perish but may have eternal life. (John 3:16)

The three statements explain that the resurrection of Jesus was part of the command of God, the Father. Resurrection is part of the total purpose of God that aims to bring life to the world. This life is now able to be understood as an eternal life. Such a life combines mortality and eternity. The actions of the physical and the spiritual Christ are to be seen as one. Both are held together in the crucifixion and the resurrection. Through the crucifixion we are saved for the life of resurrection.

The three statements explain that the purpose of God for both Christ and us is that we should not perish, but have eternal life. Our salvation and our eternity are made clear for us in these three statements.

❯❯·◉·❮❮

47

John 11:32–44

[32]When Mary came where Jesus was and saw him, she knelt at his feet and said to him, 'Lord, if you had been here, my brother would not have died.' [33]When Jesus saw her weeping, and the Jews who came with her also weeping, he was greatly disturbed in spirit and deeply moved. [34]He said, 'Where have you laid him?' They said to him, 'Lord, come and see.' [35]Jesus began to weep. [36]So the Jews said, 'See how he loved him!' [37]But some of them said, 'Could not he who opened the eyes of the blind man have kept this man from dying?'

[38]Then Jesus, again greatly disturbed, came to the tomb. It was a cave, and a stone was lying against it. [39]Jesus said, 'Take away the stone.' Martha, the sister of the dead man, said to him, 'Lord, already there is a stench because he has been dead four days.' [40]Jesus said to her, 'Did I not tell you that if you believed, you would see the glory of God?' [41]So they took away the stone. And Jesus looked upward and said, 'Father, I thank you for having heard me. [42]I knew that you always hear me, but I have said this for the sake of the crowd standing here, so that they may believe

that you sent me.' ⁴³When he had said this, he cried with a loud voice, 'Lazarus, come out!' ⁴⁴The dead man came out, his hands and feet bound with strips of cloth, and his face wrapped in a cloth. Jesus said to them, 'Unbind him, and let him go.'

Context

Here is a passage in John's gospel which shows Jesus intimately concerned for a family in the crisis of the death of a loved one. Jesus shares their grief and raises Lazarus from the tomb. Christ's actions fulfil his promise to be resurrection and life to those who believe.

Sensing

Stand in front of the tomb with Martha. Hear the crying of all the mourners. Listen to the groans of grief. Watch the face of Jesus. His eyes are red with tears; his face is furrowed with sorrow. Join in the mourning for Lazarus, dead and buried.

Stand in front of the tomb with Martha. See the stone firmly shut across the entrance to the cave. Life is shut out while the process of death proceeds. Hope is as cold as stone. Only remembrance remains. Join in the mourning for Lazarus, dead and buried.

Stand in front of the tomb with Martha. Hear the firm voice of Jesus taking command of the situation. Watch him wave to the strong men, calling them to move the stone. See the look of horror on Martha's face. She is holding her scarf over her nose. Four days have passed since Lazarus' death. Decay has long begun. There is no use hoping for life. Join in the mourning for Lazarus, dead and buried.

Stand in front of the tomb with Martha. Hear the firm voice of Jesus offering a prayer to God. Here is thanksgiving; here is faith; here is revelation of the giver of life. Watch the sparks of hope rising as Martha and her friends lift their heads up to heaven. Share their trust in Jesus, the giver of hope. Join in the mourning for Lazarus, dead, buried and loved by Jesus.

Stand in front of the tomb with Martha. Hear the firm voice of Jesus calling to Lazarus: 'Come out.' Watch the amazement on the faces of Martha and her friends. From the tomb comes Lazarus, but still bound in the robes of death. Join in the mourning for Lazarus, firmly wrapped in death.

Stand in front of the tomb with Martha. Hear the firm voice of Jesus calling to the mourners: 'Unbind him, and let him go.' Watch the relief on the faces of Martha and her friends. Freed from the bonds of grief, they let Lazarus go. His life is in God's hands. Death no more detains him. Join in the rejoicing for Lazarus, free in resurrection.

Intuition

When we experience the loss of a loved one, we are torn between two strong emotions. In turn we echo the two verses: 'Jesus began to weep', and 'Unbind him and let him go.'

Can you relate to the experience of weeping when your loved one has died? When Jesus wept the people said, 'See how he loved him.' When we weep we shed our tears out of love. In our grief we want to cling to everything that will attach us to our loved one. Every piece of clothing is precious to us. Every memento of times shared together is retained. In grief we hope that time will stand still and we can stay in touch with our loved ones in death. Our continuing tears show the depth of our love. Can you relate to such an experience?

Can you relate to the experience of wanting to release your loved one into the new life of resurrection? When Jesus said, 'Unbind him and let him go,' he addressed the mourners. In the garden of resurrection Jesus told Mary not to cling to him. Jesus had to be released to return to his Father and our Father. We too desire to release our loved one into the new life of resurrection. When the process of dying has been difficult, we want to let our loved one go. Our hope is for freedom from the pain and trouble of this world. We look for comfort in the promise of the Book of Revelation (21:4) that death, mourning, crying, and pain will be no more. We want our loved one to move on to the fullness of eternal life that God gives to the faithful. We too know we have to move on with our lives. Can you relate to such an experience?

Can you relate to the experience of being torn between those two emotions? One moment we are crying for the loss of the one we love. Another moment we are crying out to God to take our loved one into the care of the risen Christ. The two emotions pull us this way and that. Can you relate to such an experience?

Feeling

Step into the place of those who mourn, and share the grief of Mary, the sister who loved Lazarus so much. Mary was the sensitive one who loved to sit at the feet of Jesus to show her trust in his every word. But what was the point of such a relationship now? Alas, in death God feels so absent.

Step into the place of those who mourn, and share the grief of Jesus, the friend who loved Lazarus so much. Jesus was the sensitive one who loved to touch the sick and dying to restore them to life. But what was the point of such a relationship now? Alas, in death God seems so powerless.

Step into the place of those who mourn, and share the grief of the family friends who loved Mary, Martha and Lazarus so much. They were the sensitive ones who, out of love, gathered at the time of the funeral to give their support to the family. But what was the point of such a relationship now? Alas, in death human comfort feels so ineffectual.

Step into the place of those who mourn, and share the grief of Martha, the sister who loved Lazarus so much. Martha was the practical one who loved to see everyone's needs were met. She ordered the food for the funeral feast for the living, but there is little she could do for the dead. But what was the point of such a relationship now? Alas, in death we feel helpless that practical things cannot restore life.

Step into the place of those who mourn, and share the confidence of Jesus, the Lord of life and resurrection, who loved Lazarus so much. Share his practical trust in God that those who believe will discover that there is more to life than death. There is resurrection for both the dead and the living. 'Did I not tell you that if you believed, you would see the glory of God?' Surely there is every point in such a relationship now. In grief and in resurrection do we not feel the glory of God?

Thinking

There are some striking parallels between the account of Lazarus' freedom from the grave in John 11, and the account of Jesus' resurrection in John 20. Consider these examples.

Consider carefully the parallel between 'They thought that Mary was going to the tomb to weep there', in John 11:31, and 'But Mary stood weeping outside the tomb', in John 20:11.

Here is clear Christian teaching that the proper reaction for those who encounter death is one of grief born out of love. A time of mourning is appropriate for Christians even when they know in faith that Jesus has promised resurrection and eternal life.

Consider carefully the parallel between 'Jesus came to the tomb. It was a cave and a stone was lying against it', in John 11:38, and 'Mary Magdalene came to the tomb and saw that the stone had been removed from the tomb', in John 20:1.

Here is clear Christian teaching that the proper actions for people to take when a loved one has died is to provide a secure resting-place for their mortal remains. It is appropriate for Christians to pay respect to the body of the dead even when they believe that Jesus has promised resurrection and eternal life.

Consider carefully the parallel between 'The dead man came out, his hands and feet bound with strips of cloth, and his face wrapped in a cloth', in John 11:44, and '[Peter] saw the linen wrappings lying there, and the cloth that had been on Jesus' head . . . rolled up in a place by itself', in John 20:6–7.

Here is clear Christian teaching that the proper hope for people to hold is that resurrection is found in freedom beyond death, not in avoidance of death. We have to die in Christ so that we might rise with Christ to eternal life. Though our bodies lie bound in the tomb, our spirits will be free to live with God in eternity.

Consider carefully how the parallels from the story about Lazarus prepare us to interpret the account of the resurrection of Jesus. Resurrection applies both to the master and to the beloved disciple. Surely it also applies to all those who trust the promise of Jesus to be the resurrection and the life, even to the saints of God in every age.

48
John 12:20–33

²⁰Now among those who went up to worship at the festival were some Greeks. ²¹They came to Philip, who was from Bethsaida in Galilee, and said to him, 'Sir, we wish to see Jesus.' ²²Philip went and told Andrew; then Andrew and Philip went and told Jesus. ²³Jesus answered them, 'The hour has come for the Son of Man to be glorified. ²⁴Very truly, I tell you, unless a grain of wheat falls into the earth and dies, it remains just a single grain; but if it dies, it bears much fruit. ²⁵Those who love their life lose it, and those who hate their life in this world will keep it for eternal life. ²⁶Whoever serves me must follow me, and where I am, there will my servant be also. Whoever serves me, the Father will honour.

²⁷'Now my soul is troubled. And what should I say - "Father, save me from this hour"? No, it is for this reason that I have come to this hour. ²⁸Father, glorify your name.' Then a voice came from heaven, 'I have glorified it, and I will glorify it again.' ²⁹The crowd standing there heard it and said that it was thunder. Others said, 'An angel has spoken to him.' ³⁰Jesus answered, 'This voice has come for your sake, not for mine. ³¹Now is the judgement of this world; now the ruler of this world will be driven out. ³²And I, when I am lifted up from the earth, will draw all people to myself.' ³³He said this to indicate the kind of death he was to die.

Context

In this passage the request of the Greek pilgrims echoes the desire of all those who long to see Jesus. His work for the salvation of the world is wrought on the cross and affirmed by God in the glory of his resurrection. To 'see' Jesus is to gaze upon his cross and there find life.

Sensing

Come join the crowd going up to Jerusalem for Passover. Look around you. Most of the pilgrims share the same culture, race and religion. Hear the language of their conversation. It is the tongue of the Hebrew people. Some accents are from the rustic north;

others from sophisticated Judea. Listen to the buzz of chatter in the language of the Hebrews.

Come join the crowd going up to Jerusalem for Passover. Look around you. Some of the pilgrims are heading for the Court of the Gentiles. Hear the language of their conversation. It is the tongue of common Greek. Some accents are from Asia Minor; others from sophisticated Athens. Listen to the buzz of chatter in the language of the Greeks.

Come join the crowd going up to Jerusalem for Passover. Look around you. Many of the pilgrims cluster around Jesus from Nazareth. Listen as his own people shout out his praises for the wonderful signs he has shown to them. There is talk that he has brought someone back to life. Such a reputation spreads like wildfire in this fired-up crowd.

Come join the crowd going up to Jerusalem for Passover. Look around you. Some of the Greek-speaking pilgrims politely ask Philip for an introduction to the prophet. Listen as they put their request: 'Sir, we wish to see Jesus.' Such a reputation needs careful investigation.

Come join the crowd going up to Jerusalem for Passover. Look around you. Two disciples have brought the Greek pilgrims close to listen to the Master. What will they see in him? Watch the reaction on their faces to his words: 'Those who love their life lose it, and those who hate their life in this world will keep it for eternal life.' Such a message needs careful investigation.

Come join the crowd going up to Jerusalem for Passover. Hear the buzz among the pilgrims as they argue about what this might mean. Feel your ears tingle and your heart pound as your neighbour puts the question straight in your face: 'Are you ready to lose life to keep it for eternity?' Such a question needs a careful answer.

Intuition

How can you apply this story to the way people come to faith? For many, there are four steps in the process of evangelism. Can you trace those in your own experience of the journey? Take a look and see how you found your faith in Christ.

John's story begins with the crowds admiring Jesus. A crowd of disciples, Jews and some Greeks were going up to worship at the Passover. There was general enthusiasm for Jesus as the powerful presence of God. In your first steps towards faith, did the singing and the enthusiasm of the crowd draw you on? Did your friends' zeal encourage you to share their admiration for the work and person of Jesus? Trace your own experience and see how you first admired the Lord.

John's story proceeds to the point of enquiry. Some Greek pilgrims approached the disciple Philip, with a request to see Jesus. When you took your second step towards faith did you ask others to tell you more about Jesus? As you studied the Bible and heard believers' experiences of Jesus, how did you ask your questions of the Lord? Did a course of instruction respond to your enquiries? Trace your own experience and see how you reached the point of enquiry.

John's story proceeds to the point of revelation. Jesus responded to the opportunity for evangelism by revealing who he was and what actions he was taking. As Son of Man, Jesus revealed the presence and purpose of God by the action of dying on the cross. How did you come to see Jesus as God's own Son? How did you stand beneath the cross and behold Jesus as your saviour? Trace your own experience and see how Jesus revealed himself to you.

John's story proceeds to the point of commitment. Jesus called on his listeners to follow and to serve. How did you make your commitment as a disciple of Christ? How did you find ways to serve the Lord? What joy have you found in the company of Christ and his disciples? Trace your own experience and see how you made your commitment to Christ.

There are four steps in the process of evangelism. Trace your own experience of the journey.

Feeling

Jesus said, 'Now my soul is troubled.' Enter into the heart of Jesus as he faces the awful reality of the path he must take for the salvation of the world.

Feel for Jesus as he hears his own words: 'Unless a grain of wheat falls into the earth and dies'. It is one thing to talk about death; it is another to enter into its reality. Feel for Jesus as the hour draws closer. The opposition is already working (John 11:53). Plots have been laid by the religious authorities. Even his beloved friend Lazarus is under threats (John 12:10). Feel for Jesus as the dark clouds gather and the storm is about to break.

Feel for Jesus as his inner heart is torn between the desire to live and the willingness to die. You can empathize with his prayer: 'Should I say – Father, save me from this hour?' He had prayed to his Father to save Lazarus from the grave, should not the Father rescue his Son from the lions' claws? Feel for Jesus as the heavy clouds of doubt hover overhead.

Feel for Jesus as his will is made up and he firmly resolves to go forward on the chosen path. You can admire Jesus' courage and determination shining through his words: 'No, it is for this reason that I have come to this hour!' Jesus was sure of his mission and the way that it must be fulfilled. All his ministry had one over-arching purpose, the salvation of the world. Feel for Jesus as the light of certainty shines down on the path to the cross.

Feel for Jesus as he hears the Father's affirmation. Share his joy in knowing that he glorifies the name of God and is glorified by God as he enters his passion. Here is the sound of victory; here is the joy of fulfilment; here is the wonder of the cross. Feel for Jesus as the drum roll of thunder signals the climax of the glorious cross.

Share his doubts; share his certainty; share his courage; and share the harvest joy of his victory.

Thinking

The necessity for Christ to die on the cross has been a challenge to many people's faith. It is a matter that requires careful explanation.

Consider Jesus' mission policy as it is outlined in John's gospel. The author demonstrates who Jesus is by a series of signs and sayings. He tells us that Jesus incorporates a new reign of God by generosity and love. There is new wine and new bread. There is new sight and new light. There is living water and abundant life. There is healing for this life and for the life of eternity. He tells us that Jesus is the good shepherd, the light of the world, the resurrection and life of the faithful. Jesus is the Word made flesh, the Son of God and the Son of Man. Jesus comes to bring life to all the world. Can you explain why he needs to talk of dying?

Consider Jesus' warning about darkness. In John's gospel sharp distinction is drawn between the new way of Christ and the old ways of religion; between the light and the darkness; between God and the rulers of this world; between those who plot Jesus' downfall and those who share his mission. Jesus is not afraid of conflict. He issues the challenges. He provokes deep thought about the truth. Can you explain why Jesus constantly stirs up such opposition?

Consider Jesus' realism regarding judgement. In John's gospel the truth is highlighted, never disguised or hidden. Jesus is ready to reveal the stark reality of the necessary conflict between good and evil. While evil is allowed to pass for some sort of good, truth cannot flourish. There must be a time of judgement: 'Now is the judgement of this world; now the ruler of this world will be driven out.' The cross is the ultimate point of judgement. It is the place of decision. It is the place of truth. Evil can only be overcome by love. The death of Christ exposes the evil at the same time as it reveals God's goodness and love. Now can you explain why Christ must be lifted up on the cross?

49

John 15:1–8

[1]'I am the true vine, and my Father is the vinegrower. [2]He removes every branch in me that bears no fruit. Every branch that bears fruit he prunes to make it bear more fruit. [3]You have already been cleansed by the word that I have spoken to you. [4]Abide in me as I abide in you. Just as the branch cannot bear fruit by itself unless it abides in the vine, neither can you unless you abide in me. [5]I am the vine, you are the branches. Those who abide in me and I in them bear much fruit, because apart from me you can do nothing. [6]Whoever does not abide in me is thrown away like a branch and withers; such branches are gathered, thrown into the fire, and burned. [7]If you abide in me, and my words abide in you, ask for whatever you wish, and it will be done for you. [8]My Father is glorified by this, that you bear much fruit and become my disciples.'

Context

According to John, Jesus had brought his disciples to the supper table and washed their feet. Judas had already gone out into the night before Jesus began this important programme of teaching, immediately prior to his betrayal. In chapter 15 the teaching focuses on the vine.

Sensing

Remember where you are; remember who you are. Look around you and see the familiar faces of the eleven remaining disciples seated at the table. Gaze into their eyes and sense the expectancy and the confusion. Look around you and see Jesus presiding at the feast. Gaze into his eyes and sense the urgency and the anguish. Look around you and see the empty space vacated by Judas. Gaze through the window into the bleakness of the night where Judas now roams free. You are waiting for traumatic events to happen.

Remember where you are; remember who you are. Look around you and see the familiar signs of the Maundy Thursday meal. Gaze at the bowl of water used for the washing of feet and sense the cleansing power. Look around you. See the bread still resting on the table and sense its life-giving power. Look around you. See the red wine still gleaming in the cup, and sense its invitation to share in the Messiah's banquet. You are feasting in the kingdom of God.

Remember where you are; remember who you are. Listen carefully to the familiar words of the Maundy Thursday meal. While the red wine of the Messiah's banquet gleams in the cup, Jesus directs attention to himself. 'I am', says Jesus, 'the true vine.' Here is the vine which fills the cup. Here is both the master of the feast and the feast itself. You are in the presence of God's anointed one.

Remember where you are; remember who you are. Listen carefully to the familiar words of the Maundy Thursday meal. While the red wine of the Messiah's banquet gleams in the cup, Jesus directs attention to you and to your companions gathered around the table. 'You are', says Jesus, 'the branches.' You are the disciples who have been chosen to drink from the cup. You are the disciples who have been grafted into the true vine. You are the disciples who have been cleansed and commissioned to bear much fruit. You are both guests at the table and co-providers for the feast.

Remember where you are; remember who you are.

Intuition

The great 'I am' sayings of John's gospel are calculated to speak to the imagination. They are springboards to profound insights into deep religious truths.

Sit around the supper table and hear Jesus proclaim, 'I am the true vine.' Just pause and contemplate the simple word 'I'. How often do you assert the I-word in your conversation and in your behaviour? Perhaps it is all too easy to assert who *I am* and what *I want*, before listening to who others are and what others want. Jesus was in control of the I-word. Pray that we also may be in control of the I-word.

Sit around the supper table and hear Jesus proclaim, 'I am the true vine.' Just pause and contemplate the simple verb 'to be'. How confident are you about who you really are? Perhaps it is all too easy to lose touch with the essence of our real identity, or even to fail to discover our true being. Jesus knew who he really was. Pray that we also may come to know ourselves as we are known.

Sit around the supper table and hear Jesus proclaim, 'I am the true vine.' Just pause and contemplate the power of the word 'true'. How committed are you to seeking out the truth and remaining committed to it? Perhaps it is all too easy to make do with half-truths and half-tested claims. Jesus was firmly committed to the truth and to being true to himself and to his God. Pray that we also may be committed to the quest for what is true.

Sit around the supper table and hear Jesus proclaim, 'I am the true vine.' Just pause and contemplate the image of the vine. How well do you relate to Jesus as the vine through whom comes all your strength, purpose, and growth as a Christian. Perhaps it is all too easy to prefer a less dynamic, less nurturing God. Jesus was firmly committed to the organic union between himself as the vine and his disciples as the branches. Pray that we also may be firmly grafted into him who is the true vine.

The great 'I am' sayings of John's gospel are calculated to spark the imagination. They are springboards to profound insights into deep religious truths.

Feeling

Join those eleven trusted disciples at Jesus' last supper as they are recommissioned to do the work of the kingdom of God. Experience the range of emotions generated by Jesus' teaching.

Sitting there with the wine still fresh on the table, those eleven trusted disciples were filled with feelings of affirmation. They heard Jesus' words of clear assurance: 'Those who abide in me and I in them bear much fruit.' As you grasp the cup feel deep down how you, too, are being affirmed in the eucharistic feast.

Sitting there with the wine still fresh on the table, those eleven trusted disciples were filled with feelings of responsibility. They heard Jesus' words of firm expectation: 'My father is glorified in this, that you bear much fruit.' As you lift the cup, feel deep down how you, too, are being charged with responsibility in the eucharistic feast.

Sitting there with the wine still fresh on the table, those eleven trusted disciples were filled with feelings of trepidation. They heard Jesus' words of stark caution: 'Whoever does not abide in me is thrown away.' As you gaze at the wine in the cup, feel deep down how you, too, are filled with trepidation in the eucharistic feast.

Sitting there with the wine still fresh on the table, those eleven trusted disciples were filled with feelings of inadequacy. They heard Jesus' words of profound realism: 'Apart from me you can do nothing.' As you press your lips to the wine in the cup, feel deep down how you, too, are confronted with your personal inadequacy in the eucharistic feast.

Sitting there with the wine still fresh on the table, those eleven trusted disciples were filled with feelings of confidence. They heard Jesus' words of eternal faithfulness: 'Those who abide in me and I in them bear much fruit.' As you sip the wine from the cup, feel deep down how you, too, have confidence in Christ's eternal faithfulness renewed in the eucharistic feast.

Thinking

Clearly the communion service stands at the heart of the Christian tradition, and the words of institution at the last supper stand at the heart of the communion service. Jesus took bread and said, 'This is my body.' Jesus took wine and said, 'This is my blood.' Yet, in John's gospel there is no reference to such straightforward institution of the eucharist. So what do you think is going on?

While for Matthew, Mark and Luke, eucharistic theology is left to the very eve of the betrayal and crucifixion, John's gospel seems vibrant with eucharistic imagery right from the start. Right there in chapter 2 Jesus presides over a wedding feast at Cana in Galilee. Is it mere accident that the wedding feast takes place on the third day, for the third day is itself the day of the Messiah's resurrection? Is it mere accident that Jesus himself provides wine for the feast? Is it mere accident that the steward of the feast finds the wine to be of an outstanding vintage? Is it mere accident that through this outpouring at the wedding feast Jesus manifested his glory and his disciples believed in him? So what do you think is going on?

While for Matthew, Mark and Luke, eucharistic theology is left to the very eve of the betrayal and crucifixion, John's gospel seems vibrant with eucharistic imagery right from the start. Right there in chapter 6 Jesus presides over the feeding of the five thousand in quite a different way from the account in the three synoptic gospels. Is it mere accident that the dramatic feeding takes place when the Passover was at hand, for in John's gospel the last supper, too, takes place when the Passover is at hand? Is it mere accident that Jesus himself provides bread for the feast? Is it mere accident that the people perceived Jesus' power and wished to anoint him as king? Is it mere accident that, while the bread is still fresh in the twelve baskets on the grass, Jesus proclaims, 'I am the bread of life'? So what do you think is going on?

While for Matthew, Mark and Luke, eucharistic theology is left to the very eve of the betrayal and crucifixion, John's gospel seems vibrant with eucharistic imagery right from the start. Right here in chapter 15 Jesus presides over the farewell supper with his chosen and trusted disciples. Is it mere accident that, while the wine is still fresh in the twelve glasses on the table, Jesus proclaims, 'I am the true vine'? So what do you think is going on?

So perhaps the communion service really does stand at the heart of John's gospel and the sacred words of institution are presupposed throughout.

50
John 15:9–17

[9]'As the Father has loved me, so I have loved you; abide in my love. [10]If you keep my commandments, you will abide in my love, just as I have kept my Father's commandments and abide in his love. [11]I have said these things to you so that my joy may be in you, and that your joy may be complete.

[12]'This is my commandment, that you love one another as I have loved you. [13]No one has greater love than this, to lay down one's life for one's friends. [14]You are my friends if you do what I command you. [15]I do not call you servants any longer, because

the servant does not know what the master is doing; but I have called you friends, because I have made known to you everything that I have heard from my Father. [16]You did not choose me but I chose you. And I appointed you to go and bear fruit, fruit that will last, so that the Father will give you whatever you ask him in my name. [17]I am giving you these commands so that you may love one another.'

Context

At the supper table immediately prior to his betrayal, Jesus says to his disciples, 'I am the vine and you are the branches.' It is the Christian qualities of love and friendship which characterize life within the true vine.

Sensing

So often it is impossible to interpret the words unless we can first picture the context.

Once again we need to go back to that first Maundy Thursday, the eve before that first Good Friday. We need to go back to the supper table with those eleven chosen disciples, after Judas had gone out into the dark dark night. We need to hear Jesus say, 'You are my friends.'

Once again we need to go back to that first Maundy Thursday, the eve before that first Good Friday. We need to see Jesus, our Lord and master, take the clean towel and adopt the role of the slave. We need to hear the water splashing in the bowl. We need to feel the cleansing and cooling streams run through our toes. We need to hear Jesus say, 'You are my friends.'

Once again we need to go back to that first Maundy Thursday, the eve before that first Good Friday. We need to see Jesus, our Lord and master, take the fresh baked loaf and break it open for all to share. We need to smell the rich aroma of the bread. We need to taste the nourishing and satisfying morsel in our mouth. We need to hear Jesus say, 'You are my friends.'

Once again we need to go back to that first Maundy Thursday, the eve before that first Good Friday. We need to see Jesus, our Lord and master, take the flagon and pour it for all to drink. We need to hear the wine splashing in the goblets. We need to taste the rich and refreshing liquid on our tongues. We need to hear Jesus say, 'You are my friends.'

Once again we need to go back to that first Maundy Thursday, and look forward to the world-changing events of that first Good Friday. With the water still in the bowl, with the bread still broken on the table, with the wine still fresh in the cup, we need to hear Jesus say, 'No one has greater love than this, to lay down one's life for one's friends. You are my friends.'

So often it is impossible to interpret the words unless we can first picture the context.

Intuition

So what do you like doing most with your best friends? What is real friendship?

Do you like sitting around a table and sharing a well-chosen and carefully prepared meal? Do you enjoy providing and receiving good food with friends? Could you agree that real friendship is eating together?

Do you like sitting around a table and sharing a well-chosen and generously poured bottle of wine? Do you enjoy providing and receiving good wine with friends? Could you agree that real friendship is drinking together?

Do you like sitting around a table and sharing well-chosen and interesting topics? Do you enjoy listening to and contributing to good conversation? Could you agree that real friendship is talking together?

Do you like going out and sharing in a useful and helpful task? Do you enjoy setting up and participating in good projects? Could you agree that real friendship is working together?

Do you like going out and sharing in an enjoyable and pleasant recreation? Do you enjoy devising and taking part in good hobbies, sports and pastimes? Could you agree that real friendship is playing together?

Do you like going out and sharing in services of praise, thanksgiving and intercession? Do you enjoy leading and responding to good acts of worship? Could you agree that real friendship is praying together?

So what do you like doing most with your best friends? What is real friendship?

Feeling

When Jesus calls us his friends, he is also calling us to belong to a community of friends. The church of Christ should be one of those rare places in life where it is possible to forge friendships across those divisions which so often separate people.

In the world, age is a great divider of people. Children live in one world and adults live in another world. Yet the church of Christ should be able to offer children and adults equal status in their Christian journey. The church of Christ should be able to offer children the opportunity to learn from adults and adults the opportunity to learn from children. Here friendships can be formed across the generation gap on the basis of mutual respect.

In the world, sex is a great divider of people. Women live in one world and men live in another world. Yet the church of Christ should be able to offer men and women equal recognition in their Christian journey. The church of Christ should be able to offer women the opportunity to minister to men and men the opportunity to minister to women. Here friendships can be formed between men and women on the basis of mutual respect.

In the world, race is a great divider of people. People from one ethnic group live in one world and people from a different ethnic group live in another world. Yet the church of Christ should be able to offer people of different races equal status in their Christian journey. The church of Christ should be able to offer people from different parts of the world the opportunity to enrich one another. Here friendships can be formed between people from different ethnic and cultural backgrounds on the basis of mutual respect.

When Jesus calls us his friends, he is also calling us to belong to a community of friends which knows no distinctions on the basis of age, sex, race, or other divisions.

Thinking

There is an old saying which goes like this: 'Show me your friends and I will understand your character.' What do you learn, then, about Jesus' character from how he treats his friends?

Suppose we take Judas as the first test case. Here was a man with a real flaw in his character. At least in hindsight, we know that Judas could be duplicitous and two-faced. Judas could sit at the supper table and smile at the friend he was about to betray. Judas could pervert the kiss, the sign of friendship, to become the sign of betrayal. What do you learn, then, about Jesus' character from how he treats Judas?

Suppose we take Peter as the second test case. Here was a man with a real flaw in his character. At least in hindsight, we know that Peter could be both impetuous and cowardly. Peter could sit at the supper table and listen to the gospel of peace, and yet the same Peter could carry a sword into the garden of Gethsemane. Peter could sit at the supper table and listen to the predictions of betrayal, and yet the same Peter could deny his Lord three times in the courtyard of the trial. What do you learn, then, about Jesus' character from how he treats Peter?

Suppose we take James and John as the third test case. Here was a pair of brothers with a real flaw in their family character. Jesus knew from the outset of their irascible and fiery nature, and named them Boanerges, 'the sons of thunder'. What do you learn, then, about Jesus' character from how he treats James and John?

Suppose we take Levi the tax collector as the fourth test case. Here was a man with a real flaw in his character. Jesus knew from the outset that he was a man from a deeply religious background who had turned his back on his family heritage in order to work for the occupying Roman forces. What do you learn, then, about Jesus' character from how he treats Levi?

There is an old adage which goes like this: 'Show me your friends and I will understand your character.' What do you learn, then, about Jesus' character from choosing you and me to stand among his friends and from the generous way in which he continually forgives us and constantly offers us new hope in his kingdom?

51

John 15:26–27; 16:4b–15

²⁶'When the Advocate comes, whom I will send to you from the Father, the Spirit of truth who comes from the Father, he will testify on my behalf. ²⁷You also are to testify because you have been with me from the beginning.

^{4b}'I did not say these things to you from the beginning, because I was with you. ⁵But now I am going to him who sent me; yet none of you asks me, "Where are you going?" ⁶But because I

have said these things to you, sorrow has filled your hearts. [7]Nevertheless I tell you the truth: it is to your advantage that I go away, for if I do not go away, the Advocate will not come to you; but if I go, I will send him to you. [8]And when he comes, he will prove the world wrong about sin and righteousness and judgement: [9]about sin, because they do not believe in me; [10]about righteousness, because I am going to the Father and you will see me no longer; [11]about judgement, because the ruler of this world has been condemned.

[12]'I still have many things to say to you, but you cannot bear them now. [13]When the Spirit of truth comes, he will guide you into all the truth; for he will not speak on his own, but will speak whatever he hears, and he will declare to you the things that are to come. [14]He will glorify me, because he will take what is mine and declare it to you. [15]All that the Father has is mine. For this reason I said that he will take what is mine and declare it to you.'

Context

At the supper table immediately prior to his betrayal, Jesus promised his disciples that, after he is taken away from them, he will send to them the Spirit of truth, the Advocate, the Holy Spirit. The promise was fulfilled on Pentecost Sunday.

Sensing

Sometimes a good picture can say so much more than a whole book full of words. On that first Pentecost Sunday, the church was given a profound picture concerning the nature of God the Holy Spirit. The Holy Spirit came to those eleven disciples like a mighty rushing wind. Forget the words, and for now just live for the picture.

The Spirit came like a mighty rushing wind, and the wind is right here. Open your eyes and look for the wind. At first you see nothing. Then you remember how you see the wind blow the washing on the line, how the clothes hanging there are brought to life. You remember how you see the wind pick up sheets of paper and blow them along the street. In the same way, you can see the effects of the Holy Spirit on the lives of people.

The Spirit came like a mighty rushing wind, and the wind is right here. Stretch out your hands and touch the wind. At first you feel nothing. Then you remember how you feel the wind blow you along the promenade on a blustery day, transforming your whole experience. You remember how the wind blows sailing boats through the sea and tugs the child's kite into the sky. In the same way, you can feel the effects of the Holy Spirit on the lives of people.

The Spirit came like a mighty rushing wind, and the wind is right here. Prick up your ears and listen to the wind. At first you hear nothing. Then you remember how you hear the wind rustle through the trees and give voice to the voiceless branches. You remember how you hear the wind slams doors shut and rattles the dustbin lids. In the same way, you can hear the effects of the Holy Spirit on the lives of people.

Sometimes a good picture can say so much more than a whole book full of words. Forget the words, and for now just live the picture.

Intuition

Sometimes a good image can stimulate the imagination and spark ideas so much better than a whole book full of words. On that first Pentecost Sunday the church was given a profound image concerning the nature of God the Holy Spirit. The Holy Spirit came to those chosen disciples like tongues of fire. Now what ideas does that image start running in your mind?

Imagine the ancient world without the discovery of fire, for fire gives light in the darkness. Without fire, when the sun goes down, the world is left in darkness. Does not the Holy Spirit bring light into our lives? Then pray that this fire may illuminate the whole world!

Imagine the ancient world without the discovery of fire, for fire brings warmth in the coldness. Without fire, when the snow falls and the ice sits thick on the lake, the world is left shivering in the cold. Does not the Holy Spirit bring warmth into our hearts? Then pray that this fire may warm the hearts of all people!

Imagine the ancient world without the discovery of fire, for fire cooks our food and kills unwelcome bacteria. Without fire, bread cannot be baked, fish cannot be grilled, vegetables cannot be transformed. Does not the Holy Spirit feed our souls with the food of immortality? Then pray that this fire may feed the spiritual quest of all nations!

Imagine the ancient world without the discovery of fire, for fire refines the metals from the rich deposits in the earth. Without fire, gold and silver cannot be fashioned into artefacts of beauty; iron and bronze cannot be forged into objects of utility. Does not the Holy

Spirit refine the base metal of our lives for the greater glory of God? Then pray that this refiners' fire may transform the human race!

The Holy Spirit came to those chosen disciples like tongues of fire. Now what ideas does that image start running in your mind?

Feeling

Jesus offered his disciples many different images through which they could explore their experience of God the Holy Spirit. The image of the *Paraclete* is one of the most encouraging and enheartening. Sometimes translated as 'Advocate', the word Paraclete means literally 'the one who is called to stand alongside'.

Ever since that first Pentecost Sunday, Christian men and women have been very conscious of God the Holy Spirit being called alongside them as Paraclete in their time of need. Listen to the accounts of the early disciples in the Acts of the Apostles. Remember how, when they were in prison, the Paraclete came to stand alongside them. Remember how, when they were on trial for their faith, the Paraclete came to put words into their mouths. Remember how, when they were martyred, the Paraclete brought them comfort.

Ever since that first Pentecost Sunday, Christian men and women have been very conscious of God the Holy Spirit being called alongside them as Paraclete in their time of need. Listen to the accounts of Christian disciples across the world today. Hear how, when followers of Jesus are imprisoned for their faith, the Paraclete still comes to stand alongside them. Hear how, when they are on trial for their faith, the Paraclete still puts words into their mouths. Hear how, when they face death for the sake of their faith, the Paraclete still brings them comfort.

Ever since that first Pentecost Sunday, Christian men and women have been very conscious of God the Holy Spirit being called alongside them as Paraclete in their time of need. Listen to the accounts of Christian disciples in your own congregation. Hear how, when followers of Jesus are under stress and fatigue, they become aware of the Paraclete called to stand alongside them. Hear how, when they are sick and in great pain, they become aware of the Paraclete called to stand alongside them. Hear how, when they face the hour of death, they become aware of the Paraclete called to stand alongside them.

The image of the Holy Spirit as Paraclete is both encouraging and enheartening.

Thinking

Jesus offered his disciples many different images through which they could express their understanding of God the Holy Spirit. The image of the *Spirit of truth* is one of the most challenging and controversial.

Throughout the ages, from that very first Pentecost Sunday, the church of Christ has been committed to truth. The danger is that we sometimes imagine that we have got it right from the very beginning, that all truth has been established and communicated in the past. But listen carefully to the words of scripture.

Listen carefully to Jesus' promise to his disciples. Jesus said, 'When the Spirit of truth comes, he will guide you into all the truth.' The verb 'guide' is of extreme interest and great significance. It seems unlikely, therefore, that the Spirit of truth plans to reveal or to present all the answers complete and final for human acceptance. A guide may show the way, but nonetheless still expects us to make the journey of discovery for ourselves. It is worth taking the verb very seriously.

Listen carefully to Jesus' promise to the disciples. Jesus said, 'When the Spirit of truth comes, he will guide you into all the truth.' The future tense 'will' is of extreme interest and great significance. It seems unlikely, therefore, that the Spirit of truth intended to have retired from the appointed task as guide shortly after the first Pentecost Sunday. A guide who remains active in the church is day by day leading the people of God to grasp new insights and new truths of the kingdom. It is worth taking the tense seriously.

Listen carefully to Jesus' promise to his disciples. Jesus said, 'When the Spirit of truth comes, he will guide you into all the truth.' The qualifier 'all' is of extreme interest and great significance. The church continues to struggle with issues of huge significance, issues of doctrine, issues of practice and issues of morality. On many of these issues, is it not arrogance and foolishness to claim that our view of the truth is complete? Our guide remains with us as the quest for all truth goes on. It is worth taking the qualifier seriously.

The image of the Holy Spirit as the Spirit of truth is one of the most challenging and controversial.

52
John 17:6–19

[6]'I have made your name known to those whom you gave me from the world. They were yours, and you gave them to me, and they have kept your word. [7]Now they know that everything you have given me is from you; [8]for the words that you gave to me I have given to them, and they have received them and know in truth that I came from you; and they have believed that you sent me. [9]I am asking on their behalf; I am not asking on behalf of the world, but on behalf of those whom you gave me, because they are yours. [10]All mine are yours, and yours are mine; and I have been glorified in them. [11]And now I am no longer in the world, but they are in the world, and I am coming to you. Holy Father, protect them in your name that you have given me, so that they may be one, as we are one. [12]While I was with them, I protected them in your name that you have given me. I guarded them, and not one of them was lost except the one destined to be lost, so that the scripture might be fulfilled. [13]But now I am coming to you, and I speak these things in the world so that they may have my joy made complete in themselves. [14]I have given them your word, and the world has hated them because they do not belong to the world, just as I do not belong to the world. [15]I am not asking you to take them out of the world, but I ask you to protect them from the evil one. [16]They do not belong to the world, just as I do not belong to the world. [17]Sanctify them in the truth; your word is truth. [18]As you have sent me into the world, so I have sent them into the world. [19]And for their sakes I sanctify myself, so that they also may be sanctified in truth.'

Context

At the supper table immediately prior to his betrayal, Jesus concludes his teaching with a great prayer which begins, 'Father, the hour has come.' Jesus prays for his followers that they may be one.

Sensing

There are many key themes in Jesus' high priestly prayer. Take, for example, the theme of mission. Paint pictures in your mind of the great missions of the church.

See those twelve chosen disciples sent out two by two in Mark's gospel. Picture them as they go on their first missionary journey around the villages, commissioned to proclaim the good news of God's kingdom and to heal the sick. Hear Jesus pray, 'As you, O Father, have sent me into the world, so I have sent them into the world.'

See Paul sent out on his great missionary journeys in the Acts of the Apostles. Picture him as he travels over land and across seas to bring the good news of God's kingdom to the centre of the civilized world, to the city of Rome itself. Hear Jesus pray, 'As you, O Father, have sent me into the world, so I have sent them into the world.'

See the early missionaries sent out on their great journeys to bring the Christian faith to your own land. Picture them as they travel over land and across seas to establish Christian churches for the first time in new places. Hear Jesus pray, 'As you, O Father, have sent me into the world, so I have sent them into the world.'

See today's missionaries sent out from their homelands to witness to the Christian faith in every corner of the globe. Picture them as mission partners set in diverse cultures working side by side with local congregations, healing, teaching, proclaiming the gospel. Hear Jesus pray, 'As you, O Father, have sent me into the world, so I have sent them into the world.'

See the men and women of your own congregation sent out on their great journeys to witness to their faith in Christ in your own vicinity. Picture them as they go about their business in the shops, in the offices, in the factories, in the schools, and in the hospitals of your home area. Picture them as they travel on their business on foot, by car, by train, by bus, by bicycle, knowing that with each journey they may, knowingly or unknowingly, be engaged in proclaiming the gospel of Christ through their deeds and through their words. Hear Jesus pray, 'As you, O Father, have sent me into the world, so I have sent them into the world.'

Intuition

There are many key themes in Jesus' high priestly prayer. Take, for example, the theme of revelation through the Son. What do you learn about the nature of God through the activity of Jesus?

According to John's gospel, Jesus begins his ministry at the wedding at Cana in Galilee. There Jesus turns water into wine and could properly pray, 'Father, I have made your name known.' So what does that say about the nature of God?

According to John's gospel, Jesus goes from the wedding at Cana in Galilee to the temple in Jerusalem. There Jesus overturns the tables of the money changers and could properly pray, 'Father, I have made your name known.' So what does that say about the nature of God?

According to John's gospel, Jesus returns to Cana in Galilee. There Jesus is met by an official whose son was ill. Jesus gives health to the boy and could properly pray, 'Father I have made your name known.' So what does that say about the nature of God?

According to John's gospel, Jesus once again goes from Cana in Galilee to Jerusalem, this time to the pool by the sheep gate. There Jesus finds the man who had been ill for thirty-eight years. He gives new strength to the man and could properly pray, 'Father, I have made your name known.' So what does that say about the nature of God?

According to John's gospel, Jesus goes to the other side of the Sea of Galilee. There Jesus sees a great and hungry crowd. He breaks five loaves and shares two small fishes to feed five thousand people and could properly pray, 'Father, I have made your name known.' So what does that say about the nature of God?

According to John's gospel, Jesus sees a man blind from his birth. There he anoints the man's eyes with clay. The blindness was healed and Jesus could properly pray, 'Father, I have made your name known.' So what does that say about the nature of God?

According to John's gospel, Jesus goes to Bethany. There Jesus finds that his friend Lazarus has died and is already laid in the tomb. There he calls the dead man back to life and could properly pray, 'Father, I have made your name known.' So what does that say about the nature of God?

Feeling

There are many key themes in Jesus' high priestly prayer. Take, for example, the theme of intercession. Be conscious of those for whom you should pray.

Open your hearts to any children in your community who are deprived of true parental love. With them on your heart, pray Jesus' prayer, 'Holy Father, protect them in your name.'

Open your hearts to any teenagers in your community who have fallen captive to substance abuse. With them on your heart, pray Jesus' prayer, 'Holy Father, protect them in your name.'

Open your hearts to any young unemployed in your community for whom time hangs heavily and whose self-esteem is fragile. With them on your heart, pray Jesus' prayer, 'Holy Father, protect them in your name.'

Open your hearts to any men and women in your community who have built up debts from which they cannot escape. With them on your heart, pray Jesus' prayer, 'Holy Father, protect them in your name.'

Open your hearts to any outsiders, foreigners, strangers or asylum seekers in your community who are lonely and isolated from their family and from their friends. With them on your heart, pray Jesus' prayer, 'Holy Father, protect them in your name.'

Open your hearts to any individuals in your community who are suffering from depression, despair or suicidal thoughts. With them on your heart, pray Jesus' prayer, 'Holy Father, protect them in your name.'

Open your hearts to any individuals in your community who are suffering from physical pain, disease or injury. With them on your heart, pray Jesus' prayer, 'Holy Father, protect them in your name.'

Open your hearts to those in your community who are at the point of death. With them on your heart, pray Jesus' prayer, 'Holy Father, protect them in your name.'

Thinking

There are many key themes in Jesus' high priestly prayer. Take, for example, the theme of unity. What kind of unity do you think the church should be seeking in our generation?

Some argue strongly that the presence of different churches

and chapels in the same town is a stark contradiction of Christ's high priestly prayer, 'that they may be one'. Surely the different denominations should come together to worship in one place? Do you think that is a fair judgement?

Some argue strongly that the idea of a priest travelling around to several different churches in the same benefice on a Sunday morning is a stark contradiction of Christ's high priestly prayer, 'that they may be one'. Surely the different churches should come together in one place? Do you think that is a fair judgement?

Some argue strongly that holding different types of services in the same church for different congregations is a stark contradiction of Christ's priestly prayer, 'that they may be one'. Surely the different congregations should come together for one big service? Do you think that is a fair judgement?

Others listen carefully to the second clause of Jesus' high priestly prayer when he prays that 'they may be one as we are one'. Now the unity between the Father and the Son presents an interesting theological model, for Christian doctrine reminds us to respect and protect the difference of the persons as much as to respect and protect the unity of the substance.

So, perhaps, there may be a good theological case for valuing some of the differences so well displayed between different denominations? Perhaps there may be a good theological case for respecting the claim of each church to its own Sunday services? Perhaps there may be a good theological case for maintaining very different congregations within the same church. After all, Jesus did pray, 'that they may be one as we are one'. Where do you think a fair judgement lies?

53
John 18:33–37

³³Then Pilate entered the headquarters again, summoned Jesus, and asked him, 'Are you the King of the Jews?' ³⁴Jesus answered, 'Do you ask this on your own, or did others tell you about me?' ³⁵Pilate replied, 'I am not a Jew, am I? Your own nation and the chief priests have handed you over to me. What have you done?' ³⁶Jesus answered, 'My kingdom is not from this world. If my kingdom were from this world, my followers would be fighting to keep me from being handed over to the Jews. But as it is, my kingdom is not from here.' ³⁷Pilate asked him, 'So you are a king?' Jesus answered, 'You say that I am a king. For this I was born, and for this I came into the world, to testify to the truth. Everyone who belongs to the truth listens to my voice.'

Context

In John's gospel Jesus' trial before Pilate focuses on understanding and dismissing the political threat which Jesus could have posed to Roman rule. Jesus explains that his kingdom is not from this world.

Sensing

The encounter between Jesus and Pilate has such dramatic qualities. Come into the theatre and take your seats. The drama is called 'King Jesus'. There are five acts.

Act One takes place in a garden across the Kidron valley. It is night. See a pool of light from lanterns and torches. Hear the coarse chatter of the soldiers as their pool of light gets closer and closer to Jesus. Witness the arrest as Jesus is led away captive. Behold your king!

Act Two takes places in the Jewish court. It is still night. See the fires burning in the courtyard to illuminate the darkness and to warm the chill air. Hear the high priest question Jesus and see the guard strike Jesus on the face. Witness Jesus' passive acceptance. Behold your king!

Act Three takes place outside Pilate's headquarters. By now the dawn is breaking. See the Jewish authorities press their case before Pilate. Hear Pilate try to pass the buck, saying, 'Take him yourselves and judge him according to your law.' Witness their implacable insistence that Jesus should be tried by Pilate. Behold your king!

Act Four takes place inside Pilate's headquarters. It is still early morning. See Jesus and Pilate confront each other, and stand amazed at their conversation. Hear Pilate ask the first test question, 'Are you the King of the Jews?' Then contemplate Jesus' perceptive reply, 'Do you ask this on your own, or did others tell you about me?' Hear Pilate ask the second test question, 'What have you done?' Then contemplate Jesus' full response, 'My kingdom is not from this world.' Witness Pilate formulate his judgement, 'I find no case against him.' Behold your king!

Act Five takes place outside at Golgotha, the place of a skull. The sun is now well up in the sky. See three crosses raised against the hillside, and read the simple text, 'Jesus of Nazareth, the King of the Jews.' Behold your king!

After Act Five it is you who goes out into the night. You remain unconvinced that Pilate has had the last word. Clearly, the drama requires Act Six. On Easter Sunday, behold your risen king!

Intuition

The encounter between Jesus and Pilate has so much to spark the imagination. So what insights can you find?

Take the idea that Pilate was able to summon Jesus to his court. Here is an example of the state exercising control over religion and regulating religious teachers. In parts of the world Christianity is still regulated in this way. Pray for religious tolerance and for religious freedom.

Take the idea that Pilate so completely failed to understand how religious language was being used. Here is an example of someone taking a religious concept (the kingdom of God) and misinterpreting what was being said. In our land so many people are failing to give a proper hearing to the gospel because they have never been taught to appreciate the grammar of religious discourse. Pray for religious education and for literacy about religious matters.

Take the idea that Pilate so completely failed to understand how the minds of the Jewish leaders worked. Here is an example of political leadership in a multiracial, multicultural, and multi-religious environment which had failed to grasp the significance of faith for shaping the whole of life. In our own world so many misunderstandings, problems and fatal conflicts can be traced to the failure to be properly informed about matters of faith. Pray for dialogue between the great religions of the world and for politicians to take religious diversity seriously.

Take the idea that Pilate so completely failed to ensure that justice was done. Here is an example of a judicial system being perverted by political expediency. Across the world the course of justice continues to be perverted by incompetence, by ignorance, by prejudice and by corruption. Pray for all who hold responsibility to administer justice.

Take the idea that Jesus so completely refused to use force to ensure the victory of his cause. Here is an example of committed pacifism facing certain death rather than compromising fundamental principles. Across the world brave individuals continue to maintain the pacifist cause for a variety of ideological reasons. Pray for all who remain committed to peace in the face of conflict.

The encounter between Jesus and Pilate has so much to spark the imagination. See what insights you can find.

Feeling

That encounter between Jesus and Pilate has so much to say about the qualities of human leadership, about the dignity, and about the vulnerability.

Put yourself in Pilate's official robes and feel the dignity. The Jewish leaders have come to you because to you alone has been given ultimate authority over their affairs. You alone have complete command over matters of life and death. Feel the dignity as you pull yourself to your full height and see the prisoner stand so helpless before you. Stand on your dignity as you pose the questions and demand the answers. Here is the dignity which comes with the office.

Now put yourself in Jesus' shoes and feel a very different form of dignity. You know that you have right on your side and that no legitimate case can be made to stand against you. You alone have complete truth on your side. Feel the dignity as you pull yourself to your full height and see the governor stand so confused before you. Stand on your dignity as you defuse the questions and examine their assumptions. Here is the dignity which comes from being a person of integrity.

Put yourself in Pilate's official robes and feel the vulnerability. The Jewish leaders have come to you with a problem that you are not fully equipped to understand. Feel the vulnerability as a prisoner stands before you who clearly enjoys widespread support and who possesses considerable miraculous powers. He has healed the lame, given sight to the blind, fed the crowds, and raised the dead. Feel the vulnerability as the Jewish leaders stand before you on the eve of the most politically charged festival in their religious calendar. They could rally the crowd into insurrection at any moment. Here is the vulnerability which comes with the office.

Now put yourself in Jesus' shoes and feel a very different form of vulnerability. You are confronted by a judicial process in which neither truth nor justice is likely to prevail. Feel the vulnerability as the Jewish authorities campaign for your death. Their status is threatened by your divine authority. Feel the vulnerability as the Roman procurator struggles to keep political stability. Here is the vulnerability which comes from being a person of integrity.

That encounter between Jesus and Pilate has so much to say about the qualities of human leadership, about the dignity, and about the vulnerability.

Thinking

That encounter between Jesus and Pilate has so much to say about the potent and volatile mix between religion and politics. So, should religion and politics be kept separate, or are they two sides of the same coin?

Jesus seems clear that his kingdom was not from this world. According to Jesus, God's reign was about ensuring that the wedding party had sufficient wine for its celebration and for the living of life to the full. Do you think that this can really be achieved without confronting the political structures?

Jesus seems clear that his kingdom was not from this world. According to Jesus, God's reign was about restoring health to the sick child, and making strong the legs of the lame. Do you think that this can really be achieved without confronting the political structures?

Jesus seems clear that his kingdom was not from this world. According to Jesus, God's reign was about taking pity on the starving crowd and providing food for them to eat, even with enough to spare. Do you think that this can really be achieved without confronting the political structures?

Jesus seems clear that his kingdom was not from this world. According to Jesus, God's reign was about giving sight to the blind and about teaching wisdom to the ignorant. Do you think that this can really be achieved without confronting the political structures?

Jesus seems clear that his kingdom was not from this world. According to Jesus, God's reign was about bringing new life to the dead, and new hope to those whose will to live had died. Do you think that this can really be achieved without confronting the political structures?

That encounter between Jesus and Pilate has so much to say about the potent and volatile mix between religion and politics. So should religion and politics be kept separate, or are they two sides of the same coin?

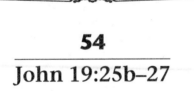

54

John 19:25b–27

²⁵ᵇMeanwhile, standing near the cross of Jesus were his mother, and his mother's sister, Mary the wife of Clopas, and Mary Magdalene. ²⁶When Jesus saw his mother and the disciple whom he loved standing beside her, he said to his mother, 'Woman, here is your son.' ²⁷Then he said to the disciple, 'Here is your mother.' And from that hour the disciple took her into his own home.

Context

At the scene of the crucifixion John describes how Jesus' mother Mary stood with other women near the cross where Jesus hung. Among these women was Mary Magdalene and Mary the wife of Clopas.

Sensing

There are two main occasions in John's gospel where Mary, the mother of Jesus, takes centre stage. On the first occasion Mary takes control and Jesus responds to her request. On the second occasion Jesus takes control and Mary responds to his request. Come, let us explore and contrast these two occasions.

The first occasion took place at Cana in Galilee. Go back to Cana and experience all that is going on. You are in the middle of a wedding banquet. Look round at the faces and pick out those whom you recognize. See Mary deep in conversation with the steward of the feast. See Jesus standing some distance off huddled with his friends.

The first occasion took place on the third day, and for Christians the third day symbolizes the day of resurrection. You are in the middle of a wedding banquet, a foretaste of the Messiah's celebration at the end of the ages. See the troubled faces as the supply of wine threatens to fail. Then hear Mary draw Jesus' attention to the problem, saying to him, 'They have no wine.' Hear also Mary's confidence as she instructs the servants, 'Do whatever he tells you.' This was an occasion when Mary was clearly in charge and Jesus responded by turning water into wine.

The second occasion took place at Golgotha outside Jerusalem. Go back to Golgotha and experience all that is going on. You are in the middle of a crucifixion. Look round at the faces and pick out those whom you recognize. See Jesus alone and hanging on the cross. See Mary standing nearby huddled with her friends.

The second occasion took place three days before the resurrection, three days before anyone knew with certainty how the story would end. You are in the middle of a crucifixion. See the troubled faces as Jesus' grasp on life runs thin. Hear Jesus plan for the future. Turning to the disciple whom he loved, he said to Mary, 'Here is your son.' Turning to Mary, he said to that disciple, 'Here is your mother.' This was an occasion when Jesus was clearly in charge and Mary responded by returning to that disciple's home.

Intuition

The account of Mary standing by the cross on the day of crucifixion has been an inspiration to painters, to poets and to musicians. What kind of inspiration does it bring to you?

Start with the most obvious aspect of the account, the pain in Mary's heart as she witnesses and shares her son's suffering and humiliating death. All of us in our own way will have brought pain to our parents. May God forgive.

Then look deeper into Mary's heart and see alongside the pain those precious memories of joy, contentment and pride, as she has witnessed her son bringing new wine to the wedding and new life to the diseased and disabled. All of us in our own way will have brought joy to our parents. May God be praised.

See how Mary is being supported in her time of sorrow by a close member of family, her very own sister. Our parents, too, may be supported by close family at times of need, pressure or sickness. May God be praised.

See how Mary benefits from the companionship of other wise and holy women, for here are Mary the wife of Clopas and Mary Magdalene. Our parents, too, may be supported by close friends at times of need, pressure or sickness. May God be praised.

See how Jesus makes sensible provision for his mother's future, to ensure that she is looked after in her old age. Our parents, too, may need our care and provision when the roles are reversed, and when they become dependent on us. May God guide us.

See how the other disciple opens his home to receive Jesus' mother. In our society, too, there are ageing, single, widowed and separated men and women who have no family to care for them. May God guide us.

The account of Mary standing by the cross on the day of crucifixion has been an inspiration to painters, to poets and to musicians. What kind of inspiration does it bring to you?

Feeling

The account of Mary standing by the cross on the day of crucifixion is a story of great heroism and of great tragedy. Can you grasp what the pain must have been like for her?

By this stage Mary must already have endured all sorts of pain on account of her unusual son. Most boys would have been content to grow up and to stay close enough to home. But, by the age of thirty, Jesus had wandered off to far-flung places. Mary bore the pain of never knowing where he was.

By this stage Mary must already have endured all sorts of pain on account of her unusual son. Most boys would have been content to take a wife and to rear a family. But Jesus had preferred the company of a disparate crew of men and women. Mary bore the pain of never enjoying being a grandmother to his children.

By this stage Mary must already have endured all sorts of pain on account of her unusual son. Most boys would have been content to follow in their father's footsteps and to learn their father's trade. But Jesus had exchanged the steady income of the carpenter's shop for the uncertain reward of the peripatetic preacher. Mary bore the pain of insecurity in her old age.

By this stage Mary must already have endured all sorts of pain on account of her unusual son. Most boys who had his outstanding powers would have turned them to good effect. Properly managed, her Jesus could have been worth a fortune. But Jesus used his outstanding powers only to outrage the authorities. Mary bore the pain of seeing her son ostracized and threatened.

By this stage Mary must already have endured all sorts of pain on account of her unusual son. Most boys who had made a name for themselves in the wider world would have been proud to come back to their own village to show off in front of family and neighbours. But, when Jesus came to Nazareth, he did no great things there at all. Mary bore the pain of being let down in front of the people that mattered to her most.

Now Mary comes to face what must be the greatest pain a mother can bear, as she witnesses the execution of her son by the barbaric tools of crucifixion. The account of Mary standing by the cross is a story of great heroism and of great tragedy. Can you grasp what the pain must have been like for her?

Thinking

The account of Mary standing by the cross on the day of crucifixion is a very powerful theological witness to the true humanity of Jesus. So do you understand why it may have been particularly important for John the gospel writer to make that point?

When Luke began his gospel, he took the story back to the point of conception. The angel Gabriel confronts Mary with the gospel that she is to be the mother of Jesus. Luke leads us to Bethlehem for the birth. The cradle and the swaddling clothes are discussed. The shepherds are brought along as witnesses to the humanity of Jesus. Surely Luke has left no room to doubt the humanity of Jesus.

When Matthew began his gospel, he took the story back through the Davidic ancestry. The angel confronts Joseph with the gospel that Mary is to be the mother of Jesus. Matthew leads us to Bethlehem for the birth. The wise men from the east are brought along as witnesses to the humanity of Jesus. Surely Matthew has left no room to doubt the humanity of Jesus.

When John began his gospel, however, he began in a very different place. John begins not with a clear witness to the humanity of Jesus, but with a clear witness to the divinity of Jesus. For John the story begins right back before the beginning of time, right back before the primordial act of creation. 'In the beginning,' says John, 'was the Word, and the Word was with God, and the Word was God.' Surely John has left every room to be uncertain about the humanity of Jesus.

When John concluded his gospel, however, he wanted to ensure that any room for doubt had been removed. The crucifixion which John proclaims is real death, and the resurrection which John proclaims is real life. There, at the point of death, waits Mary the mother who brought Jesus into the world, and she has by her side, as an additional witness, her sister. Surely, after all, John has left no room to doubt the humanity of Jesus.

The account of Mary standing by the cross on the day of crucifixion is a very powerful theological witness to the true humanity of Jesus.

55
John 20:19–31

¹⁹When it was evening on that day, the first day of the week, and the doors of the house where the disciples had met were locked for fear of the Jews, Jesus came and stood among them and said, 'Peace be with you.' ²⁰After he said this, he showed them his hands and his side. Then the disciples rejoiced when they saw the Lord. ²¹Jesus said to them again, 'Peace be with you. As the Father has sent me, so I send you.' ²²When he had said this, he breathed on them and said to them, 'Receive the Holy Spirit. ²³If you forgive the sins of any, they are forgiven them; if you retain the sins of any, they are retained.'

²⁴But Thomas (who was called the Twin), one of the twelve, was not with them when Jesus came. ²⁵So the other disciples told him, 'We have seen the Lord.' But he said to them, 'Unless I see the mark of the nails in his hands, and put my finger in the mark of the nails and my hand in his side, I will not believe.'

²⁶A week later his disciples were again in the house, and Thomas was with them. Although the doors were shut, Jesus came and stood among them and said, 'Peace be with you.' ²⁷Then he said to Thomas, 'Put your finger here and see my hands. Reach out your hand and put it in my side. Do not doubt but believe.' ²⁸Thomas answered him, 'My Lord and my God!' ²⁹Jesus said to him, 'Have you believed because you have seen me? Blessed are those who have not seen and yet have come to believe.'

³⁰Now Jesus did many other signs in the presence of his disciples, which are not written in this book. ³¹But these are written so that you may come to believe that Jesus is the Messiah, the Son of God, and that through believing you may have life in his name.

Context

John's gospel tells of two meetings with the risen Jesus on Easter day. Early in the morning Mary meets Jesus near the empty tomb. In the evening the disciples meet Jesus in their locked house. So with confidence they can say, 'We have seen the Lord.'

Sensing

It is important to know what happened on that first Easter day. Listen carefully as the story unfolds. There are two facts that John wants to establish.

The first fact concerns the body in the tomb. There were objective witnesses to the fact that Jesus was really dead. Listen to the evidence. When the soldiers inspected the three criminals hanging on the crosses, they verified that Jesus was already dead. Then they pierced his side with a spear. With the witness of the soldiers, no residue of doubt could remain. Jesus was dead.

The first fact concerns the body in the tomb. There were objective witnesses to the fact that Jesus was really dead. Listen to the evidence. When the soldiers had finished their work, it was Joseph of Arimathea who took the body away. Joseph of Arimathea knew Jesus well; his witness can be trusted. Then Nicodemus, who had known Jesus from the very beginning of John's gospel, came to help prepare the body for burial; his witness, too, can be trusted. With the witness of Joseph and of Nicodemus, no residue of doubt could remain. Jesus was dead.

The second fact concerns the resurrection from the dead. There were objective witnesses to the fact that Jesus was really fully alive. Listen to the evidence. On the first day of the week, when it was still dark, Mary Magdalene saw Jesus walking through the garden. Jesus spoke. Mary Magdalene knew his voice; her witness can be trusted. This close disciple went away and proclaimed with confidence, 'I have seen the Lord!' But with only one witness, the residue of doubt could still remain.

The second fact concerns the resurrection from the dead. There were objective witnesses to the fact that Jesus was really fully alive. Listen to the evidence. On the first day of the week, when it was evening, the main body of the disciples saw Jesus walking through the house. Jesus spoke. The disciples knew his voice; their witness can be trusted. These close disciples went away and proclaimed with confidence, 'We have seen the Lord!' With the witness of so many, no residue of doubt could remain. Jesus is alive. Alleluia!

It is important to know what happened on that first Easter day.

Intuition

The story which John tells about the disciples' encounter with the risen Lord on the first Easter Sunday, when it was evening, contains the key ingredients of our Christian liturgy. Do you see what I mean?

When we come together to commemorate our Lord's death and resurrection, we begin our liturgy with the words of salutation. Do you not immediately link the salutation with Jesus' words to his disciples, 'Peace be with you'?

When we come together to commemorate our Lord's death and resurrection, we come with the mood of penitence and with the need for confession. Do you not immediately link this confession with Jesus' words to his disciples, 'If you forgive the sins of any they are forgiven'?

When we come together to commemorate our Lord's death and resurrection, we come with the intention of renewing and reaffirming our faith. Do you not immediately link this credal affirmation with the disciples' words to Jesus, 'My Lord and my God'?

When we come together to commemorate our Lord's death and resurrection, we come to be nourished and strengthened through the Eucharist with the power and grace of the Holy Spirit. Do you not immediately link these holy gifts with Jesus' words to his disciples, 'Receive the Holy Spirit'?

When we come together to commemorate our Lord's death and resurrection, we conclude our liturgy with the words of dismissal. Do you not immediately link the dismissal with Jesus' words to his disciples, 'As the Father has sent me, so I send you'?

When we are dispersed again to the four corners of the world, having met to commemorate our Lord's death and resurrection, we are commissioned to proclaim our faith to all and sundry through word and deed. Do you not immediately link the call to witness to the disciples' proclamation, 'We have seen the Lord'?

Today, when we repeat these liturgical words and actions in the eucharistic community, the risen Lord continues to stand in our company. Do you see what I mean?

Feeling

Here is a story about how some very different people came to find faith in the risen Christ. The people are very different; their pathways to faith are quite distinct; and yet there is a clear pattern to their different personal experiences.

Get to know Mary Magdalene. Share her experiences from the inside. On the Friday, Mary Magdalene shared the anguish of standing at the foot of Jesus' cross. She had felt her hopes drain right away. On the Sunday morning, Mary Magdalene had come to the tomb, not knowing what to expect. But she had put herself in a position from which Jesus could take the initiative. Share in Mary Magdalene's joy as Jesus addresses her by name, 'Mary'. With her cry, 'Rabbouni' faith is announced and commitment proclaimed. Here is Mary Magdalene's journey to faith.

Get to know Peter. Share his experiences from the inside. On the Friday, Peter had shared the anguish of seeing Jesus led away to Golgotha and nailed to the cross. He had felt his hopes drain right away. On the Sunday morning, Peter had come to the tomb, not knowing what to expect. His mistake was to leave too quickly and not to put himself in a position from which Jesus could respond.

Get to know Peter better. Share his experiences from the inside. On that Sunday evening, he had met with the other disciples behind locked doors. Now, Peter had put himself in a position from which Jesus could take the initiative. Share in Peter's joy as Jesus addresses the disciples by name, 'Peace be with you.' With their cry, 'We have seen the Lord,' faith is announced and commitment proclaimed. Here is Peter's journey to faith.

Get to know Thomas. Share his experience from the inside. Like the other disciples, Thomas had shared the anguish of seeing Jesus led away to Golgotha and nailed to the cross. Like the other disciples, on the Friday Thomas had felt his hopes drain away. On the Easter Sunday evening his mistake was not to place himself in a position from which Jesus could respond. The following week, however, Thomas was there with the others. Share in Thomas's joy as Jesus addresses him by name, 'Do not doubt but believe.' With his cry, 'My Lord and my God,' faith is announced and commitment proclaimed. Here is Thomas's journey to faith.

Here is a story about how some very different people came to find faith in the risen Christ. Share their experiences and learn from their examples.

Thinking

For some of us faith does not come easily. We look at life with a proper caution. We are wary of enthusiasm. We are suspicious of those who are convinced too easily. Sceptical Thomas is a disciple after our own hearts.

Surely Thomas was right to be sceptical. There was so much to be sceptical about. The whole of Jerusalem knew by now what had taken place on the Friday. They knew about the trial. They knew about the crucifixion. They knew about the death. The soldiers could not keep quiet about the final thrust of their spear. Can talk of resurrection make any logical sense? Is it not better to be sceptical than gullible?

Surely Thomas was right to be sceptical. There was so much to be sceptical about. Already from early in the day the network of Jesus' followers had been buzzing with excitement and with rumour. Peter and that other disciple whom Jesus loved had been to see the tomb. They had found the stone rolled away, but they had found no body. They had seen no risen Lord. On the basis of such slim evidence, can talk of resurrection make any logical sense? Is it not better to be sceptical than gullible?

Surely Thomas was right to be sceptical. There was so much to be sceptical about. When Mary Magdalene returned from the tomb, she came proclaiming, 'I have seen the risen Lord.' But the evidence of one person testifying alone would never stand up in court. When pressed, Mary Magdalene could not say that she had actually touched Jesus. On the basis of such slim evidence, can talk of resurrection make any logical sense? Is it not better to be sceptical than gullible?

Surely Thomas was right to be sceptical. There was so much to be sceptical about. The other disciples came proclaiming, 'We have seen the risen Lord.' But they brought no real physical evidence of what they had seen, no finger prints or plaster cast of the wounds. On the basis of such slim evidence, can talk of resurrection make any logical sense? Is it not better to be sceptical than gullible?

Sceptical Thomas is a disciple after our own heart. But once Thomas saw for himself, Thomas believed. Maybe it would be just too sceptical not to trust his judgement now.

Further reading

The following books provide further insight into the theory of psychological type underpinning the Myers-Briggs Type Indicator and the relevance of type theory for the Christian community.

Baab, L. M., *Personality Type in Congregations*, Washington DC, Alban Institute, 1998.

Bayne, R., *The Myers-Briggs Type Indicator: A Critical Review and Practical Guide*, London, Chapman and Hall, 1995.

Briggs-Myers, I. and Myers, P. B., *Gifts Differing*, Palo Alto, California, Consulting Psychologists Press, 1980.

Bryant, C., *Jung and the Christian Way*, London, Darton, Longman and Todd, 1983.

Butler, A., *Personality and Communicating the Gospel*, Cambridge, Grove Books, 1999.

Davis, S. and Handschin, B., *Reinventing Yourself: Life Planning After 50*, Palo Alto, California, Consulting Psychologists Press, 1998.

Duncan, B., *Pray Your Way: Your Personality and God*, London, Darton, Longman and Todd, 1993.

Dwyer, M. T., *Wake Up the Sun: An Exploration of Personality Types and Spiritual Growth*, Thornbury, Victoria, Desbooks, 1988.

Dwyer, M. T., *No Light without Shadow: An Exploration of Personality Types*, Thornbury, Victoria, Desbooks, 1995.

Edwards, L., *How We Belong, Fight and Pray: The MBTI as a Key to Congregational Dynamics*, Washington DC, Alban Institute, 1993.

Faucett, R. and Faucett, C. A., *Personality and Spiritual Freedom: Growing in the Christian Life through Understanding Personality Type and the Myers-Briggs Type Indicator*, New York, Doubleday, 1987.

Francis, L. J. and Atkins, P., *Exploring Luke's Gospel: A Guide to the Gospel Readings in the Revised Common Lectionary*, London, Mowbray, 2000.

Francis, L. J. and Atkins, P., *Exploring Matthew's Gospel: A Guide to the Gospel Readings in the Revised Common Lectionary*, London, Mowbray, 2001.

Goldsmith, M., *Knowing Me, Knowing God*, London, Triangle, 1994.

Goldsmith, M. and Wharton, M., *Knowing Me, Knowing You*, London, SPCK, 1993.

Grant, W. H., Thompson, M. and Clarke, T. E., *From Image to Likeness: A Jungian Path in the Gospel Journey*, New York, Paulist Press, 1983.

Harbaugh, G., *God's Gifted People: Discovering Your Personality as a Gift*, Minneapolis, Augsburg Publishing House, 1990.

Hedges, P., *Understanding Your Personality: With Myers-Briggs and More*, London, Sheldon Press, 1993.

Hirsh, S. and Kise, J. A. G., *Looking at Type and Spirituality*, Gainesville, Florida, Centre for Application of Psychological Type, 1997.

Hirsh, S. and Kummerow, J., *Life Types*, New York, Warner Books, 1989.

Innes, R., *Personality Indicators and the Spiritual Life*, Cambridge, Grove Books, 1996.

Johnson, R., *Your Personality and the Spiritual Life*, Crowbridge, Monarch, 1995.

Keating, C. J., *Who We Are is How We Pray*, Mystic, Connecticut, Twenty-Third Publications, 1987.

Keirsey, D., *Please Understand Me: 2*, Del Mar, California, Prometheus Nemesis Book Company, 1998.

Kelsey, M., *Prophetic Ministry: The Psychology and Spirituality of Pastoral Care*, Rockport, Massachusetts, Element, 1991.

Kroeger, O. and Thuesen, J. M., *Type Talk*, New York, Delta, 1988.

Kroeger, O. and Thuesen, J. M., *Type Talk at Work*, New York, Delacorte Press, 1992.

Michael, C. P. and Morrisey, M. C., *Prayer and Temperament*, Charlottesville, Virginia, The Open Book, 1984.

Moore, R. L. (ed.), *Carl Jung and Christian Spirituality*, Mahwah, New Jersey, Paulist Press, 1988.

Moss, S., *Jungian Typology*, Melbourne, Collins Dove, 1989.

Osborn, L. and Osborn, D., *God's Diverse People*, London, Daybreak, 1991.

Oswald, R. M. and Kroeger, O., *Personality Type and Religious Leadership*, Washington DC, Alban Institute, 1988.

Quenk, N. L., *Beside Ourselves: Our Hidden Personality in Everyday Life*, Palo Alto, California, Davies-Black, 1993.

Richardson, P. T., *Four Spiritualities: Expressions of Self, Expressions of Spirit*, Palo Alto, California, Davies-Black, 1996.

Spoto, A., *Jung's Typology in Perspective*, Boston, Massachusetts, Sigo Press, 1989.

Thorne, A. and Gough, H., *Portraits of Type*, Palo Alto, California, Consulting Psychologists Press, 1991.

Williams, I., *Prayer and My Personality*, Bramcote, Grove Books, 1987.